A HISTORY TEACHING TOOLBOX

Practical strategies for the secondary classroom

Russel Tarr

ACTIVEHISTORY
BOOKS

books.activehistory.co.uk

RUSSEL TARR

First published 2022
Typeset in Garamond
All photographs by the author
Copyright © 2022 Russel Tarr
Published by ActiveHistory Books
books.activehistory.co.uk

ISBN-13: 9781838181413

DEDICATION

To all my students, past and present, who have made history teaching such an enjoyable vocation.

RUSSEL TARR

Praise for *A History Teaching Toolbox*

Russel has created and curated an enviable collection of strategies and techniques to achieve specific learning outcomes in consistently engaging and intellectually challenging ways. By identifying and categorising the broad objectives, and grouping his suggested strategies accordingly, he has produced a well-organised book that should be on every history teacher's desk. Whether you are planning a new unit of work, or looking for a different angle from which to approach a particular aspect of the course, the Toolbox will provide a wealth of practical ideas that can be implemented immediately.

Scott Allsop

This collection of teaching strategies is highly recommended for anyone seeking to improve their teaching – there's just so many good ideas to develop to fit the needs of your students.

Ian Dawson

This book is jam-packed full of great, simple to implement ideas which would enhance any lesson. If you are a history teacher, then this book is an essential purchase. I cannot recommend it highly enough!

John Mitchell

A History Teaching Toolbox really is the go-to guide for innovative and engaging History lessons. It really is a fantastic book. It's rare to find such creative, adaptable ideas which are clearly explained.

Alex Fairlamb

This truly is the type of book that provides activities and suggestions that any social studies teacher could implement tomorrow. It is also a great book for history departments – go through a chapter together, try out a few of the ideas, and come back together to tweak and adapt.

Glenn Wiebe

This creative compendium of strategies is rooted in real-life classroom practice. The Toolbox is structured around outcomes allowing the teacher to immediately select the right tool. The no-nonsense approach is perfect for busy teachers.

Carmel Bones

As Professor Robert Coe has pointed out it is entirely possible to have engagement without any learning going on. On the other hand it is also possible to have engagement and learning going on. This is particularly the case, when, as in this book, there is a clear intellectual and conceptual underpinning which gives the activities and ideas meaning and purpose. This is a collection of great ideas and resources.

Ben Walsh

RUSSEL TARR

CONTENTS

HOW TO USE THIS BOOK

This book provides history teachers in secondary schools with simple, practical and creative strategies to improve engagement and subject mastery in the classroom. It is broken into key sections to broadly reflect various stages in the learning process. Although the case studies I outline will refer to examples from the history classroom, many of the strategies behind them will, I hope, be easily transferable to other subjects.

As a simple target, I suggest you aim to use one key idea from each of the chapters within the academic year, preferably with different year groups. The following year, decide which ones to keep, which to refine, and which to ditch – as well as which fresh ideas you would like to try out.

All of the templates I refer to within the book can be downloaded via my blog "Tarr's Toolbox" (**www.tarrstoolbox.net**) where I share teaching strategies that have worked particularly well in my own classroom. The book also draws heavily on resources I have shared on my training courses and developed on my websites **www.activehistory.co.uk** and **www.classtools.net**, through which you can contact me directly for further support.

Russel Tarr

RUSSEL TARR

1
IMPARTING KNOWLEDGE TO STUDENTS

Rigorously imparting subject knowledge to students is a fundamental priority. This chapter outlines means of doing so which keep students actively engaged rather than relying solely on 'chalk and talk' teacher lectures.

Chronological narratives

At the start of a new topic, it's often useful to provide students with an essential chronology of events before analysing this timeline in terms of key questions. Simply delivering a narrative lecture to the class gives the students too much opportunity to lose attention. The following strategies help students engage with and absorb the narrative, and can be used in sequence or in isolation.

1. Running dictation
The running dictation is an efficient and energetic way of teaching students about dramatic moments in history.

- Before the lesson, anticipate dividing the class into teams of about five students and print off a timeline of key events for each team. This timeline should be written in the present tense (e.g. "The Spanish Armada has just set sail for England!") to give it a sense of immediacy.
- Cut the first timeline into slips and place these neatly into an envelope with the first event at the top of the pile. Repeat for the other timelines.
- When the class arrives, divide the students into their groups. Each group member should be given a number (1, 2, 3…)
- When the activity begins, position yourself at the far end of the classroom (even better, go outside where there is more space).
- Upon your signal, the first person from each team should run up to you and collect their first slip from their timeline.
- They should run back to their teams and read the slip out to their group. The rest of the team writes quick notes. The speaker can repeat details, but cannot show the slip.
- When you get the impression that the teams have had almost enough time, announce that the next slip of information is available. The second person from each team should run to you, bringing the original slip with them. They exchange this for the next slip from the timeline, and return to their teams.

- The process is then repeated until all the slips have been used up, with responsibility for 'running' looping through the students in each group for as long as necessary.
- When the process is completed, students should return to the classroom and spend some time in their groups comparing and completing their notes: after all, each member of the team will not have notes relating to events that they read to the rest of the group.

2. What do you think they should do next?

The running dictation is less effective for detailed, slow-paced stories which take place over many years. A better method in this case is a teacher-led lecture using the 'What should they do next?' format. This is particularly good for topics based around the assessment of a particular individual's handling of a situation. For example, when studying how far the Russian Provisional Government was responsible for its own downfall in October 1917, I introduce a dilemma that they face upon taking power on a PowerPoint slide. I then discuss with the class what the appropriate response should be to increase support for the government (sometimes providing them with several options):

1. February

- The Tsar has been arrested and placed under house arrest, but **The PG lacks real power**. The Petrograd Soviet has issued "Order Number 1" which asserts control over the armed forces. The Minister of War has stated that "The PG has no real power...it exists only as long as it is permitted to do so by the Soviet".

- *To the PG:*
- *You must decide who should be your Prime Minister. Do you select*
- *(a) Kerensky (a member of both the Soviet and the Duma) or*
- *(b) Prince Lvov, a moderate aristocrat?*
- *Why?*

Remember: your objective is to decide which choice would increase your level of popular support!

I then move to the next slide which reveals what the government actually did. Based on the earlier discussion, students then make brief notes on how successfully they think the situation was handled, using a grid which is already getting them to think in terms of themes rather than a chronological narrative:

As the teacher leads this exercise, organise notes under these four headings.
Note: To save time, you should just note the NUMBER of each event first (with explanation of why placed in that cell if necessary). At the end of the exercise you can then be given the PowerPoint presentation to develop your notes in more detail.

	Bolsheviks = "Methods"		Provisional Government = "Conditions"	
	Lenin		Kerensky	
	a. Evidence of Popularity [Fitzpatrick]	b. Evidence of Unpopularity [Pipes]	c. Evidence of Popularity [Pipes]	d. Evidence of Unpopularity [Fitzpatrick]
Military: The Soldiers				
Socio-Economic: The Soviets, Peasants				
Political: Other parties (Mensheviks, SRs etc)				

The process is repeated for other events – sometimes calling upon students to consider how the Provisional Government should act, and sometimes considering how the Bolsheviks should react.

After the teacher-led element is finished, students can be provided with the complete PowerPoint presentation to develop their tables further: if students are aware that you are going to do this from the outset, this is an efficient strategy to ensure that during the lesson they are focusing on formulating and writing judgments, rather than furiously trying to copy the factual information in each slide word for word.

3. Re-assemble a timeline in the correct order

This strategy is most effective for simpler timelines with relatively few events. I use it frequently with younger classes in a quiz format to get them engaged. Start by providing students with a list of events running down the page. To the right of the events are columns like this:

	Event	My Guess	Correct Answer	Difference
William has himself crowned as King of England				
Godwineson swears to support William's claim				
Edward the Confessor dies childless				

In "my guess" students number each event to reflect the chronological order in which they think they occurred (with "1" being the first event, and so on). Afterwards, the teacher then tells the class what the "correct answer" is for each event. Students then calculate the difference between the two numbers (note: this will always be a positive number – e.g. 5-3 would be a difference of 2, and 3-5 would also be a difference of 2). They then add up the total of the "difference" column to get an overall score: the student with the lowest overall difference is the winner!

One important point with this technique is that some thought should be given to providing some contextual clues within each "event" about what happened previously, or what is about to happen next (e.g. "Because Harold promised to support William, he was then allowed to go home to England").

4. Categorise, colour-code, elaborate and chunk

Following on from the above (or, with timelines that are too complex or detailed, starting at this point) introduce the key question for investigation (e.g. "What was the most important cause of the Spanish Civil War?"). Provide students with a timeline of events. They then have to tick the appropriate column to indicate which category the event fits into. Such columns might indicate positive or negative developments for the stability of the regime. If students are working on a word processor they can simply cut and paste the event into the appropriate column.

Next, students can highlight different events in different colours according to a key (for example, social, economic and military factors) and explain their reasoning for placing the event in that particular column in that particular colour. Finally, students consider the key turning points in the narrative and chunk the timeline into appropriate titled chapters. This is a useful way to help students see a bigger picture.

Causes of the Spanish Civil War: Overview Timeline		

Task 1

Each of the events listed in this table belongs in either the left hand ("Positives") column or the right hand ("Negatives") column. Your job is to
(a) CUT and PASTE each event into the second column if it needs to be moved;
(b) HIGHLIGHT different events into the appropriate colour using the following key:

Socio-Economic	Religious	Military	Regional

NOTE: different parts of the same sentence may be highlighted in different colours.
NOTE: The events up to 1921 have been done for you.

Date	Positives for Spain: signs of stability, success, improvement	Negatives for Spain: signs of instability, failure, decline (EXPLAIN AS NECESSARY)
The Monarchy		
1851		Religiously, the Catholic Church had a stranglehold over education since the 1851 Concordat. This was dangerous since Church support could not be relied upon and this would offend the large minority of non-Catholics and anticlericals in Spain.
1898		Militarily, the army was overstaffed and overpowerful after the loss of Cuba in 1898. This was a source of instability as the army now lacked a role and increasingly looked for activity within Spain's own borders.
1909		Socially, problems of poverty for the peasantry and the proletariat had led to bloodshed in "Tragic Week" (1909). This created a situation where the proletariat increasingly saw the government as being against their interests.
1920		Regionally, Catalonia and the Basque region wanted independence. The refusal of the monarchy to countenance devolution meant that these regions remained disaffected with the government – increasingly so as they became the industrial

Categorised and colour-coded timeline on the Spanish Civil War

5. How do we measure/prove this?

Many of the points in the timeline will require substantiation. In the example relating to the causes of the Spanish Civil War shown above, the statement is made that "The army was overstaffed and powerful". But how do we prove this? How can this be measured? Students should identify as many of these statements as possible, turn them into questions for research ("How do we measure whether the army was overstaffed?") and then set about finding the answer. This is particularly valuable to teach students the importance of substantiating their arguments. It also helps students formulate proper questions for research, in a form that cannot be answered by a straightforward 'Google Search'.

6. What questions does this timeline raise?

To lead students into an independent research activity, discuss the sorts of questions that the timeline leaves unanswered. These can be in the form of "describe" (what, who, where, when), "explain" (why?) and "assess" (to what extent?).

7. Add captioned images and extra points from the video clips for key points in the story

In the lesson from which the following image is taken, students read through the first part of the timeline together, watch a short video clip from a documentary covering this period. They then make extra notes and added an appropriate image alongside each event. In this instance, this was leading towards students making a video documentary.

What were the main causes of the American Civil War?
Your Task: To Create a Video Documentary on the Causes of the Civil War

Task 1: Gathering the material for your documentary

1. As a class, read through the first batch events in the timeline overleaf, and then watch the first video clip carefully at the suggested point (TIP: note carefully how Ken Burns uses music, silence, gentle panning of images, changes in the narrative voice and a focus on personal stories to generate interest and emotion).
2. Next, find BOTH a picture AND an extra point of information about each of the events so far described. In this way you will be building up the raw material for your video documentary.
3. Repeat this process (reading, watching, research and note-taking) for the rest of the timeline.

Discussion Point: At what point did the civil war become inevitable?

Date	Event	Picture	Extra points of information from the video clip / web research
1776	In 1776, the American Declaration of Independence united all the separate states of America. It said each state in "The United States" could decide whether to allow slavery. Half the states became "slave" states, the other half became "free" states.	JOIN, or DIE.	
1780	The "slave" states were based around the cotton plantations of the south. The "free" states were based around the factories of the north.		
1790	The "slave" states wanted the US government to respect the customs of each state (a loose "Confederacy"). The "free" states wanted the US government to forge a national identity (a tight "Union").		
	Video Clip "1" from Episode 1 of Ken Burns		
1793	The invention of a new machine, the "Cotton Gin", made the cotton plantations in the South very profitable. As the cotton plantations grew, so did the number of slaves – and their conditions became increasingly unpleasant.		
1820	The "Missouri Compromise", kept a voting balance of a slave state (Missouri) and a free		

Opening section of the timeline on the American Civil War

Character cards

Providing each student with a character card at different points in a historical study is a great way to engage the class with the motives of individuals and the nature and extent of change and continuity.

Method 1: Using "before" role cards to anticipate how key characters will react to circumstances

Before studying a key moment or event in history, give the class a list of the main characters involved and encourage students to consider such things as what they might believe, say and do (or what they anticipate they will gain or lose) as the story unfolds. These could be delivered as role-play presentations or imagined dialogues.

As a result of this initial activity, students will study the event in question with a much greater interest in how different people and groups were actually involved, and will be much more engaged in discussing such things as who had the most effective reactions, whose beliefs changed the most, whose reputation was enhanced or tarnished, or whatever other issues are pertinent for the topic in question.

Case study: The Little Rock Nine
When studying the desegregation of American schools in the 1950s, the case of Little Rock in Arkansas is an essential case study. In 1957, nine black students were enrolled in the school, and this sparked off riots.

After doing the necessary background reading which enabled me to identify the key characters and how they fitted into the story, I was able to provide each of my students with a different role corresponding to different key characters involved, as shown overleaf:

The Little Rock 9: Role play / Anticipation Task

You are: Governor Faubus of Arkansas. The local school board has made you aware that nine students will be admitted early next week and they have asked you to make a statement to the press outlining your position and how you are preparing for this. You are a relative moderate, but you are aware that many of your voters have deep misgivings.What will you say?

You are: President Eisenhower. You are aware that the tension in the South is explosive and that the Little Rock situation could easily escalate into violence. You are also aware that the world's media will be focused on you. Describe how you expect things could unfold and how you will react to various scenarios.

You are: The father of a black student who has been selected – due to his/her excellent grades – to be one of 9 students to attend Little Rock High School. Try to persuade your wife that your child should take up the offer.

You are: The mother of a black student who has been selected – due to his/her excellent grades – to be one of 9 students to attend Little Rock High School. Try to persuade your husband that your child should not take up the offer.

You are: A student who has decided to take up the offer to go to Little Rock. Explain why you have chosen to do so.

You are: The leading member of the National Guard outside Little Rock School. A number of the black students have made their way into the building, but a mob is now gathering outside. What will you do to bring the situation under control and prevent it escalating further?

You are: Elizabeth Eckford, one of the black students. It is the first day of school at Little Rock. Due to a misunderstanding, you find yourself separated from the rest of the group and in the middle of an aggressive white mob. What do you do?

You are: A white student at Little Rock High. A journalist has asked for your opinion of the situation: (Who is to blame? Do you think the schools can and should be integrated?) What is your reply?

You are: Minniejean Brown, one of the black students. You have now been at the school for several weeks. You are standing in the lunch queue and you are being continually insulted, taunted and bullied by a fellow (white) student behind you. What (if anything) do you do?

You are: Ernest Green, one of the black students. You have finally graduated from Little Rock, but in the graduation ceremony you are confronted by a sea of hostile faces when you take your seat. What do you do, and what is your attitude, when your name is called out and you are expected to walk up to the stage to receive your diploma?

Role cards for the Little Rock case study

After students had delivered their presentations and we had discussed issues arising, they then watched the extract from the classic "Eyes on the Prize" TV documentary to make notes on how events actually unfolded and how each character actually reacted and was affected. By speculating and anticipating in advance, students were much more interested and much more engaged in the discussion that followed

("Do the cases of Minnijean Brown, Ernest Green and Melba Petillo suggest that the Little Rock campaign was regarded as successful by the children involved?", "How effectively did you think (a) President Eisenhower and (b) Governor Faubus dealt with the situation at Little Rock?" and so on).

Method 2: Using "before" and "after" role cards to study the nature and impact of change and continuity

Step 1: At the start of the unit

Another simple way to use role cards in the classroom is to produce pairs of cards for key individuals from different walks of life. The "before" card is provided to each student at the outset of a dramatic period of study (for example, Nazi Germany 1933-39, World War One 1914-1918, The Black Death 1347-1350). This first card outlines, in a first-person narrative, such things as his/her situation, beliefs, hopes and concerns at the start of the period. These may be real individuals or represent generic types.

The first student reads out their character card, and the rest of the class notes down whether the character appears to be doing well in the current circumstances, and whether they are hopeful for the future. Based on the answers to these questions, the name of the character is then placed into a matrix grid (page 172) based on these two criteria, or a debate takes place about where they should be placed in this grid using a game of 'Interpretation Battleships' (page 173). The process is repeated for the remaining characters, and then students then use the completed matrix grid to reflect on the overall situation on the eve of the event in question.

Step 2: At the end of the unit

At the end of the study, each student is provided with the "after" card for their character, which outlines how the character's life and outlook has been affected over the course of the period in question. For example, some people will have become more optimistic; some more pessimistic; some will have found their situation has improved, got worse, or stayed the same; some will find that their attitudes on key issues will have changed. General conclusions and comparisons can then be drawn and key questions can start to be addressed ("To what extent did World War One lead to a social revolution?").

Using maps effectively

Maps can provide the basis of some very effective and interesting classroom activities. The following methods for the history classroom are transferable to other topics and subjects.

1. Convert a narrative into a Google Earth Tour

Students can be provided with a timeline of key events, and challenged to plot these on a map or in Google Earth to give them a fresh perspective and gain some geographical awareness of the topic in question. For example, I have designed such a tour to teach students about Tsarist Russia on the Eve of World War One. It is illustrated with original colour photographs from the Prokudin-Gorskii archives, organised around six groups of issues: political, economic, social, military and religious.

2. Place one map inside another to stress the scale of territory or impact

It is easy for students to overlook the vast scale of a territory being studied, despite the fact that in some instances this provides a crucial means of understanding the process of change and continuity. In this sense, placing one feature inside another can provide a quick but effective means of illustrating scale. For example:
• Provide students with a map of their own country (e.g. Great Britain). Then provide students with a map of imperial Russia. Ask them to draw a rectangle inside it somewhere to indicate the size of Great Britain. Then, provide students with an actual scaled map of Britain. Is it smaller than expected (likely)? What challenges would this provide to a ruler? A simpler method is to get students to guess how many kilometres are represent per centimetre before telling them the correct figure.

- Provide students with a map of their own locality. Ask them to draw around this the borders of another region, city, battle-lines or event. Then they should compare this to the reality. For example, students could overlay a map showing the impact of the atomic bombs dropped on Japan onto their own locality to bring home the scale of destruction.
- Provide student with a 'then and now' overlay to demonstrate the scale of change or impact. For example, when studying World War One, I use a Google Earth Tour to zoom in on the area corresponding today to the Western Front. I ask students to anticipate where, and how many, allied graveyards can be found in this area. Then, I tick the box which reveals a folder of placemarks showing each cemetery as a small white cross. It is an absolute blizzard and generates an audible sharp intake of breath around the class. It's a very simple, but profoundly moving, map-based starter activity.

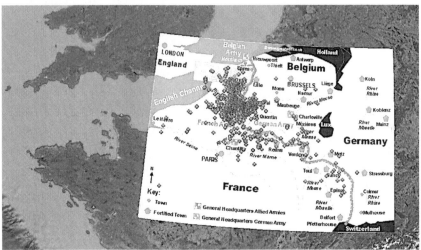

A Google Earth visualisation of Commonwealth war cemeteries

3. Anticipate and research key features on a blank outline map at the start of the topic

Rather than providing students with a detailed map as a reference resource - which, more likely than not, will end up filed away and neglected - give students a blank outline map and challenge them to label key cities, borders and natural features using whatever sources they can find. This is particularly useful when the study of the topic will require frequent reference to particular regions, cities and natural features.

Stage 1: Anticipation

This phase is particularly useful if students have studied this place before. Provide students with a blank outline map and then ask them, from their existing knowledge and through their own powers of deduction, where they anticipate certain borders and places are located. Some examples might be:

- "Here is a map of Europe in 1914. Draw a line to represent where you think the Western Front started and ended by Christmas 1914"
- "Here is a map of Austro-Hungary at the end of World War One with the national minorities highlighted. Divide the territory into new states (Hungary, Austria, Czechoslovakia, Yugoslavia…)"
- "Here is a map of Germany after World War Two. Label the location of Berlin, then draw the anticipated borders of the French, British, Soviet and US zones of occupation based on what you know about the Soviet occupation and the debates at Yalta and Potsdam"

Stage 2: Research

Students should start by comparing their maps with a partner and as a class (the teacher could even try to reach a class consensus on a final, whole-class map). Then, when they conduct their research to complete a master copy, they will be much more engaged in the process and willing to answer such questions as "Were the borders substantially larger or smaller than you expected?".

If the topic is a new one, it is unlikely that the anticipation stage will be worthwhile and so students could proceed straight to this research phase. For example, I start my study of the Spanish Civil War with a homework exercise in which students are challenged to label an outline map of the Iberian peninsula with key features, cities and regions (in particular, noting where separatist movements were particularly strong, and the north-south divide in terms of agriculture and industry).

4. Use classroom debate to decide upon the most appropriate / likely border changes partway through a topic

This technique is similar to the anticipation exercise outlined above, but lends itself particularly well to topics involving debate between different parties about the most appropriate border changes. Students are arranged into small teams, with each person representing a different interest group, and they are then challenged to agree upon the fairest possible division of territory. For example:

- Provide students with a map of Palestine after World War Two. Key geographical features should be labelled in terms of population distribution, water sources and fertile land. In teams of three (representing Arabs, Jews and the Western powers), students have to divide the territory into three areas (Palestine, Israel and International Zones) in a way which they think is most likely to bring lasting peace to the region. You should stress that you will cast a vote in favour of the best plan. Therefore, although students should aim to defend their interest group's objectives, they should be aware that being too greedy will likely mean that their plan will be thrown out altogether as being too controversial. At the end of this particular exercise, students can compare their maps to the various genuine proposals put forward before and after World War Two by the British and by the UN and discuss the merits of each.

- Another topic which lends itself well to this approach are the negotiations at Versailles (1918) and Yalta/Potsdam (1944-45) about the future of Germany. If there is time, a 'compare and contrast' exercise based on Germany's treatment after both World Wars is particularly valuable.

5. Plot the movement of individuals along a path

This approach is useful when charting the journey of a particular person over time. As an added challenge, students could be provided with a jumbled timeline and reconstruct it into the correct order by plotting the places mentioned on a map and thereby deducing the most likely order in which they happened. Google Earth is particularly effective for creating these tours, and I have created several which can be freely downloaded from www.activehistory.co.uk. Possible topics might include:

- The circumnavigation of Sir Francis Drake
- The Long March of Mao Zedong
- The voyages of Marco Polo
- The invasion of Russia by Napoleon's armies
- The journeys of Olaudah Equiano
- Medieval pilgrimage routes

6. Chart the expansion/contraction of an idea, an empire or a catastrophe

a. Empires
The growth and decline of Empires lends itself well to map work. Students should shade different territories in different colours to represent the different time periods that they were absorbed into the Empire. For added challenge:

- Provide students with a timeline listing when various territories were incorporated, but don't label these on the map itself: instead, students have to identify where these territories are themselves before drawing the borders on the map and shading them in.
- Ensure that students are provided with follow-up questions to reflect upon so it doesn't become a meaningless colouring-in exercise: for example "Which was the period of greatest expansion?", "Can you find out who was Emperor at this time?", "Why did the empire not expand any further?", "What benefits and drawbacks would continued expansion bring?"

b. Diseases and Ideas

The spread of a pandemic like The Black Death can be charted on a map very effectively. Data exists for the time when the disease was first and last recorded in various cities all over Europe, and plotting this information on a map in various colours to represent various dates is an enlightening exercise when trying to get students to appreciate the scale and speed of how the disease spread.

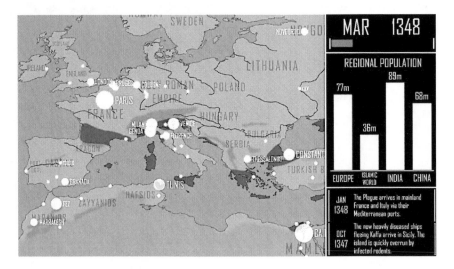

c. Crime – geographic profiling

Geographic profiling is an activity I use when studying Jack the Ripper at www.activehistory.co.uk. It is the name we give to the technique used by the police to work out where a killer might live. It is usually the case that

- The murders will be committed close to home (to allow a quick 'return to base') and
- The murders will take place increasingly close to home as the police step up their presence in the area.

With this in mind, I instruct students to plot the location of each murder on the map. Then, based on the information, students are asked to speculate where they think that the murderer is most likely to live and to shade this area on the map. Finally, we look at what the most recent 'Ripperologists' have concluded before discussing the limitations of this evidence.

History mysteries

These investigations are designed as stand-alone projects lasting three to four hours. They teach skills of deductive reasoning, independent research, group work and structured writing.

My students complete at least one mystery project each year. Because the mark scheme stays the same, they provide a particularly useful way of measuring student progress over time. More importantly, they start each year's studies with a sharp and interesting focus.

Stage 1: The role-play

The first part of the History Mystery consists of a role-play element led by the teacher, usually involving some props. This is deliberately designed to pique the curiosity of the students. The role card for the "Iceman mystery" which the Geography and History departments use as a secondary school induction project looks like this:

Role Card Starter Activity

Cast: Teacher

Props: "Crime Scene" tape. A blanket, covering up something which is as much like the shape of a body as possible. A full-body white overall to be worn by the teacher.

The teacher should have the 'body' covered with a blanket before students get to the room. Crime Scene Tape should be placed across the classroom door. The teacher should be wearing the white coat and be carrying a clipboard to look officious. When the students are lined up outside the class, outline that over the next few lessons they will be investigating a genuine mystery. They will need to use detective skills to form their own conclusions.

Cut the tape away and instruct them to sit down away from the 'body'.

1. Point out the body to the students. Students then have to come up with a series of questions in the WHO / WHY / WHEN / WHERE / WHAT format. Write each of these into the record grid as outlined in the teacher lesson plan.

2. With the initial questions now outlined, draw a line halfway down the board underneath the questions. This is where we will start listing some 'answers'. Ask the students to hypothesize the answers to the questions as far as possible (some answers will be impossible as we have no evidence yet).

Based on this initial introductory role-play, the class is then invited to come up with a series of preliminary questions for investigation (e.g. "Who is this?", "Why did they...?", "When did...?", "What is...?", "Where are we?"). In the case of the "Iceman mystery", the questions that students came up with as a starting point included the following:

- Are we at the scene of a murder, or an accident?
- How did this person die?
- Was this person pushed or did they jump?
- Was the victim a child (the body seems very small)?
- Are we high up? On a balcony? In the forest? On a rooftop?

Investigators Tarr and Podbury introduce the 'iceman' mystery

Stage 2: The images

The next part of the investigation involves showing the students a series of images on the whiteboard. Each image helps the students to formulate fresh questions, amend existing ones or even form some provisional answers.

Stage 3: Deciding upon the five key questions

On scrap paper, students work individually to identify what they think are the five "Big Questions" that require further investigation. Note: some of these questions may be taken directly from the list; it is more likely though that students will form broader questions which aim to encompass several "mini-questions" from the list.

The teacher then leads a classroom discussion to gather a list of 'big questions' and to narrow these down to what we consider to be the most popular five questions overall.

The students then write these five questions down in their sheets. They should also write a provisional answer against each one to reflect what they think is currently the most likely answer.

During this times the teacher can be cutting up the evidence slips ready for the next part of the investigation.

Stage 4: The information slips

This question formulation and resolution process then continues with a series of information slips shared amongst the class. One slip is handed out to each student and they use this to come up with a fresh question or (even better) to provide a possible answer to one of the "five big questions".

There are lots of these slips, so students who work more quickly than others can be given a second or even a third slip. Once all the slips have been handed out and analysed in this way, the students are put into groups to compare their findings.

I then use the jigsaw group approach (page 202) after this feedback phase: in other words, I create a new set of groups, with each new group containing one member from each of the old groups. The feedback phase is then repeated. In this way, every single slip has the opportunity to be discussed. This is usually a very lively phase and contains quite a few 'Eureka!' moments.

Stage 5: Individual research and write-up phase

Finally, each student produces a written report which is graded against a standardised mark scheme. Specific credit is given to students who demonstrate evidence of independent research: to this end, the teacher could construct a QR treasure hunt (page 30) to accompany the exercise for students to complete at break times.

Sweets to measure change over time

Any topic that focuses on changing fortunes over time could adopt this approach, which uses a large bag of sweets to represent a key theme being measured (for example, success or satisfaction).

A selection of students sit at the front of the class to represent different individuals or themes. The rest of the class decides how many sweets they should have at the start of the time period in question. Then a series of events is read out. For each one, a different member of the class is called upon to decide who gained and who lost out as a result, and redistribute, take away or provide more sweets to the appropriate characters after discussion and agreement.

A log should be kept (e.g. in an Excel spreadsheet) of the sweets held by each person as the simulation proceeds. At the end of the simulation, the sweets should be shared among the group. Students can be asked to spot the most important turning points for different groups and to produce an annotated infographic explaining the most pertinent points.

Possible examples

- **Rule of Mao - sweets represent 'satisfaction'** (of groups in China such as women, children, factory workers).
- **Rise of Castro - sweets represent 'support'** (of groups and individuals from 1953 onwards in Cuba).
- **Causes of Spanish Civil War** - sweets represent 'stability' (in different areas such as politics, economics, religion).
- **Consequences of World War One** - sweets represent 'success' (for different themes such as medicine, technology, workers' rights). Each one of these people as a homework exercise has to explain why they gained, and why somebody else lost, as a result of World War One. In the lesson, these presentations / debates can take place before the rest of the class, acting as judges, allocate out the sweets. For added sophistication, the presentations could take place in three phases: (a) short-term effects; (b) mid-term; (c) long-term.

Case study: The rise of Stalin

Five students take the role of key members of the Politburo at the end of 1922 who could feasibly have taken power after Lenin's death (Stalin,

Trotsky, Bukharin, Kamenev and Zinoviev). Prior to the lesson each one prepares a short speech explaining why they are the best person to lead the Soviet Union. In the lesson, the five candidates sit at the front of the class whilst the rest of the students form the audience. A large bag of sweets is split between the audience members and then the five campaign speeches are delivered as persuasively as possible.

When the speeches are over, each member of the audience splits his or her sweets between the candidates in proportions to reflect the respective political strength of each individual, explaining their reasoning to the rest of the class as they do so. Each candidate counts the sweets they have and we record this in a spreadsheet. Then, the teacher outlines the first key event that takes place: Lenin's funeral, and in particular Trotsky's failure to attend and Stalin delivering the funeral oration. Discuss whose reputation will clearly benefit from this, and whose will suffer, after looking more closely at the details behind these developments in the form of primary source readings. After discussion, one student is nominated to decide who should lose sweets, how many they should lose, and who should gain them.

The new numbers are added into the spreadsheet along with an explanation. This process is repeated to cover subsequent key events until Stalin is left in an unassailable position in 1929. The students then convert the spreadsheet into a graph to spot the key turning points, and categorise the key causes for Stalin's rise to provide the basis of an essay.

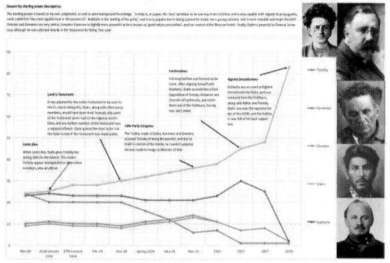

A graph to show the shift in power over time of several Politburo members

Hexagon learning

The hexagon approach involves providing students with key pieces of information on hexagons. Their job is to organise these into categories of their choice, with hexagons being placed adjacent to each other to highlight links between them.

These groups are then glued down onto sugar paper and then the diagram is developed with titles being written over each category, and arrows being used to connect the different categories and thereby chart a 'path' through the diagram. The annotations over these arrows ultimately provide the opening topic sentences for each paragraph in the essay that will be the concrete outcome of the activity.

Case study: The rise of Stalin

How Stalin was able to emerge as leader of the USSR against apparently overwhelming odds is one of the most intriguing questions in history. In the years that following the Bolshevik Revolution, due to a series of blunders and miscalculations, Stalin had lost the support of the party leadership: so much so that on his deathbed, Lenin dictated a formal 'Testament' describing Stalin as a liability who needed to be removed from his post. He was also hated by Lenin's closest ally, Leon Trotsky, who was widely expected to step into the leadership position after Lenin's death. Yet just five years later Stalin was undisputed leader of the USSR and Trotsky was in exile.

The story of how Stalin transformed his fortunes so dramatically is a great story revolving around his treachery, cunning and downright charm. But the danger of this is that the essays that are then written by students become mere narrative, storybook accounts which do little more than give a step-by-step account of the main events between 1924-1929.

After a study of the events culminating in Stalin emerging as leader of the party, I made a list of factors which could be used to explain why Stalin became dictator of the USSR. I then put these into the

Hexagons Generator I have developed at www.classtools.net to create two single-page documents containing a total of 40 hexagons.

Stage 1: Selection and Categorisation

The class was divided into pairs for the activity. Each pair of students was given a copy of the first sheet of hexagons, which they cut up and started to organise on their desks into categories of their choice. This process, involving the categorisation of 20 hexagons, took about 15 minutes. Students were encouraged to come up with no more than five categories overall. They could also choose to leave some of the hexagons to one side if they were considered less important than the others.

We then spent five minutes comparing the different categories that students had identified. Each pair of students took turns to suggest one idea for a category heading until all the ideas had been shared.

Following this, I gave each students a blank sheet of hexagons. The challenge was to identify other factors which could help to explain Stalin's rise to power and write these directly into the hexagons. After five minutes, each pair of students took it in turns to suggest an idea. If this was a valid (and fresh) idea, then the other students copied it into their pair's version of the sheet, and the students who shared the idea were each given a sweet - we had a bag of these left over as a result of our 'Rise of Stalin through sweet-eating' lesson (page 22) which had preceded this lesson! This process was repeated until the students had run out of ideas.

Each pair of students then cut up this new sheet of factors and used them to develop their existing diagrams. In some instances this involved merely adding fresh evidence into existing categories. Sometimes though it involved adding new categories, or amending earlier categories.

Finally, each pair of students was given the second sheet of hexagons and the process of categorisation continued.

Stage 2: Linkage and Prioritisation

By this stage, the students had decided upon the main factors to explain Stalin's rise to power, organised into key categories. Each of these categories could form the basis of a paragraph in an essay. However, it was still necessary to decide two things.

Firstly, students would need to determine the order in which to deal with the points in each paragraph. It would not be enough to simply introduce the category title, then randomly write about each piece of evidence from that group. This is where the hexagons are particularly useful.   The six sides mean that factors can be placed alongside each other in various combinations to highlight connections between batches of factors within categories. After students rearranged their factors in this way, they stuck them down onto sugar paper with a glue stick. They could then write the title of each category over each batch of hexagons, and annotate around each group of hexagons to explain why they were arranged in that particular way.

Secondly, students had to decide how to connect their main categories together to create an overall thread of argument. They did this by drawing arrows between the factors and explaining their connections over them. For example:
"Economic problems > *created* > Divisions in the party > *exploited by* > Stalin's Cunning > *which contrasted with* > Opposition weakness"

Stage 3: Essay preparation

The final part of the process was to use the completed diagrams as an essay plan. I photographed each of the diagrams and shared them with the students. Their task was to use the diagrams as the basis of their essay answering "Why did Stalin become leader of the USSR?". Each paragraph was to focus on separate categories of hexagons, and the points made in each paragraph should have some logical order and flow. Moreover, the order of the paragraphs was dictated by the arrows linking the categories, with the opening sentence of each paragraph after the first one being based on the explanation over each arrow.

Concluding points

Hexagon learning steers students away from a narrative approach and into an analytical frame of mind. It helps them frame categories of analysis, build up their command of the material step-by-step. It provides them with the opportunity to easily change their initial assumptions, connect factors together both within and between categories, and give them a very effective basis of an accomplished written piece.

It is also a very simple approach that can be transferred to other topics and other curriculum subjects. All that is needed is an initial list of factors – contributed either by the teacher or the students – which can then be written into a blank hexagons template or turned into hexagons automatically using my www.classtools.net Hexagons Generator. Thereafter, all that is needed are scissors, sugar paper and a glue stick.

A hexagon exercise investigating why the Union won the American Civil War. Orange hexagons were added by students using additional notes from a video documentary halfway through the process. The rectangles are primary source extracts added as a final task.

Taking it further

The hexagons approach can be developed in a variety of ways, for example:

- Provide students with a blank sheet of hexagons (preferably in a different colour) and challenge them to add at least one further point in each of their categories from further research.
- Provide students with (or ask them to find) some primary source extracts (written or visual) and challenge them to add a selection of these alongside some of the categories they have developed.
- Ask students to highlight the 'most important / interesting' factor in each category and be prepared to explain their choices to the rest of the class.

The hexagon essay writing approach also overlaps effectively with the visual essay writing approach (page 293) and the sticky-note approach (page 204).

Spiced-up "cloze" exercises

"Fill the Gaps" ("Cloze") exercises help students build up vocabulary and to learn fresh information through focused, methodical reading. Here are several ways to 'spice up' cloze exercises.

1. Don't immediately provide students with the missing words.
• Instead, challenge students to fill the gaps purely from their own background knowledge.

2. Include extra 'rogue' words in the list of possible words that students can use to fill the gaps.
• Use familiar key terms from earlier topics: this is a nice way to remind students of earlier vocabulary that they have learned!).
• Use new key terms that students will learn in the new topic, and then challenge students to research the meaning of each of these.

3. Don't just remove nouns – cloze exercises can also be used to help students enrich their vocabulary in other ways.
• Remove adjectives from the account and challenge students to insert the appropriate term from their own judgment or from a list.
• Remove linking words and phrases (e.g. However, Therefore, Nevertheless, Additionally, Hence) from the start of paragraphs to help students think more carefully about how writers join paragraphs:

Nevertheless | Moreover | In some ways | However | On the other hand

> **Could you get justice in the Middle Ages?**
> In the Middle Ages, the guilt of somebody accused of a crime was determined in a range of ways.
>   these methods were unfair and they are no longer used. For example, was unfair because . In addition, was unfair because [etc]
>   , we should not be too harsh on people in the Middle Ages, because they did not have the sort of science and technology that we have today to help them. For example, in the Middle Ages they did not have which helps catch criminals today by [etc]
>   , in other ways, these methods were fair and are still used today. For example, was fair because . [etc]

Using cloze exercises to develop style, not just factual knowledge

QR code treasure hunts

A QR-Code treasure hunt involves getting students using their mobile devices to continue learning and running around outside of lesson time. A series of questions are converted into QR codes and hidden around the school. Points are awarded to students who find, decode and answer each question.

1. The background

For several lessons, the students had been engaged in a "History Mystery" exercise (page 19) focusing on the disappearance of the Franklin Expedition. Through pictures, snippets of evidence, and a role play exercise, the students formulated their own questions for investigation, framed provisional answers, and then reframed their assumptions as more evidence was progressively provided to them.

At the end of the research phase, students were required to produce an essay introducing the mystery and answering the five key questions they settled upon as being the most important to solve. The standardised mark scheme, which is provided to students in advance, gives specific credit to students who show evidence of wider research - which is where the QR code treasure hunt comes in.

2. The treasure hunt

With students just about to start their essay assignment, a series of 20 codes were hidden in random locations around the school. These were created using the www.classtools.net QR Treasure Hunt Generator.

Students were put into small teams: each of these teams contained at least one person that owned a smartphone which could decode the QR codes using one of the many free downloadable apps for this purpose.

In break times over a two-day period, the teams of students hunted around for the codes, copied down the numbered questions as each one was decoded, and then researched and recorded the answers. The completed answer sheets were then handed in at the end of the school week and the team with the most correct questions and answers was awarded a prize.

The following week, the sheets were photocopied and returned to the members of the teams. Each student could then use the fresh information they had gathered in the treasure hunt to develop their essay project in more depth.

3. Five tips for a successful treasure hunt

1) Make sure the students are arranged into teams so that students without mobile devices are not disadvantaged.
2) Make it clear that the treasure hunt will feed directly into their essay assignment and thereby help them get a good mark.
3) Provide a mix of questions - some of which test existing knowledge, some of which require further independent research.
4) Keep a record of where you place each code - so they can easily be removed after the exercise has finished.
5) When you mark the completed sheets, award one point for each correctly copied question, and one mark for each correct answer, and declare the winning team on this basis.

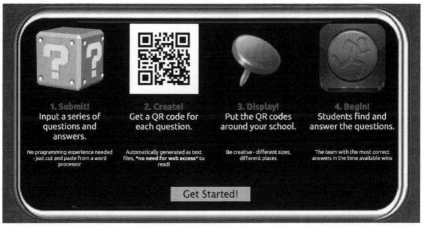

Create your own QR Treasure Hunt using the generator at www.classtools.net

Taking it further

The treasure hunt approach to learning can be developed on a larger scale across an entire locality as a local scavenger hunt (page 333).

Escape the room!

An "Escape the room" lesson is an adventure game where students are given a historical scenario in which they are trapped in a dangerous place. They work against the clock to engineer their escape by finding mission slips hidden around the room and completing these using the sources provided.

Three dates from clues will crack the three padlocks to obtain the next mission

These lessons, which can be set up to run for any length of time between thirty minutes and a couple of hours, are fantastic for introducing a new topic, consolidating existing knowledge and/or introducing fresh learning into the classroom in a highly engaging way.

Although they have great potential for creating memorable learning experiences in the classroom and are particularly valuable as team-building exercises, they can easily become a time-consuming gimmick where plenty of fun is had but very little genuine learning is taking place. I have therefore established an easily replicable format which allows teachers to set these activities up quickly, and which keeps genuine subject mastery at the heart of the excitement.

The approach I recommend is outlined below and and works well in a lesson lasting 45-60 minutes.

Step 1: Pre-class preparation

- Formulate an engaging scenario based on the topic explaining why they need to "Escape the Room".

- Construct a timeline of ten events relating to the topic and cut this into ten slips. Students will be rewarded with one of these slips each time they complete a mission to develop their knowledge.

- Decide upon a "final clue" which will enable them to "escape". This will be read out to the class by the teacher only after they have obtained the last piece of the timeline, and will require them to make use of it. For example: "The date of the fourth event in the timeline is the key to escape!" These four digits can then be used to open a combination lock to a box containing the key to the cell; alternatively, the digits could complete a phone number which then needs to be dialled to get through to a rescuer!

- Gather a series of sources: written accounts, images, props and artefacts relating to the topic in question.

- Produce ten questions / tasks requiring use of some of these sources and write these on separate 'mission slips'. These missions could be named after key individuals and events ("Mission Roosevelt", "Mission Fascism" and so on) which might later be researched in their own right as an extension activity.

- Hide these mission slips around the room in various places (under desks, stuck to the ceiling, inside some of the books and objects...)

- Prepare some hint questions which can be answered using the sources in the room. If students get stuck at finding or completing a mission, you can pose one of these questions and reward a correct answer with a hint to keep things moving.

- <u>Spread the various sources all over the room</u>, along with other random objects and artefacts to add further interest and confusion.
- <u>Have some appropriate music playing</u> to create some atmosphere.

Step 2: Conducting the activity

- Greet students outside the classroom and introduce the scenario before they are allowed inside.
- Students enter the classroom, are provided with the scenario and a few minutes to look around the room without touching anything.
- The class is then challenged to start looking for the hidden mission slips. Whenever one is found, the teacher halts the class and reads out the mission. It is up to the students to decide who should complete this mission and who should continue looking for the remaining mission slips.
- Each time students feel a 'mission' is completed, they should alert the teacher. The teacher asks all students to pay attention as the mission is read out and the answer is provided.

- If the answer is correct, the next piece of the timeline (starting with the earliest) is then read out and given to the class on a slip of paper.
- Once the class has the final piece of the timeline, the final clue will be given by the teacher which enables them to use this timeline to complete the final mission and escape (see Step 1).
- In this way it is only possible for students to "escape" once ALL of the missions have been successfully completed.

Step 3: Debriefing

After the activity is finished (successfully or otherwise), students should be asked to reflect on the activity with the following sorts of questions:

- What sorts of things did you learn through this activity?
- How did your group work well together?
- How might you have worked together better?
- What might you do differently next time?

Other points to note:

- As the mission progresses, there are inevitably fewer missions left to solve. This makes it a good idea to have 'hint' questions available (see Step 1) so that 'spare' students can keep busy and help the rest of the team complete the remaining mission(s).
- There is no problem in having more missions hidden in the room than there are pieces of the timeline. As long as students find and complete ten missions, they will obtain their ten timeline pieces and can complete the mission. Indeed, it's a good idea to have more missions than you need in the first instance: this will enable you to work out which ones are particularly easy to find / complete so that the next time you do it you can adjust accordingly.

Case study: "Mission Galileo, 1610"

The scenario

"It is 1610. the Renaissance ('Rebirth') of arts and sciences has transformed Europe. You are students of the great scientist Galileo in

Padua, Italy. You have all been put in jail by the church for insisting that the earth goes round the sun! You will all be taken away to be executed in 45 minutes - unless you can find the key to escape! The location of the key is provided in the coded message in the middle of the room".

Conducting the lesson

Students are then encouraged to engineer their escape by finding mission slips, completing the tasks and reconstructing the timeline in the manner described earlier. From this point the activity should pretty much run itself - students will hunt around the room trying to find missions, then completing them, and slowly building up the timeline. As the teacher, all you need to do is have your own copy of the mission slips printed onto a sheet so you can tick off which ones have been located, and which ones have been completed, so that useful hints can be provided as necessary later on. It's one of those occasions where it's a positive advantage for the teacher to stay as quiet as possible!

Taking it further

For lots more ideas and resources for creating your own escape room, go to: www.activehistory.co.uk/escape_room.

Hand gestures to reflect changing relations between groups

In any topic involving the changing relations between two factors (countries, parties, ideologies or individuals), get students to act out the sequence of events using their hands to help them.

In her final speech to the House of Commons, British Prime Minister Margaret Thatcher placed her hands one above the other to represent the gap between rich and poor. She then slowly lowered both hands, bringing them closer together as she did so, to illustrate her claim that socialists are quite happy to see both rich and poor get worse off as long as the gap is being closed. She then raised both hands, restoring a larger gap as she did so, to claim that Conservatives instead are happy seeing the gap get bigger, as long as everyone on the whole was seeing a rising standard of living.

The same method can be used in a variety of classroom contexts. For example, get students to make fists out of their two hands and hold these in front of them. Tell them each hand represents a different party or ideology. Next, give them a series of events referring to changes in the policies, membership or actions of the two main parties. They then decide how to move their fists based on the idea that further away from each other means diverging views; closer together closer co-operation and agreement.

To make the activity more challenging, other dimensions can be added. For example, to illustrate the fact that both major UK political parties 'veered to the left' in the years immediately following World War Two, the fists could not only move closer together, but could both move to the left. Conversely, the breakdown of 'consensus' politics under Thatcher could see both fists not just move wide apart, but one go sharply to the left and the other sharply to the right; whilst the advent of Tony Blair might see the "Labour" fist move towards the right.

As well as using the horizontal axis, the fists could move up and down to represent another measurement such as success or failure, popularity or unpopularity. Consider using different hand shapes at different points in the timeline. A fist could represent aggression; a peace sign, compromise. Your students will probably come up with some other gestures which you may consider more or less appropriate!

Three effective role-play techniques

Although role-play and simulation exercises in the classroom are an entertaining way of bringing history to life, they are also perfectly compatible with rigorously efficient academic topic coverage: especially important for older students under pressure to cover syllabus content.

I set myself the target of teaching some major units of the examination syllabus entirely through role-play over several weeks of lessons, focusing especially on topics that students had found comparatively dry in previous years. Textbooks were put away, worksheets went back into the filing cabinet, and teacher-talk came off the menu. Instead, we all immersed ourselves in the topic by imagining ourselves back into the past as key characters in the story. We thereby explored some of the key events, debates and developments as they unfolded over time.

Method 1: Teacher in role as one character

Case study: Tsar Alexander III
The most straightforward way to construct a role-play-only teaching unit is for the students to adopt generic roles and for the teacher to be the only person to adopt the role of a specific character. This involves minimal preparation for the students and keeps things tightly structured.

For example, a study of Tsar Alexander III is framed around the question "Was he more of a reactionary than a reformer?". I take on the role of the Tsar himself, and the students merely have to imagine themselves as nameless 'ministers' – half of whom should always aim to provide 'progressive' advice, whilst the others should be 'traditional' in outlook.

I start by introducing myself as the new Tsar and remind my 'ministers' that I have come to the throne as a result of my father's assassination by terrorists. I then immediately chair a debate between the 'reformers' and the 'reactionaries' on the subject of whether my coronation speech should pledge revenge for my father's murder, or strike a more conciliatory tone – maybe even offering an amnesty to the killers. I also make the point that at the time of his death, my father was planning to call a new parliamentary assembly: should I announce that this is still going ahead, or not? Finally, what title should I give to my coronation speech?

After talking the issues through and hearing the arguments for and against the different options available, I thank them for their input and read out the actual coronation speech that I have decided upon, which I have entitled "The Manifesto on Unshakeable Autocracy". This is the point when students busily take notes about the issue at hand, the decision the Tsar took, their judgment about whether this policy suggests he was a reformer or a reactionary, and whether he had acted most appropriately.

This format is then repeated for other key policies, with homework time used to write up findings and to conduct research relating to the issues due for discussion at the next 'meeting'.

Method 2: Students in role as several characters

Case study: Lenin's Russia

Role-play is even more ambitious and academically rewarding when it requires each student to take on the role of a specific historical character for several lessons, and the teacher takes more of a back seat. This approach enables students to obtain an exceptionally sophisticated understanding of historical causation and change over time: the interplay and respective contributions of different individuals to the unfolding of events is brought alive in a particularly vivid way.

For example, in our investigation about how successfully Lenin ruled Russia between 1918-1924, each student takes on the role of a different member of the government (Trotsky, Lenin, Kamenev, Zinoviev, Stalin and Bukharin form the core of this group). As an initial homework task, each student researches 'their' position on key issues facing the new Soviet state – for example whether they favour an immediate end to World War One, working with other parties and employing terror as a means of control.

In the lessons, I take the role of President Kalinin, acting as chairperson. Each lesson then works through issues "as they arise" between 1918-24 in a similar format to the study of Alexander III, but with the added benefit that the discussions are not merely generic arguments for and against different policy positions, but sometimes a five-way argument between key characters using genuine quotes from their own writings on the issue (additional students can act as 'advisors' to the main players).

As Lenin's decisions on issues are revealed at the end of each discussion, students can make detailed notes not just on 'what happened' but on how controversial these decisions were and how far Lenin was abandoning his communist ideology in favour of pragmatism.

Perhaps most importantly of all, the role-play approach allows students to appreciate that the question of Lenin's success or failure works on an assumption that Lenin was actually the key decision maker in this period – one which is increasingly questionable as his health deteriorated (in later role-play sessions, Lenin is unable to speak as he is 'recovering' first from an assassination attempt, and then from a series of strokes).

"Lenin" (wounded, on the left) and "Dzerzhinsky" during a Politburo meeting

Method 3: Students and teacher in role to represent different groups

Case study: Marxism through arm-wrestling

The most complex role-play approach I have used is designed to teach political ideology rather than key events. My 'Marxism through arm-wrestling' unit not only provides an essential ideological introduction to a proper understanding of the 1917 October Revolution, but also helps students to form their own judgments about the respective merits of left- and right-wing ideas about how society and economy should be organised.

Students act out a role-play over several rounds which is deliberately designed to illustrate the Marxist conception of how free market economies function. Each student starts with the same amount of capital (sweets), but through rounds of arm-wrestling and coin flips between randomly paired students, they gain or lose capital unfairly and inequalities quickly emerge.

Thereafter, each of the newly wealthier 'bourgeois' students is given the opportunity to increase their capital by engaging in production – they 'buy' some paper and scissors from the teacher and employ members of the poorer 'proletariat' to cut this into neat circles (proletarians who demand the highest wages end up being unemployed and leaving the game, a rule which means that wages are kept low). The teacher will buy a certain amount of the goods that come out of each 'factory' (as long as they are of a decent quality) on a 'first come, first served' basis. This ensures that the bourgeoisie demand more and more from their disaffected workforce.

This process is repeated over several rounds, with subtle twists each time: for example, factory owners can confer and discuss a wage strategy to keep wages down (in other words, create a cartel); the teacher can offer a credit system at a low rate of interest (to encourage entrepreneurialism); workers can form a 'trade union' with a nominated representative to negotiate with the owners, or pool their resources to create a 'strike fund'.

As the game proceeds, attempts to maximise profits drives down wages, discriminates against smaller traders and generally creates a class of disaffected, exploited proletarians. The outcome of the unit is that each student produces a 'Beginner's Guide to Marxism' that they can refer back to at different points in the course.

Chapter 4: Marx and His Remedy for Capitalism

Some of you may be asking, what is the whole point of *The Communist Manifesto*? And THAT'S OK! Read on to find out! The Communist Manifesto contains a school of thought called (coincidence?) Marxism, which is basically a glorified set of Google Maps directions to Communism:

The road from feudalism to communism is unfortunately very convoluted

On this metaphorical road you will pass by some interesting landmarks (keep an eye out!):

Feudalism Fountain: On your left you will see some serfs. They are not happy because they are serving some lords which then, in turn, serve a tyrant. They have no belongings except for a small plot of land they receive in return for agricultural labor. They will most likely jack your car so floor it!

Capitalism Castle: On your right you will see a banana tree. If you skipped ahead to get to the "good bits" in this guide, I apologize, please rewind to page 3.

Socialism Snack Shack: Straight ahead you will see Socialism Snack Shack. This restaurant is very special; its management is currently under renovation! Here all ingredients have been taken under the control of a small group of flavor-revolutionaries, and they will distribute these flavors evenly in all of their dishes! Coming soon: Communist Cupcakes!

"A beginner's guide to Marxism"

In subsequent lessons students produce a critique of Marxism, produce a defence of capitalism and thereby form their own independent judgment.

Image flash

Rather than just present students with an image on the screen and discuss what it might mean, provide them instead with a completely blank screen. Then tell the class that you are about to show them an image for exactly one second before discussing what they can remember about it.

Proceed to show the image for just one second and then turn the screen off again. Students have to discuss with a partner, then in groups, what details stick in their memory. There might be particular questions about the source that might be asked by the teacher ('did the image create a negative or positive impression about…?', 'when/where/by whom/for whom do you think this image was produced?' and so on). Finally, bring the image back onto the screen to determine how accurate their memories were, and to focus on remaining details which were overlooked. At this stage students can be provided with further information to help them understand it fully.

This works well for political cartoons, photographs, and works of art. The central point is that rather than look at these images from the outset at leisure, a sense of anticipation is built up and students study them briefly but with intense focus from the outset.

Taking it further

• Before showing the image, the class could be arranged in groups, with different people given a different thing to think about (**Who** is shown?, **When** was it produced?, **Why** was it produced?, **Where** was it produced?, **What** is its essential message?). After the image is shown, each student then feeds back to the rest of the group.

• Students could be challenged to sketch the picture directly after seeing it, rather than simply discuss it. These sketches could be compared with other members in the same group to produce a team version, with credit given to the team which includes the most detail and provides the best interpretation.

Unlock the box!

To encourage some out-of-classroom learning, obtain a date padlock (day / month / year) and set it to the exact date of a particular historical event. Place a sheet of information about this event inside a box, and lock it using the padlock. Place the box in a prominent place and make it clear that the first student to unlock it will be eligible for a prize.

Next, place a notice next to the locked chest informing students that a fresh clue will be provided each day hinting at the correct combination, and that the first student to crack the code should bring the contents of the box to the teacher to claim their prize.

Between Monday and Friday, at the start of morning break, add a fresh clue onto or next to the box, making it progressively easier to crack the code. The first student to open the box will obtain the information sheet and should study it before bringing it to you. Ask the successful contender a series of simple questions to test what they have learned. Award a prize if they answer correctly: sweets for each correct answer to share with friends if you run the competition every week, or a larger prize like a book token if it's a special event and if they answer all the questions successfully.

Daily : The Murder of Gandhi (1948)

Here are five clues I used in one of my recent challenges:
1. [Monday]: He was a graduate of Oxford University
2. [Tuesday]: He wrote a letter to Hitler in 1939 trying to prevent World War Two

3. [Wednesday]: The event did not take place in Europe
4. [Thursday]: He believed in the power of nonviolent resistance
5. [Friday]: The murder took place somewhere in Asia

Taking it further: Multiple Padlocks!

A second approach I have tried – and which I now prefer – involves adding several padlocks to the box. Each day, a new clue is provided, the answer to which will unlock one of the padlocks.

When the final clue is made available, any student trying to open the box has to do so in my presence and will have 60 seconds to open all of the locks. If they fail, they will not be allowed to try again for a minimum of 5 minutes: so they need to be sure to have answers ready. If they succeed, they are then asked some simple factual questions based on what they have hopefully learned by researching the answers to the puzzles. Correct answers to these questions wins the prize!

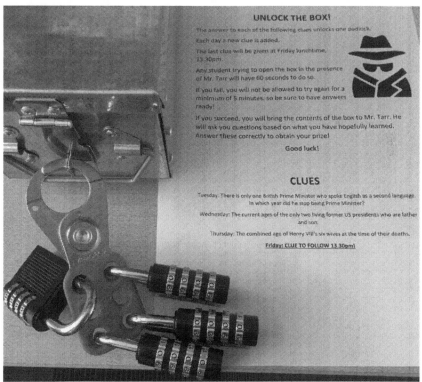

"Unlock the box!" – four clues are provided, one per day,
the answer to each one of which unlock one of the padlocks.

Time wipes

To avoid anachronism and to help students more deeply understand a particular time and place, challenge them to list key features of the modern world first and then remove all those which would have been alien to people from the earlier period.

Case study: Why was the church so popular in the Middle Ages?

Understanding the importance of religion in Early Modern Europe can be difficult for students of our modern - and increasingly secular - world to grasp. The church was not merely feared and respected due to its power over our the fate of souls; it also attracted genuine love, enthusiasm and support as the glue which bound communities together here on earth.

To illustrate this centrally important point, start the lesson (without giving the class any clue about what topic they are about to start studying) by giving students a few minutes to discuss with each other what they enjoy doing most the most in their spare time before listing all these hobbies and interests on the whiteboard.

Next, explain to the students that the next challenge is to work out how many of these would have been familiar as hobbies and pastimes in the Middle Ages. Starting with the first one on the list, the class should vote on whether they think it should stay on the board or needs to be wiped off because it was did not exist (or would not have been regarded) as a leisure activity in the Middle Ages. Some of these (computer gaming, watching TV) will be obvious; others might require more discussion.

After the "time-wipe" is finished, the board will be left with things like art, stories, food and drink, music, drama and football. At this point, tell the students that in a medieval village there was one person who was responsible for providing all of these things (and who, as a result, was very popular). After they have tried guessing who it was (the Lord of the Manor, perhaps) tell them if they fail to get the correct answer that it was in fact the parish priest. You can then go back through each of the items in the list to provide further detail:

Art	Murals, stained glass (useful teaching aids for the priest)
Music	Choir, hymns
Fashion	Everyone wore their 'Sunday best'
Feasting	Harvest festival, Church Ales
Drama	Sermons, Mumming Plays
Games	Archery, Football competitions between parishes
Holidays	Comes from "Holy Day"

To draw things together, get students to produce a poster encouraging the local villagers to "Come to Church!" which includes as many of these ideas as possible (see picture).

Taking it further

• Consider how the time-wipe approach could be used for other topics you teach. For example, older students could begin by listing all the features of modern society which help to provide and protect rights and freedoms to citizens regardless of gender, race or religion. The time-wipe could then be applied to determine how many of these were a feature of Mussolini's Italy, Stalin's Russia or the UK at the turn of the 20th century.

Sample poster produced after the 'timewipe'.

Convert an essay into a magazine article

It's always good practice for teachers to write a timed essay at the same time, and in the same conditions, as their students. In this way students can immediately appreciate that you can 'walk the walk' and not just 'talk the talk'.

Moreover, they will then be able to compare their essays, and the comments they receive, with a model piece of writing which is superb for developing their own writing with concrete feedback. To ensure that students read the essay carefully, engage them in the reading process by challenging them to convert it into a magazine article.

Case Study: The domestic policy of Richard Nixon

After writing a timed essay on the subject "Analyse the successes and failures of Nixon's domestic policies", I provide students with a model essay on my own on the same topic. After doing some of the more standard reading tasks – for example, reading the opening topic sentences, highlighting key facts, identifying any use of historiography – I then challenge them to reflect more deeply on the piece by considering how a magazine editor would take this 'raw copy' and turn it into a proper article.

I then provide students with a selection of magazines so they can look more closely at the most common features, including:

- An opinionated title
- A brief thesis statement
- Subheadings to clarify the structure
- Key quotes in marginal boxes
- A timeline
- A glossary of key terms
- Recommended further reading
- Illustrations with captions
- Footnotes with additional information

The students then proceed to pore over the article to determine what these things should consist of for the essay in question. By reading the introduction, conclusion and topic sentences, they should be able to produce an opinionated title ("Richard Nixon: The Quiet Reformer") and a thesis statement ("Russel Tarr argues that despite harsh rhetoric at a time of economic crisis, Nixon was both liberal and successful in his domestic policies"). They could also extract what they think are the most arresting statements made within some of the paragraphs and insert suitable subheadings at appropriate points.

The timeline can be constructed by identifying all the dates mentioned in the piece; the glossary can be put together after making a list of all topic-specific terminology; recommended further reading can be identified after researching the works of any historians named in the piece; and illustrations should be chosen to illustrate particular points made in the article rather than for decoration.

The end result is that students will have considered the piece from a variety of angles, engaged with it directly to turn it into a more accessible article, and thereby created for themselves a useful revision resources as well as reflecting more deeply on what constitutes good writing.

Taking it further

There are a great deal of online tools which are arguably even better. At the time of writing www.canva.com is my favourite.

Codebreaking

When studying topics involving intrigue, secrets or subterfuge, present students with the essence of the story in the form of a coded message familiar at the time. Challenge them to decode the message to engage them effectively from the outset.

Case Studies

Lady Jane Grey (Caesar Cipher)

The famous "nine days' queen" is Lady Jane Grey who briefly thwarted Mary Tudor from claiming her rightful inheritance following the death of her brother, Edward VI. When studying this curious chapter in British history, I provide students with an encoded (fictional) communication from the lead conspirator, the Duke of Northumberland (Jane's uncle) outlining that Edward has died, explaining why it's necessary to ensure the Protestant succession against the Catholic Mary given recent events, and asking for support.

The "Mid-Tudor" Period: Edward VI (1547-1553)

You are the powerful Earl of Warwick. Henry VIII died in 1547. His young son Edward then became your King. With the help of his uncle, the Duke of Somerset, he tried to turn England into a Protestant country. It is now 1553. The King has been ill for some time, and his Catholic sister – Princess Mary – is next in line to the throne. You have just had this top-secret message delivered to you! Translate it and answer the questions which follow.

From: The Duke of Northumberland, servant to King Edward VI
(Note: words might break over more than one line):

				e			a			,								e	a	t					t	e		t
ȯ	ц	A	š		ç	þ	Ÿ	!	†	þ	,		Ž	ȯ	†		š	†	ç	!	æ		Š	†	Ž	æ	ç	Œ	æ
a		t						,			a					e					t			e				
!	A	æ		ȯ	ц	A	š	.		b	!		Œ		þ	ц	ç	þ		Ž	ß		æ	ȯ	Ö	ç	†	»	ȯ	Ð
			.					a		e		a			e	a				e		e			t	e		
Ž	Œ	ц	Œ	.		ц		b	!	Ï	ç			!	Ð	†	ç	!		þ	ç		ç	¿	ç	»	ȯ	æ	ç	þ
							e			a					e			a					e					,			a		
þ	ц	Œ		ȯ	A	»	Ð	ç	.		ç	þ	Ÿ	!	†	þ		Œ	ç	ç	Ø	Ž	ȯ	†			!	A	þ
		a				e										t				a				a		e

You can quickly encode such messages using the online tool I have written for this purpose (www.activehistory.co.uk/codebreaker). I then explain to them the principle of the "Caesar Shift Cipher", which involves encoding each letter by shifting a set number of places along by a certain number of letters, looping back to the start of the alphabet if necessary (e.g. "+3" would mean A became D, Z became C and so on). The method is named after Julius Caesar, who apparently used it to communicate with his generals.

Babington Conspiracy (frequency analysis)

Later on, when students are studying the Elizabethan period, I enjoy teaching them about the Babington Conspiracy, an attempt this time to replace the rightful Queen of England with the Catholic Mary Queen of Scots. The difference here is that the code used wasn't a simple Caesar Shift (which only has 25 possible permutations and so is relatively easy to 'crack') but involved substituting each and every letter of the alphabet with a unique symbol. The possible amount of permutations is therefore: 25 X 24 X 23 X22...all the way to X1. It's good fun getting students to guess how large this number will be! To crack the code this time, students can be introduced to the concept of frequency analysis, pioneered by the Arab polymath Al-Qindi of Baghdad (800-873AD). He realised that certain letters occurred more frequently within language than others. In English, for example, "E" is the most common, followed by "T".

Therefore, the symbols in the encoded message will appear in the same proportions, and in this way the code can be cracked (a simple way to demonstrate the principle of frequency analysis is to ask everyone in the class to raise their hand if they have the letter 'E' in their name. Then get all those with a 'Z' to raise their hand).

I then proceed to give students an encoded version of the essence of Babington's murderous proposal to Mary Queen of Scots (in reality several letters were sent between them whilst she was under house arrest, which were all intercepted by Elizabeth's spymaster, Sir Francis Walsingham). The simplest way to do this is to type your message into a word processor and then choose a nonsensical font such as 'Wingdings' which will instantly create your own coded message. Give students a little while to identify the most common symbols and start to decode it. When the momentum starts to run out, give them a little hint: for example, there are only two one-letter words in English - 'A' and 'I' - so a lone symbol between two spaces must be one of those two things. Similarly, the most common words of three letters in English are 'the' and 'and'.

Samuel Pepys (shorthand)

Moving forward a little more in time once again, I love introducing students to Samuel Pepys, the great chronicler of the Great Plague and the Fire of London. The secret code he used for his wonderfully evocative diary was simply a form of shorthand, which is a brilliant skill to share with students to help them with their note-taking. I show the students first of all an image of one of the pages of his diary so they have an idea of how he wrote. I then explain how the basic principles of shorthand operate. First of all, remove all vowels from the words, unless the word starts with a vowel. In this way, the amount of writing has been substantially reduced at a stroke, and yet "y wll fnd tht th mssg is stll qt esy t undrstnd". Next, each letter is converted into a simpler symbol, and the message is then written in joined writing to create a message.

At this point, I display a message on the board using the system and challenge them to decipher it; then to write their own messages using the system and swap them around to see if they can decipher those of each other. Invariably the students get thoroughly drawn into the exercise and some of them have reported to me that they proceeded to keep a secret diary for some time afterwards using the code, and still use it to take notes during lectures. History and study skills joined up perfectly!

Taking it further

- I have limited the history of codes and codebreaking here to examples from the 16th and 17th centuries. Students could then be asked to find other examples from other periods: for example, older students could research Room 40, Britain's top secret codebreaking department in the First World War, responsible for decoding the Zimmerman Telegram which helped to bring the USA into the war.
- Similarly, the cracking of the Enigma codes by the codebreakers at Bletchley Park is a fantastic subject of study (and allows for some LGBTQ History if then expanded into a study of the life and career of the genius Alan Turing). The Navajo code talkers are another great subject of study from World War Two.
- Students could also use the study of codes in history as a way of looking at other languages and communications systems: for example Braille and Morse Codes; Mayan, Babylonian and Roman number systems; Egyptian hieroglyphs.

2

DEBATE AND DISCUSSION STRATEGIES

Questions of interpretation are the lifeblood of a lively history classroom. This chapter provides useful techniques for promoting interesting classroom discussions and vigorous debates. Some of these may even be the primary method through which the topic is studied rather than merely a concluding exercise at the end of a unit.

Socratic seminars

Classroom discussions can easily end up as teacher-talk with occasional student input. The Socratic Seminar, in contrast, puts students in control, pushes teachers to the side, generates its own momentum and produces insights which might not otherwise have emerged.

Stage 1: Set the initial reading / viewing as a homework exercise

The first step is to set an initial research task as a homework exercise, along with questions for discussion, so that the students will turn up for the session ready to contribute to discussion. For example, I recently set a viewing of "Dr Strangelove" as a homework task as part of our Cold War studies, along with some questions for consideration, including:

- Did you think that President Muffley, as portrayed in the movie, provided good leadership? (TIP: Consider what defines good leadership)
- Do you think the humour in the film underscores, or undermines, the serious message of the film? (TIP: Refer to a specific incident of humour in the film)
- Based on the lessons of history, and on the conclusions we can draw from the film, what can be done about preventing the on-going threat of nuclear holocaust? (TIP: Try to find out what attempts have been made by politicians since 1945 to address this issue so that you have a specific proposal to share).

Stage 2: Conducting the Socratic Seminar

The seminar itself proceeds in the following manner.
- The class should arrange itself into a circle.

- One student will be appointed as class moderator. This student runs the activity, interjects in discussions, and keeps track of each student's participation.
- Each student should be prepared to answer the questions that formed the homework task.
- The student moderator will begin by posing the first question to the class. Anyone willing to answer should raise their hand. Nobody can speak unless called upon to do so by the moderator. The moderator should never call on a student for a second time before recognizing another student for the first time (thereby ensuring that all students' opinions may be heard).
- Students should aim to respond to points raised by other people so that the tone of the meeting becomes more of a conversation than simply a series of isolated contributions. The moderator can facilitate this by using questions like "Has anyone got any questions for X based on what they just said? Does everyone agree with X? Would anyone like to take the point made by X any further?". The moderator should also encourage contributors to explain and substantiate their points more clearly if this is necessary.
- Students may ask one of their own questions when if allowed to do so by the moderator if discussion over the previous question has faded off and the moderator allows it.
- To keep the discussion centred on the students, the teacher may only take part in discussion to clear up a factual point or to contribute an additional question.
- Students may or may not take notes as the discussion proceeds and develop their earlier answers after the session with any fresh perspectives provided by other students.

If the class is rather large, then you can arrange two circles of students, one inside the other. The inner circle conducts the seminar. The students in the outer circle must be silent and should take notes, pass on questions and provide evidence to the speakers as they occur. Pair students together so that each 'speaker' in the inner circle has one 'supporter' in the outer circle.

Balloon debates

Balloon debates start from the premise that a hot air balloon in which we are travelling is losing height rapidly. It will soon crash into the side of a mountain unless all but one person is thrown overboard. Each person on the balloon will try to persuade the class that they deserve to be saved due to their unique importance.

Lesson 1: Students research a character and prepare their presentations

In the first lesson, each student needs to choose (or will be allocated) a character relating to the topic of study - for example, eminent Victorians or the greatest women in history. Names can be allocated randomly to the students using the www.classtools.net Random Name Picker. Each student should then be given a template which they can use to frame their research:

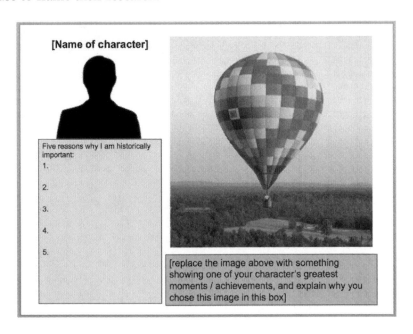

> *Note: Defining "Importance"*
> To be historically important, a person must do some or all of the following:
> When? Had an impact both in the short- and the long-term
> Who? Had an impact on a lot of people's lives
> Where? Had an impact over many countries
> What? Had an impact on many areas of life

Lesson 2: Conducting the Balloon Debate

A. Getting Ready for the First Round – focusing on 'positives'
- Give the students 10 minutes to refresh their memories and to revise the material.
- Get the presentations saved into a public area of the school network so they can be shown on the whiteboard.

B. Round one of the debate – focusing on 'positives'
- Four or five randomly selected students stand at the front of the class. The first student's presentation is displayed on the screen. The student is not allowed to read the slide – it's there only for the benefit of the audience – and they can only speak for a limited amount of time (two minutes is usually enough), explaining what they did and why they deserve to stay in the balloon.
- At the end of their speech, invite questions from the audience. These can be answered directly, or (more likely) the student concerned can nominate a 'researcher' to make a note of these questions and immediately start finding the answers to them.
- Repeat this format for the other four students.
- Go back to each of the nominated 'researchers', one after the other, to get answers to the questions raised during the debate.
- Each member of the audience then has to vote for just one character to be thrown out of the balloon.
- The two characters who get the most votes are then eliminated from the competition (more can be eliminated if you wish, depending on the size of the class and the time available).
- This process is repeated with the remaining people in the class.

C. Getting ready for the final round of the debate – focusing on 'negatives'

- Each finalist now works with a team consisting of the people they defeated in the first round of the debate.
- Their task is to gather evidence against the other finalists, for example suggesting that they were insignificant or corrupt.
- In this way, the focus of the whole debate is changed, everybody remains engaged, and the final will not merely consist of rehearsing the same old points a second time!

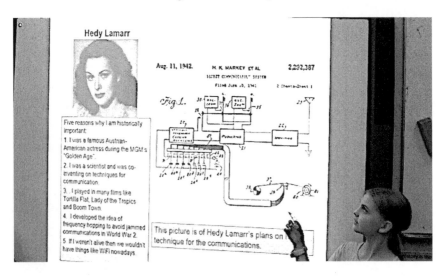

D. The final round of the debate – focusing on 'negatives'

- The finalists should line up at the front of the class.
- The first finalist should explain why the person to their left does not deserve to stay in the balloon. The person criticised in this way should be given a chance to respond before they in turn criticise the person to their left. The person at the end of the line should criticise the person who started the discussion.
- The audience then has to vote who should be thrown out. It is important that they don't vote for who should stay in – because there is too much of a tendency for students to vote in favour of the finalist whose team they belong to.
- The 'two hands / one hand" voting system works well here: in this format, students raise two hands (i.e. two votes against) their least favourite character, and one hand against the second

least-favoured. This makes for a slightly more sophisticated voting outcome.

E. Written outcomes

As a written "outcome" you could get students to answer the questions:

- Who were the last three people to survive in the balloon, and why were they considered so important?
- How could you argue that your character was more important than any one of the three finalists?

Taking it further

- Get students to make a mask to wear during the debate. An image of the character's face, scaled up to fill the page and printed out on A4, is the ideal size.
- Students could produce a Diamond 9 diagram (page 167) ranking the importance of different characters.
- Students could produce a 'Paper People' project (page 134) to connect the various characters discussed during the debate.

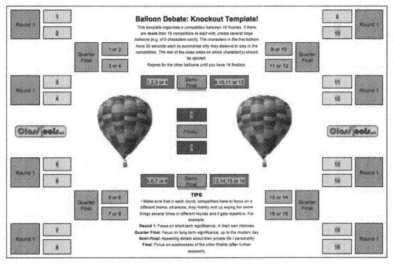

Template available at www.tarrstoolbox.net

Silent discussion

This helps conduct close reading of detailed sources, which are placed at different points around the room. Students move between the sources in pairs, in silence, annotating with observations, questions and answers to help them answer a key question.

Stage 1: Analysing the first source

Prior to the lesson, the teacher will print off a range of sources and place them on different tables. The class will be divided into pairs, and each pair will be directed to a different table with a different source.

2 minutes: Each pair of students reads their source in silence.

3 minutes: Still in silence, students annotate their sources by underlining key phrases and either making observations, or asking questions, in the margin. Each partner can answer these questions if they wish. During this time, the teacher will move between the groups jotting down further questions and writing brief answers.

Stage 2: Moving around the other sources

All pairs will now be moved around the class to look at a different source. Repeat Stage 1 for as long as time allows. At the end of the process the teacher will lead a discussion about what has been learned. The completed sheets should be put on display where they can be compared. Students should consolidate by answering the key question for discussion.

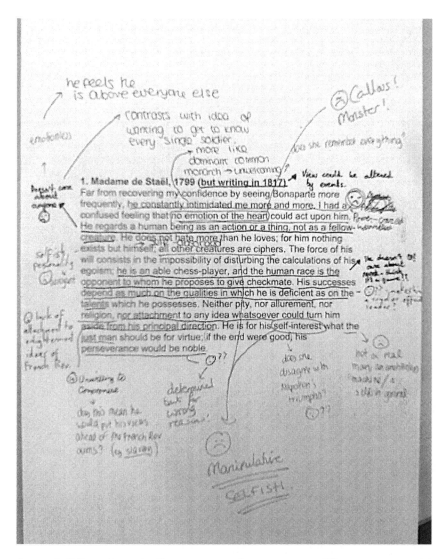

A sample "silent discussion" outcome: students annotate different sources with positive and negative observations about Napoleon, and also ask questions about such things as the reliability of the witnesses. Subsequent students can then answer those questions and react to the earlier observations.

Case Study: Vietnam war protest songs

As part of an investigation into the domestic causes for the US withdrawal from the Vietnam War, I print out and spread around the room the lyrics of a dozen or songs, such as "Eve of Destruction" by Barry McGuire, "For What It's Worth" by Buffalo Springfield and "Universal Soldier" by Buffy Saint Marie.

Students then engage in the silent discussion activity, annotating the sources, asking questions and answering those raised by other students as the exercise proceeds. I usually have the ClassTools timer on the screen (www.classtools.net/timer) which rings an alarm every two minutes to prompt the students to move to the next source.

At the end of the process, when students have had time to consider all of the lyrics, I then ask them to stand next to the song lyrics that they found the most insightful, and we then discuss some of those songs which have the largest clusters of students around them.

Next comes my favourite part of the exercise: I ask students to anticipate what style of music they expect each song to be in (rock? Folk? Pop? Soul? Jazz?) and then I play extracts from each one using Spotify or YouTube.

Finally, after considering both the quality of the lyrics for each song and the appeal of its music, students vote for what they consider to be the best songs overall. I then create a playlist and share it.

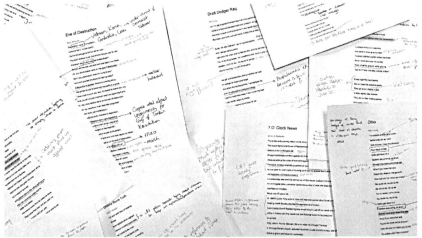

Vietnam War protest songs analysed as part of a 'silent discussion'.

Mysterious moments

This approach engages students at the beginning of a lesson and generates some interesting questions. It involves giving students an intriguing, mysterious and deliberately incomplete story based on the study topic by taking away key details, then challenging teams to ask yes/no questions to the teacher to fill the gaps and deduce what is going on.

Points are awarded to the team which first mentions keywords identified in advance by the teacher and which thereby demonstrate that they are edging towards the complete story. Finally, each student is asked to produce their own fuller account of the story, including all of the key words, using a range of sources provided by the teacher, as well as an answer to the question "What do you think historians use this event to illustrate?".

Case study: the US civil rights struggle

Start by nominating up to three "judges". Divide the rest of the class into two teams. Then proceed to read out the "Mysterious Moment":

> "In 1954, a 14-year old from out of town entered a shop: even though his friends begged him not to. The person behind the counter was deeply upset by what then happened and told her family about it. At the funeral several weeks later, attended by hundreds of people and reported nationally, the coffin was left open for everyone to look inside. Nobody went to jail".

The teacher should then conduct a discussion to gather answers to the query "What are the most intriguing questions arising from this story?". These might include, in this case, "Why were the teenager's friends so desperate that he didn't enter the shop?", "What happened that upset the person behind the counter?", "Why did the funeral only take place several weeks later?", "Whose funeral was it?", "Why was the coffin left open?".

The next step is for each group to frame questions that can only be answered with a 'yes' or a 'no' to start obtaining the most important answers to these queries. For example, "Why did nobody go to jail as a result of this story?" could be converted into "Is it the case that nobody went to jail because no crime had been committed?"

Whilst these questions are being framed, the judge(s) should be finding the answers to some of the key questions identified earlier using sources provided by the teacher or by using the internet. If they have time they should also start considering the question "What do you think historians use this event to illustrate?"

After a few minutes, when each team has had time to frame its questions, the first team asks a question designed to draw out a further key detail of the story. The judge(s) will answer this question with "Yes" or "No". In addition, if the question itself contains one of the key words or phrases decided in advance by the teacher, the team wins a point for getting closer to the final, completed story. In the given example, the keywords might be:

Murder   **Racism**   **Black**   **USA**   **Shock**   **Corruption**

This process continues, with each team taking it in turn to ask its questions, until they have run out of questions, all the key words have been correctly identified, or the teacher decides enough time has been taken.

Finally, each team is invited to provide its overall conclusion on what they think happened before the judges give bonus points to the team who came closest to the truth. The full list of key words can then be displayed so they can reflect on whether they appear to be on the right track.

The judges can then share the complete story as far as they know it, or alternatively the teacher can set this as a independent research exercise (in this instance, the infamous case of Emmett Till).

To round off the classroom-based part of the activity, the teacher should lead a discussion – starting with the judges – around the question "What do you think historians use this event to illustrate?".

Taking it further

- The judge(s) could be invited to add further key words to the initial list as part of their preparation phase using their research to help. These might be a lot more specific and unlikely to be guessed in advance. However, the purpose they serve is that all these key words will need to be included in the final account of the completed story produced by each student following the exercise. Alternatively, the teacher can provide these words as part of the original list:

"Bye, Baby"   **Mississippi**   **Moses Wright**   **civil rights**

Other examples

A particularly great thing about the "mysterious moment" approach is how quickly it can be put together. All you need to do is identify an memorable moment within a topic, reduce the story to its bare essentials, decide what additional terms are needed to bring the story to a point of comprehension, and you're ready to go. For example, consider the following:

> "Following the Pope's orders, the King took off his robes and dressed in a rough tunic made of sack cloth. He then walked barefoot through the cobbled streets until he reached the cathedral. When he arrived, he fell to his knees and was then whipped three times by each of the 80 monks at the Cathedral. He then had to spend the night sleeping in the crypt of the Cathedral before returning home to his palace"
> *(Key terms: Henry II / Becket / Canterbury / Excommunicated / Murder / Knights / "Will nobody rid me of this troublesome priest?")*

> "Sir John Franklin sails abroad from England on an expedition. He is highly experienced, but his entire expedition vanishes without trace. Ten years later a woman pays a private investigator to find out what happened. When he returns, his conclusions are so shocking that she accuses him of being a liar. Over 100 years later scientists dug up a body buried at the scene – still perfectly preserved - and conducted tests which shockingly confirmed that the investigator was right all along"

(Key terms: Arctic / Poison / Innuit / Permafrost / Cannibalism / HMS Terror / HMS Erebus).

To try out the technique for yourself, consider constructing your own "Mysterious Moment" exercise based around one of the following ideas or any other questions appropriate to your studies:

- Why did Nero commit suicide?
- Why did Archbishop Cranmer thrust his own hand into the fire?
- Why did Pepys bury his cheese?
- How did the War of Jenkins' Ear get its name?
- Why did Rossetti dig up the body of his dead wife?
- Why did Virginia Woolf dress up in a beard and say 'bunga bunga'?
- How did the War of the Stray Dog get its name?
- Why was Charlie Chaplin not allowed to return to the USA?
- Why did Lenin end up embalmed?

Students as teachers, not presenters

Consider ditching the word 'presentation' in favour of 'mini-lesson'. Instead of standing passively at the front of the class reading a PowerPoint slide, each student is instead required to engage the other students in some sort of activity, task or exercise to teach the class about the topic.

I adopted this approach with my historians during their study of "What was the most significant event of the 20th Century?". The closing phase of this unit involves each student researching a topic for themselves, then traditionally turning this into an imaginary DVD documentary inlay (a template for which can be downloaded from www.tarrstoolbox.net). On this occasion, though, I asked each student instead to prepare a plan and accompanying materials for a mini-lesson lasting 10-15 minutes. I made it clear that these would be collected in and marked, and that the best five would form the basis of a one-hour lesson run by the winning students.

Taking it further

An additional bonus of this approach, which I did not immediately anticipate, is that it is a great way to get students thinking about what makes a good lesson, and the sort of thought and effort that goes into lesson preparation by their teachers. I gave the class ten minutes to discuss in groups what lessons - from any subject - particularly stuck in their memory, and why. We came up with such things as the element of competition; team work; a hands-on practical exercise; incentives and rewards; a clear outcome; and so on. The discussion was very valuable not just for the students but also for me, since it provided some great ideas about what my colleagues around the school did to engage their students in lessons which I could emulate.

Put the teacher on trial

This method motivates students to conduct vigorous research in preparation for a debate about the success or failure of a particular individual. The incentive is that the teacher will be on trial as a historical character (e.g. Henry VIII, Louis XVI, Neville Chamberlain) defending his or her reputation in the 'court of history' against a prosecuting team made up of students in the class.

This trial can be conducted either as a way of revising and consolidating topic knowledge at the end of a unit, or as an intensive means of studying the topic for the very first time.

Sample motions:
- Napoleon betrayed the spirit of the French Revolution
- Stalin betrayed the spirit of communism
- Chamberlain pursued appeasement due to spinelessness

Stage 1: students prepare their case
Each student will be given responsibility for a particular area of policy (e.g. women's rights, economic development, religion) and should try to discover a key piece of evidence that can be used to condemn the character in question. It may be the case that several students will be allocated the same policy; in this case, they can compare their findings later and decide upon who has the strongest evidence to use in the trial. This can then be turned into a question in the following "Is it not true that..." format:

Sample questions:
- "Herr Hitler, is it not true that your policies towards women were sexist, as proven by the fact that the League of German Maidens taught girls that their role in life was 'Kinder, Kirche, Küche'?"

- "Comrade Stalin, is it not true that your Five Year Plans betrayed communist principles, as proven by the fact that you offered cash incentives to the best workers via the Stakhanovite scheme?"

If time allows, each question should be accompanied by an 'exhibit' in the form of source material – for example a written extract, political cartoon, or statistics.

Stage 2: the teacher in the dock

Ideally, the teacher should collect in the questions prior to the lesson, and collate these in a worksheet so that students can easily take notes as the trial proceeds without having to worry about writing down each question. More to the point, it allows the teacher some time to prepare their defence!

Each student should proceed to ask their question, and the teacher should give a vigorous response to it – for example, the evidence provided by the questioner might be incomplete or unreliable. Students should take notes as appropriate.

Stage 3: the verdict

Because the students have been in full 'prosecution' mode, they are unlikely to deliver an 'innocent' verdict under any circumstances! To combat this problem, tell the students that they need to decide the charges on which the accused is least guilty. For example, if the charges focused on five different counts (e.g. religion, economics, society, politics, military affairs) then each member of the class will raise two hands for the issue where evidence of guilt appears weakest, and one hand for the second-weakest area. These votes can then be added up and the charges ranked in terms of how convincing the case against the accused appears to be. I find this works better than asking students to vote for the most guilty areas – in these cases, they inevitable vote strongly for the area they campaigned for in the trial and the results become rather predictable.

Stage 4: the judgment

Each student should conclude the exercise by producing a write-up answering the key question. For older students this will most likely be in the form of an essay.

Ditch debates, adopt arbitration

The adversarial nature of a standard debate often leads to an unsatisfactory stalemate or a simplistic declaration for or against a given motion. By moving instead to an arbitration format, students are challenged to construct a synthesis from the best points made by each side.

Overview of the traditional group debate

Classroom debates can be an effective way of getting students to think about the pros and cons of different viewpoints ("Was Hitler a planner or a gambler in foreign affairs?", "Henry VIII: Hero or Villain?"). The standard way I do this is to divide the class into two teams (the 'prosecution' and the 'defence'). Each member of each team gathers evidence for one side of the argument, then converts this into a question for their opponents ("Is it not true that...which is illustrated by the fact that..."). The best questions are then allocated to members of the opposing team at the end of the lesson, with homework time being set aside for them to formulate their rebuttals (based usually on the fact that the evidence behind the question is either incomplete or unreliable). The debate then takes place in a subsequent lesson, with the teacher acting as a chairperson and everybody busy taking notes as the debate unfolds.

Problems of this approach

The sorts of debates outline above are rigorous, engaging and thorough - but they have their limitations.

- Firstly, they can be slow to conduct (notes need to be taken by all students as the debate proceeds, which takes time).
- Secondly, the adversarial nature of a debate does not lend itself to a reasoned, synthesised conclusion – indeed, there is a danger that students could end up with the death-knell, fence-sitting judgment that "there are arguments on both sides".

The solution: arbitration, not debate

With these problems in mind, I sometimes adopt a slightly different approach which is both quicker, and more sophisticated in terms of the conclusions produced.

Step 1: Create a fresh team of 'adjudicators'

In the first lesson - the research and preparation phase - create three equally sized teams rather than just two: the prosecution and defence are now joined by a team of arbitrators. A central question like "Was Hitler a gambler or a planner in foreign affairs?" is broken down into several issues for consideration ("did Hitler's speeches suggest he was a planner rather than a gambler?", "do his actions demonstrate purpose rather than drift?", "have historians since agreed that he was a planner rather than a gambler?"). Each of these issues is allocated to a team of three people, consisting of one member of the defence, one member of the prosecution, and one adjudicator.

While the members of the defence and prosecution teams are busy gathering their evidence and formulating their questions for their allocated issue, the arbitrators are responsible for anticipating the arguments and counter-arguments on each side, and working towards a synthesis position which they hope both sides will be happy to accept (for this reason, it's best if the adjudicators are the more able members of the class).

Step 2: intimate arbitration, not open debate!

In the second lesson (the debate phase), the format of the discussion is made much more efficient by getting each team of three (prosecution, defence and adjudicator) to conduct their debates simultaneously and on separate tables. Each adjudicator listens to the questions asked by each side to the other, and to the answers provided, and makes notes. Then, with the debate element over, the adjudicator works with the pair of them to design a synthesis statement which both sides are happy to accept (e.g. "Although Hitler's speeches create an impression of drift and inconsistency, these were deliberately designed to throw up a diplomatic smokescreen around his naked ambition to ensure that the appeasers continued giving in to his demands").

In this way, with all of the issues being debated all at once and with the objective being a reasoned judgment rather than the mere 'victory' of one argument over another, the process is not only made much more efficient, but much more intellectually sophisticated.

Step 3: The adjudicators confer and conclude
In the closing phase of the process, which usually takes place in a third and final lesson after the adjudicators have polished their judgments, all of the adjudicators sit around one central table and start talking through their findings one by one, with the teacher acting as a chairperson. The rest of the class are not allowed to speak, but should make detailed notes from what each adjudicator says about what the thesis made by the prosecution, the antithesis made by the defence, and the synthesis reached thereafter. Each of these discussions should take no more than a few minutes. If any member of the rest of the class wishes to contribute, they are only permitted to do so by passing a note to the adjudicator who was in their original team of three.

Taking it further

This approach could be used as an alternative or a follow-up to a balloon debate (page 58). Instead of the objective being to find an overall winner in a balloon debate (for example, on 'Who was the greatest figure of the Industrial Revolution?'), teams of people could sit around a table and find try a statement which acknowledges how all deserve to be regarded as winners but in different ways ("In the short term...but in the longer term...and for women especially...").

Chat-show challenges

Substantiating assertions with evidence is a crucial skill for young historians to develop. The "chat-show challenge" forces them to do so by drawing them in an apparently simple "yes/no" question, then throwing them out of their comfort zone by immediately demanding that they justify their answer with a second, connected question.

Case study: the Middle East crisis

Step 1: Framing the questions in advance of the lesson

Few subjects are as contentious as the Middle East crisis, which makes it all the more important that students clearly substantiate their viewpoints with reasoned arguments and carefully selected evidence. After studying the roots of the conflict, I therefore constructed a series of "Yes/No" questions covering different aspects of the topic. I then produced two accompanying questions to follow each one designed to force students to explain their reasoning in more depth:

Initial Question	Follow-up question	
	If they answer "no"...	If they answer "yes"...
The Jews were promised territory in the Balfour Declaration, but were not then given it. Do you agree that the British acted dishonorably?	How do you justify the fact that the British promised territory to these people when they needed their help, then abandoned them directly afterwards?	Aren't you being naïve here? The British were fighting a war of survival against Germany, and made promises to both sides which simply couldn't be fulfilled.
Do you agree that the Holocaust established the unquestionable necessity to create the state of Israel to protect Jewish interests?	How can you argue that the deaths of 6 million innocent civilians at the hands of the Nazis didn't prove that state of Israel was an urgent necessity?	But the Holocaust was the responsibility of Europeans, not Arabs in the Middle East. So how can you argue that the creation of Israel in the Middle East wasn't a gross injustice against the Arabs?

Do you agree that the Arabs were right to reject the UNSCOP partition plan?	But the Arabs completely rejected the UNSCOP proposals and massed armies on the borders of Israel even before its declaration of independence. So how can you say they're not responsible?	But the Jews had been responsible for terrorist atrocities in Palestine (Irgun, Stern Gang) and UNSCOP offered half the territory even though they only had a third of the population. Wasn't this the real act of war against the Arabs?

Step 2: Conducting the "Chat-show challenge"

With these questions now ready (along with others framed around the 1948 Civil War, the 1956 Suez Crisis, the 1967 Six-Day War and so on), the activity can commence. The first "initial question" is read out to the class and copied down by each student. They then reflect on their answer individually and in silence, and simply write down "yes" or "no".

Students then raise their hands to indicate how they voted (merely to indicate the popularity of each point of view). Then display the "follow-up" questions on the board and instruct students to copy down the one which applies to their response.

Repeat this process for the remaining "initial questions", then give students class or homework time to frame their developed responses to the follow-up questions. The best "Chat-show" dialogues could then be acted out in a subsequent lesson, with the rest of the class acting as a studio audience or a press corps taking detailed notes.

Taking it further

- To improve upon the format further, students could be given classroom time to 'pair up' with somebody else who took the same "yes/no" position for the first question to brainstorm possible responses to the follow-up question.
- Students could also be instructed to write each of their follow-up responses in the format "Although…Nevertheless…". In this way, they are forced to display an awareness of a merit in the argument they disagree with before proceeding to argue their own position.

Tell us something we don't know!

As a fresh way of motivating students to acquire and effectively share their knowledge and understanding, challenge them to "Tell us something we don't know!" in a quiz format.

Essentially, each team of students has to take it in turns to provide a fresh piece of knowledge, understanding or evaluation to answer a set question and score a point, with the teams contributing the most therefore winning the overall competition. This approach works well as a way of encouraging students to conduct some detailed research ahead of a lesson, but equally well as a revision strategy leading up to the examinations.

Case study: the origins of World War Two

To conduct the game, start by giving all the students a homework requiring them to find answers to central examination-style questions. I set each the students three increasingly challenging questions, each one building upon the other, in the following format:

- **DESCRIBE** ("What were the main events leading up to Hitler taking over the Sudetenland?")
- **EXPLAIN** ("Why did Hitler face so little opposition when he took over the Sudetenland?")
- **ASSESS** ("How far do the events of the Sudetenland Crisis demonstrate that Hitler was a gambler, not a planner, in foreign affairs?")

When the students return to class, they are divided into teams of three or four students. We then proceed with the quiz, with each student instructed to take notes as the game proceeds (alternatively, the teacher could act as scribe and make notes in a word processor, projected on the screen, and share it with students afterwards as revision material).

Round 1: "Describe"

In this round, each team can provide one fact for one point, or pass if they have no ideas. The process continues until no team has any further points to make. Everyone makes notes as the story proceeds, putting notes into the correct order, then writes up their findings afterwards.

As this is an 'events' question, a valuable added twist is that after the first two events, teams could be awarded a bonus point if they can state an event which took place *before* the event nominated by the previous team but *after* the one that immediately precedes it in the timeline that is building up. In other words, it pays for each team to start with the earliest events and move forwards as steadily and logically as they can, so that this round allows all students to see the story develop, step-by-step, in a logical chronology as far as possible.

Here's an example of what my 14-year old students produced, with no prior knowledge before their homework on this topic was set:

What were the main events leading up to the Anschluss with Austria?
• The Treaty of Versailles had forbidden any alliance between Germany and Austria.
• In addition, Austria lost half of its land after World War One (in the Treaty of St. Germain) and the prospect of unity with Germany became more appealing.
• In 1934, Hitler planned to invade Austria but backed down when Mussolini sent troops to the Brenner Pass.
• In 1936 the Rome-Berlin Axis was formed between Germany and Italy which removed the threat of Italian opposition to Anschluss.
• Hitler encouraged the Nazis in Austria to campaign for a plebiscite to secure an Anschluss. Austrian police later discovered Nazi plans for an invasion of Austria, which outraged Schuschnigg and led to him demanding a meeting with Hitler.
• In Feb. 1938 Chancellor Schuschnigg visited Hitler to try persuading him to bring the Austrian Nazis under control.
• Hitler bullied Schuschnigg at this meeting into accepting 10 demands including the appointment of leading Austrian Nazi Seyss-Inquart as a member of the government.
• Schuschnigg returned to Austria, then called a plebiscite to try to undermine Hitler's claim that most Austrians wanted an Anschluss.
• Hitler threatens violent action and hurriedly draws up proper invasion plans at short notice; Schuschnigg resigns.
• The President of Austria appointed a new, Nazi-friendly Chancellor, who cancelled the plebiscite and also invited the Nazis in to 'restore order'.
• Hitler sent troops into Austria to take the country over and announced unexpectedly – after a predictable triumph in a new Nazi-organised referendum – that Austria will now be incorporated into the Reich.

Round 2: "Explain"

Each team provides one reason (substantiated with evidence) for two points, add a further point of information to substantiate an existing reason for one point, or pass if they have no ideas. The process continues until no team has any further points to make. Everyone makes notes as the story proceeds, then writes up their findings afterwards. In this instance, my students came up with the following:

Why did Hitler encounter so little resistance when he absorbed Austria into the Third Reich?
One reason is because the Treaty of Versailles was considered too harsh on Germany: for example its economy had been badly destabilised by the reparations bill of £6.6 billion, Britain and France in particular were keen to make amends in a policy known as 'appeasement': this included being more open to a closer union between Austria and Germany for their mutual benefit.

A second reason is because the Austrians themselves were keen on the idea: they had lost half of their land after World War One and had been left landlocked (in the Treaty of St. Germain) and the prospect of unity with Germany became more appealing. In addition, the Austrians had been unified with the Germans for hundreds of years during the time of the Holy Roman Empire so there was a strong cultural link between the two countries and Hitler himself was Austrian.

Finally, because Britain, Italy and France had been neutralised: in the case of Britain, the Anglo-German Naval Agreement had taken the sting out of British opposition to the Nazis, and the Rome-Berlin Axis had made an ally of Italy. These events destroyed the Stresa Pact and left France neutralised as a result – especially as at this point France didn't even have a government following a political crisis.

Round 3: "Assess"

In each round, the first team provides one argument (substantiated with evidence) for one side of the argument, to win two points. The next team has to do the same for the opposite side of the argument, or pass if they have no ideas. The process continues until ideas are exhausted, with the final answer looking something like this:

To what extent do events in Austria show Hitler was a gambler rather than a planner?
How he was a 'gambler:' Hitler had already attempted but had failed: He had ordered Austrian Nazis to cause chaos in Austria in an attempt to overthrow the government. Italy also sent troops to the Austrian border whilst following the terms of the agreement with Austria to protect each other from outside aggression. Hitler hadn't even told his closest advisors: they were only told he wanted the Austrian government to appoint Nazis into the government and undermining their independence. He was bold, and kept his nerve: he threatened to invade Austria despite the fact that his generals told him that they had not got any invasion plans drawn out and on hand.

How he was a 'planner': Hitler made and alliance with Italy in advance: The Rome-Berlin axis was made in 1936 to ensure that Italy wouldn't risk attacking Germany once again like she'd done in Hitler's first attempt of Anschluss in 1934. In addition, he sent Philip of Hesse to smooth things over with Mussolini, who was thanked by Hitler directly afterwards in a personal telegram. The idea of expanding eastward had already been talked about in Mein Kampf: the autobiography expressing Hitler's desire to unite Germany with his birth country, Austria.

Taking it further

- Get students to design their own 'exam questions from hell' rather than provide these to the students in advance (page 245).

Protest placards: design, anticipate, react

When studying an issue, event or personality which is open to different interpretations, get students to design a placard summarising their own viewpoints. Alternatively, ask students to suggest how particular historians or observers would summarise their position in just a few words, or to anticipate the actual slogans of genuine protest groups.

Case study: the March on Washington

Present students with a blanked-out photograph of demonstrators involved in the "March on Washington" made famous by Dr. Martin Luther King's "I have a dream" speech.

Ask the class to anticipate what sorts of slogans might be on the placards based on their existing background knowledge. Discuss in small groups and as a class before showing the students the actual slogans. Alternatively, if there is more time available, put students in role as different types of people involved in the event. They need to discuss their different concerns and objectives, and agree on a 'joined up' campaign which will only use a maximum of three central slogans on its placards.

Taking it further

- Students could be asked to consider what sorts of slogans opponents of the marchers might put onto their placards. In the case of the March on Washington, figures in the emerging Black Power movement such as Malcolm X could be considered.
- As well as considering how the slogans might change depending on who was writing them, consider too how it might depend on where they are being written (different cities or even countries) and when they are being written (to highlight interpretations over time).
- Students could actually produce mini-placards for a classroom display, with further detail and explanation on the reverse of each one.

American suffragettes – what would their banner say?

Brilliance or baloney?

To help students substantiate their judgments on central issues, present them with snappy assertions and then challenge teams of students to explain, using evidence, why they think it is convincing ("brilliance!") or weak ("baloney!").

Case study: foreign policy of American presidents

As part of our revision for History of the Americas, my students conducted a series of debates on the successes and failures of US Presidents between 1945-1980. To round things off, I formulated a series of concluding statements overnight about each president. I then organised the class into three teams (A, B, C) ready for an arbitration exercise, and each team was then shown which statements it would need to focus on using this table:

Statement to consider: Brilliance, or Baloney?	Teams involved		
	A	B	C
In foreign policy, Truman talked tough but acted weak	X	X	
Truman's policy in Korea was restrained and pragmatic		X	X
Ike's foreign policy was neither new, nor successful	X		X
JFK deserves outright condemnation, not fawning credit, for his handling of the Cuban Missile Crisis	X	X	
JFK never would have got embroiled in Vietnam in the same way as did his successor		X	X
LBJ's policy in Vietnam has overshadowed his other, much more successful diplomatic achievements	X		X
LBJ deserves credit, not condemnation, for trusting the advice of his 'Wise Men'	X	X	
Nixon was the most visionary of all the post-war Presidents		X	X
Nixon was inconsistent and unpredictable in equal measure	X		X

Preparation phase

Each team is then given time in class (which could be homework) to (a) decide whether they agree with the statement or not and (b) gather substantiating evidence to support their judgment. Depending upon the time available, this can be done collaboratively, or different members of each team could focus on different statements and then share their ideas with their groups before the feedback phase for comments and suggestions. Finally, these ideas are written up neatly in a presentation slide.

Presentation phase

Starting with the first statement, Team "A" declares whether they regard it as 'brilliance' or 'baloney' and proceeds to explain why, with their presentation slide on display.

Team "B" then presents its thoughts on the same issue (again, with their slide on display – thereby ensuring that they don't simply 'steal' specific points from the first team in their presentation if they happened to be in broad agreement).

Finally, the third team aims to come up with a synthesis statement. At this stage they could plot a number '1' on a continuum line to indicate how strongly they regard the first statement as being 'brilliance' or 'baloney' and everyone should have a moment to jot down some notes before proceeding to the next statement.

Taking it further

- Get the teams themselves to prepare the statements in advance of the lesson. Statements from team "A" should be answered by "B" and "C", statements by "B" will be answered by "A" and "C" and so statements by "C" will be answered by the "A" and "B" teams.
- Divide the continuum line so that it runs from "Baloney!" at one end, "Brilliance!" at the other, with "Borderline!" in the middle. Challenge the class to come up with suitable adjectives beyond these three which can be placed along the line at appropriate points to develop their vocabulary further (the student vocabulary bookmark might be useful in this context – see page 307).

Guess the statistics

Convert key statistics into a quiz which challenges the class to guess what the numbers will be. Give a score to each student based on how close their answers were to the actual figures.

To do this, present students with a list of questions which will have statistics as their answers. After they have guessed the statistic for all the questions, students should be told the correct answer for the first question. They then calculate the difference between their guess, and the correct answer. This process is repeated for the other questions. Students are then asked to add up the sum total of the figures in the 'difference' column, with the student gaining the lowest score being the overall class winner.

Case study 1: How popular was appeasement on the eve of World War Two?

The example shown here was used at the end of a study of the Causes of World War Two and the reasons for appeasement. It is a particularly effective way to help students determine how much popularity the policy of appeasement enjoyed with the British public.

Question from Mass Observation	Option	Your Guess	Actual Figure	Difference
"Should Britain promise assistance to Czechoslovakia if Germany acts as it did towards Austria?" (Asked March 1938 at the start of the Sudeten Crisis)	Yes			
	No			
	No opinion			
"Hitler says that he has no more territorial ambitions in Europe. Do you believe him?" (Asked October 1938 shortly after the Munich Agreement)	Yes			
	No			

Is the British government right in following a policy giving guarantees to preserve the independence of small European states? (Asked April 1939 after Hitler had invaded Czechoslovakia)	Yes				
	No				
TOTAL SCORE (the lower the better!)					

The completed teacher version can be downloaded at www.tarrstoolbox.net

It is particularly worthwhile after completing the exercise to ask students which results particularly surprised them, and discuss why they were unexpected given their contextual knowledge; other students who guessed these same statistics more accurately could use their background knowledge to argue the opposite position.

Case study 2: How revolutionary was the Industrial Revolution?

This example shown below provides a particularly good illustration of the value of following up one of these exercises with a debrief. Starting with 'Population', I ask the class to guess what the figure will be in 1750 before telling them the correct answer (11 million). Then, working with a partner, they have to guess what the figure will be in 1900.

I start by asking them to decide first whether the number will go up, or down, compared to 1750. Then, they need to decide after discussion with their partner what they guess will be the answer, and why. This process is repeated for the other points in the list (the issue of public health – will it improve, or degenerate? – tends to divide opinion quite drastically and changes scores pretty suddenly, so I leave this one till last to build up some tension).

	Britain 1750	**Britain 1900**		
	(from teacher)	**Your guess**	**Actual figure**	**Difference**
Population: Millions of people in Britain				

Transport: How many days to travel from London > Edinburgh				
Work: Percentage of people living in towns				
Politics: Percentage of male adults with the vote				
Education Number of universities				
Health: Deaths per 1000 people per year				
Total (lowest score in class wins!)				

The completed teacher version can be downloaded at www.tarrstoolbox.net

Taking it further

- At the end of the exercise, instruct students to stand up as soon as they have calculated their overall score. Once the whole class is standing, count downwards from a high number in increments of ten or more as appropriate, and instruct students to sit down when the number announced is lower than their own score. The last person left standing is the overall winner and could be asked to explain how they reached their deductions on each of the answers they provided.

- After completing the 'quiz' element of this activity, ensure that students are given time to write a full answer which tries to explain the statistics in question rather than merely describe them ("What was the attitude of the British public towards appeasement? How do we explain this?", "What changed during the Industrial Revolution, and why?").

- Get students to convert the statistics they now have into infographics (page 117) or a "Rice above the statistics" display (page 272).

Sticky notes for silent presentations

To help students exchange their research findings in a particularly time-efficient way, ask each of them to summarise their points on a sticky note. With these attached to their heads, students silently circulate around the classroom taking notes from each other.

Case study: peace treaties after World War One

After concluding a detailed depth study of the Treaty of Versailles imposed upon Germany after World War One, it is challenging to maintain enthusiasm for a further in-depth study of the peace treaties dealing with the other Central Powers. My approach to this is to provide students with a list of points about how nine other countries were created by or otherwise impacted upon by the treaties (e.g. Turkey, Yugoslavia, Poland, Czechoslovakia). These points sweep across the entire twentieth century to provide a genuinely broad-brush approach to history.

Students are then challenged to categorise these in terms of positives and negatives, split 100% between "success" and "failure" as appropriate, then answer the question "How far did the peace treaties after Great War make the world more stable?".

However, as a critical part of this process I also produce a long list of further questions relating to each of these nine countries, and students choose one each to research further. Some of these are closed questions, and some much more open, so that students can choose one that suits their abilities. Some examples include:

- Why were the allies keen to recreate Poland in 1919?
- Would the multinational nature of Yugoslavia be a strength or a weakness?
- Why do you think the breakup of Czechoslovakia was more peaceful than that of Yugoslavia?
- Why did the Palestinians regard the creation of Israel with despair?
- What attempts have been made to solve the Arab-Israeli crisis?

- Why were the British so keen to have Iraq as a mandate?

Although all students make relatively detailed notes providing an answer to their question, they are then challenged at the start of the next lesson to summarise the most interesting or important point on a sticky note, then attach this to their heads.

Next, each student reads out to the class the question that they have been researching so that the all students can prioritise who they want to learn from by deciding which questions they find most intriguing. All students then have 10 or 15 minutes to silently wander around the class with a clipboard taking notes from what they can read from the sticky notes. This makes for quite a novel experience as students quickly learn that as soon as another student wishes to take notes from them, they are well advised to take notes from this partner at the same time rather than simply stand around waiting to move on. At the end of the silent period, students return to their places and develop their original answer with the additional points they have learned.

Taking it further

- It is a good idea for the teacher to take all of the sticky-notes in at the end of the lesson and use these as the basis of a factual test in a subsequent lesson.

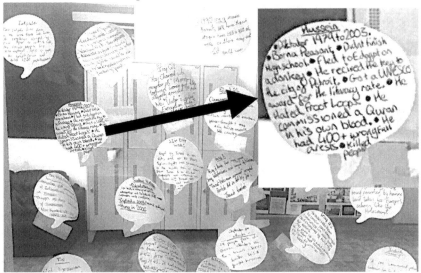

Collate the sticky notes at the end of the lesson ready to create a factual test.

What in the world?

As an engaging starter activity, provide students with an intriguing image, and challenge them to guess what it might be.

This might be connect to something currently being studied, but could alternatively be about any period or topic whatsoever. Therefore, a good starting point might be to identify one key image for each of your major topics of study, but it's also a great opportunity for bringing some additional, quirky topics and individuals into the mix from periods and places which students might not otherwise have the chance to learn about.

The image shown here, for example, will immediately raise questions about which people are depicted (they are all of course the same person). Students could then be told that they all show the same person, and that this image was given to allied soldiers as they approached Berlin at the end of World War Two. This could then lead into a discussion of who it might be, and why he is shown looking so different in each image. The answer, of course, is that it was designed to capture Hitler if he tried to escape in disguise.

Further examples

To illustrate the approach, see if you can determine what each of the following images might be (answers at the end of this section!)

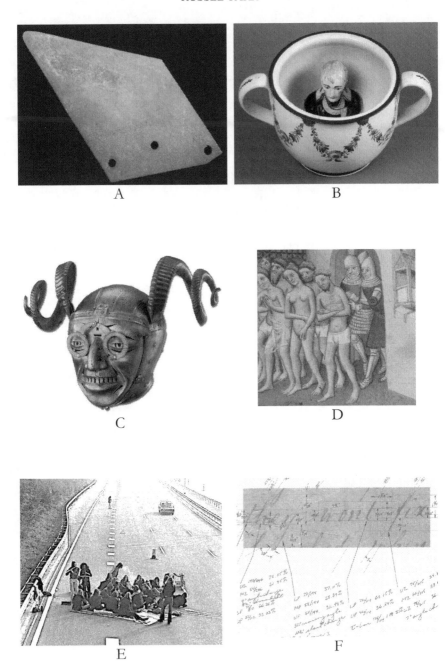

A

B

C

D

E

F

G   H

Answers

A. A blade from a French revolutionary guillotine
B. An English chamber pot with Napoleon inside
C. A helmet gifted to King Henry VIII by the Holy Roman Emperor
D. Cathars being expelled (naked) from Carcassonne
E. A picnic on a Dutch motorway in 1973
F. Handwriting analysis of a purported letter from "Jack the Ripper"
G. The gun used to assassinate President Lincoln
H. Proposed designs for World War One "Dazzleships"

Taking it further

The discussion around each image could follow the same format as the "Mysterious Moments" approach (page 65), whereby students are invited to pose questions to the teacher which can only be answered with a "yes" or a "no" (e.g. "Is this object larger than a soccer ball?", "Is it something that was used in the home?", "Was this document written by Napoleon?").

Once the identity of each image has been provided, ask students to formulate three questions raised by it, and then conduct research to find the answers to these ("Why were the Cathars ordered to strip naked?", "Why did the English hate Napoleon so much?", "Why was there so little traffic on the roads in 1973?", "What were the 'Dazzleships'?").

Boxing match debates

Boxing match debates are a fun way to help students to think more deeply about different points of view on a key issue (e.g. "Napoleon betrayed the spirit of the French Revolution").

The class is divided into two teams, with one 'supporting' the statement and the other 'opposing' it. Classroom or homework time is given for preparation.

Using the analogy of a boxing match, the 'supporting' team score one point for throwing a jab (an assertion supporting the statement) and score another point if they can follow this up with a body blow (specific substantiating evidence).

The 'opposing' team then has to block the blow to score one point (asserting an exception to / limitation of the point just given), scoring a second point if they can elaborate with substantiating evidence.

In round two, the roles are reversed, with the 'opposing' team opening the discussion, and the 'supporting' team having to react.

The "bout" can proceed for as many rounds as necessary to ensure all angles of the issue are covered.

Taking it further

- Divide the key issue into several focus points so that the different rounds have a different focus. For example, in the boxing match debate about Napoleon, divide the issue into economics, education, politics, women, children and religion.

- Work in some drama: the fighters can physically mime throwing and blocking punches as per the rules outlined above, with the loser collapsing onto the canvas at the end of the round.

- Instead of the teacher keeping a track of points, have a small group of students set aside to focus on time-keeping, taking notes of the debate, and keeping score. They can explain their scores at the end of each round, or at the end of the 'bout'.

3
TRANSFORMING AND APPLYING KNOWLEDGE

Raw historical knowledge is more effectively embedded in the memory when students apply and transform it into a personalised outcome. In its most traditional form this might take the form of an essay, but there are many other approaches that can be adopted instead or in addition.

Design a children's storybook

After studying a complex topic, challenge students to turn it into an illustrated storybook that could be understood by much younger students. Spend time in class talking through the main concepts, events and personalities that should be covered in a brief story. Consider too which images and metaphors could be used to bring the subject to life.

In themselves these books can be useful revision aids, and can be peer-assessed. Even better, arrange to read them to students in a local primary school.

Example 1: Mr. Men books: How did Hitler become Chancellor of Germany?

After completing a detailed investigation of the causes of Hitler's rise to power, secondary school students produce a 'Mr. Men' storybook which they read to primary school students. The primary students have an accompanying worksheet where their teams get points for correctly interpreting the different metaphors and identifying the key characters correctly.

A. Prior to the Activity
Pre-activity preparation for the older students
Prior to this activity, secondary students should have finished studying the Rise of Hitler. They should then spend classroom time discussing in pairs and groups how they could transform the narrative into a 'Mr. Men' story that younger students would be able to understand.
The following steps are a useful framework:
Brainstorm the key people involved (Hitler, Hindenburg, Goering, Van der Lubbe, Rohm...). Discuss their personalities / actions in relation to the topic. Bring up a picture of the Mr. Men characters on the board. Discuss which characters are the best match.

Brainstorm the key events that took place (Backstairs Intrigue, Reichstag Fire, Night of the Long Knives, Army's oath of loyalty...). Discuss how these could be turned into analogies that would fit into a Mr. Man format. At this point it is a good idea to watch one of the original Mr. Men cartoons (easily located on YouTube or purchasable online as a DVD) to get them thinking along the right lines.

Pre-activity preparation for the younger students

Primary students should have spent some time (at least an hour or two) working through the tasks and ideas in a preparatory worksheet which provides them with essential background knowledge.

B. The Activity

Setting up the class

Primary students will be divided into groups. These teams are lettered (e.g. A-G) for easy identification and a 'team leader' is nominated within each team.

On each table, place a piece of paper which will serve as a scorecard.

The older students form a 'queue' of storytellers. The person at the start of the queue should go to Team A, the second to Team B, and so on until each team has a storyteller with it. The remaining storytellers remain waiting in the queue.

The First Story

Each group listens to the story read to them by the storyteller. Each team is then asked by the storyteller to guess what the various events / Mr. Men characters represented in real life. The team GAINS a point for each correct statement they make ("We think that X in the story represents Y"). They LOSE a point for each incorrect guess.

To keep it simple, only the 'team leader' can officially make these statements (but they can discuss with the team first). Using the scorecard on the table, the 'reader' keeps a log of how many points were gained and lost overall by each team.

Subsequent Stories

When a primary school team has finished with their storyteller, the storyteller goes to the back of the queue of storytellers. The person at the front of this queue then joins this younger team so they get to hear this new story in the same format. The process continues for the time available, or until all the stories have been read to all the groups.

Close the lesson by asking the younger students which books they enjoyed most and which readers they found read the best. Scores for the teams should be added up overnight and passed back to the older students later.

Students reading their Mr. Men books about the rise of Hitler

Example 2: Henry VIII – Hero or Villain?

In this exercise, secondary school historians produce biased storybooks about Henry VIII after completing their classroom investigations. Half the class produce books from a positive perspective, and half produce books from a negative perspective. Thought should be given to which themes should form the chapters (for example his wives, his religion, his wars) and which images could be used to create a suitably partisan impression.

In a subsequent lesson, primary school students are arranged into groups and are told that their job is to reach their own judgment of Henry based on criteria like father, husband, friend, ruler and Christian. They will do this by hearing as many stories as they can in the time available and will then complete a Wheel of Life (page 170) to reach an overall judgment. Each student is given a clipboard and a record sheet.

The younger students then listen to the story and record their thoughts. When they are finished, the reader comes to a 'neutral zone' to show they are available for reading to another group. The group they have left is then allocated a fresh reader with a story from the opposite perspective. After 20 minutes we have feedback - students are lined up along the wall from "most positive" view of Henry to "least positive". Secondary students can then observe if they "won" the argument with the students they read to.

Sample storybooks about Henry VIII

Taking it further

Some time ago, the "Mr. Men" approach was subject of a heated controversy between myself and the (then) UK Secretary of State for Education, Michael Gove, which you can read more about here: www.activehistory.co.uk/gove.php

Design a museum exhibition

As a way of encouraging focused research, or an effective means of summarising or revising a topic, get students to curate their own museum or gallery exhibit rather than risk enduring a 'death by PowerPoint'. These can be displayed in a public area, scaled down to fit into a box or turned into a 3D virtual gallery using www.classtools.net.

One easy approach to design a museum gallery task involves providing students with a large range of images relating to the topic or period in question (for example, images relating to the British Empire). They have to imagine they are curating a museum exhibition on four separate walls. How will they categorise these images? How will they caption them? What is the 'big question' which this exhibition will help visitors to answer? (for example: "What are the main characteristics of…?" or "What were the strengths and weaknesses of …?").

As an added layer of interest, some of these images may be deliberately obscure – students should place these to one side. In a second phase of the exercise, the teacher provides caption slips which have to be matched to each image prior to further thought being given to the exhibition.

Portraits as propaganda: images of Napoleon and caption slips

I have also created an online "3D Gallery" application at www.classtools.net which allows students to design a virtual animated museum exhibition on any topic. There is also a mark scheme and help-sheet to accompany this facility to make it even simpler to use. Students have to choose their images and videos carefully: they have space for exactly ten exhibits. Each exhibit should be given a title and a description for maximum educational effect. When students are finished, they can save their work for future editing, and embed it into a school website to share more widely.

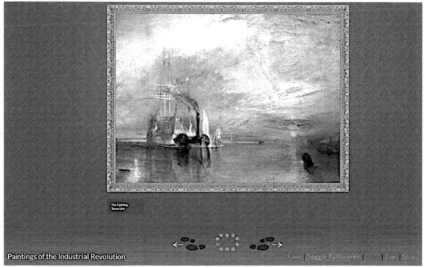

3D Gallery creator at www.classtools.net

A final approach is to give each student a different theme to investigate. For example, in my study of the culture of the Weimar Republic, students choose particular topics within broad categories including art, science, literature and music. Their job is to produce an exhibition panel for a museum exhibition, paying careful attention to the key points they wish to share and what images, artefacts or sounds will best accompany their work. These can then be shared with the rest of the class and are particularly useful for understanding some of the positive legacies of a regime which is too often dismissed as a complete failure.

Design a Hollywood film poster

Get students familiar with the key events and significance of a topic by conceptualising a Hollywood feature film about it. What will be the title of the film? What key events will it focus on? Which actors will take on which roles? What merchandise could tie-in with the film?

Stage 1: Start by outlining the central task

Provide students a timeline of key events or facts about the topic. Read this information as a class. This process can take place as the very first introductory lesson to the topic, or as a review and consolidation activity at the end of the study.

ADVERTISE A HOLLYWOOD BLOCKBUSTER!

- You are a Hollywood director producing a film about Martin Luther.
- You will produce a poster advertising your film, including:
  - A dramatic **title** for the film
  - 4 **"Screenshots"** from the film depicting the key events of his life
  - **Captions** under each screenshot describing the events
  - A **cast list** (who plays Luther? Charles V? Zwingli? Frederick?)
  - Some quotes from the film reviewers!

Task 1

Read through the following timeline as a class. Then, working individually, circle off four events that you think will work particularly well on the cinema screen. Be prepared to explain why. After a class discussion, watch the real trailer from the 2005 film. Did they choose the same events?

1505	**Luther** is training to be a lawyer. He is caught in a thunderstorm. He falls on his knees and promises God if he will become a monk if his life is spared. He keeps his promise!
1516	Luther has his "Tower experience" – locked away studying the Bible, he reads the phrase "the righteous will live by faith". From this he decides that God is more interested in whether we have real belief ("faith") than what we do ("Good Works"). He feels that a *Vernacular* Bible (i.e. one in the language of the people) is the only way of helping people find true faith in

Sample movie poster worksheet to help students study Luther's revolt

Stage 2: Completing the movie proposal form

Students are then asked to consider the following questions:

- What will be the title and strapline of your film? (decide whether you want to depict the main character/theme as a hero or a villain. Discuss as a class some famous film titles for inspiration).

- Choose five events to focus on (aim for different moods: drama, suspense, humour, violence, romance…)
- What sorts of reviews could you include?
- What sort of merchandise could you advertise as a 'tie-in' promotion?
- Choose five people from the timeline: Which famous actors would you use to play each of these characters and why?

Luther   Charles V

Matt Damon   Hugh Jackman

Frederick of Saxony

Keanu Reeves

Stage 3: Producing the poster

At this stage the students are ready to produce their poster. Provide a clear mark scheme giving credit for inclusion of each of the features mentioned earlier.

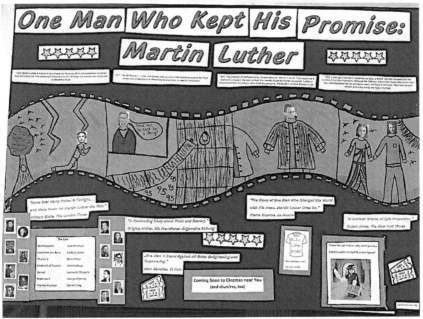

A film poster focusing on the life and significance of Martin Luther. Careful consideration was given to which characters would need to be casted, what merchandise would tie-in best with the topic, and which key events would have to be covered.

Taking it further

Allow students who wish to do so to create an actual movie trailer, complete with soundtrack and narrative. A sample trailer created by one of my students for a proposed film on Luther can be found at www.activehistory.co.uk/u/reformation.

Prejudice Maps

Get students to illustrate attitudes of people towards their world by making an "Atlas of Prejudice" as per the great examples in the book of the same name.

Overview
Start by asking students to list things we know about how the character, individual or group perceives the world around them. This could be on a local, national or global level as appropriate. Then, convert this into a map to reflect these attitudes and prejudices.

Here, for example, is a map from the Atlas of Prejudice reflecting Europe in 1555, according to Emperor Charles V. It gives a whole new meaning to the concept of 'Mind-Mapping'!

Europe according to Emperor Charles V, from the superb "Atlas of Prejudice".

Taking it further
Several maps could illustrate how attitudes changed over time.

Design a memorial

At the end of a project, challenge students to design a memorial to commemorate an event, theme, topic or individual that they have studied.

Example 1: Holocaust Memorial

Start by asking students to consider what events in international, national and personal history deserve to be 'remembered' and why (this raises the issue of how we measure significance as well as the nature of commemoration).

Then, students should be given time to research different memorials from around the world to share with the class (if time is short, the teacher could simply provide a list of these).

Next, they consider the following key questions to help them formulate their own concept for a memorial:

- What does the memorial get people to think about?
- Will it focus on the causes, or on the effects?
- Will it encourage quiet reflection, or provoke violent debate?
- What feelings does the memorial evoke?
- Regret? Guilt? Hope? Sadness? Anger? Other?
- What form does the memorial take?
- Sculpture? Mural? Gardens? Museum? Other?
- Where is it situated, and why?
- In a city (which one? why?) In the countryside (where? why?)

The final stage is to design their own memorial either on paper or as a model.

Example 2: World War One memorial / visitor centre

During my annual visit to the World War One battlefields in Belgium and France, students visit a wide and varied range of memorials and museums. Upon our return from school, they consolidate their experiences by working in teams to design their own proposed memorial and visitor centre. The following tasks are shared between the members of each group and they draw together their findings in a presentation to the rest of the class.

Group project: Design a World War One memorial and visitor centre

1. General Points

- Who or what will your project commemorate?
- What central message will your project make about war?
- What mood will it seek to evoke?
- What will be the name of your memorial?

2. The Memorial

- Where exactly would your memorial be situated? Why?
- What would be the design and material for your memorial? Why?

3. The Visitor Center

- Who is your target audience? Why?
- What would be key exhibits and features of your museum? Why?
- What would you **not** include? Why?
- What painting would you seek to borrow and why?

4. Opening ceremony

- Who would open your site and why would they be a good 'guest of honour'?
- Which poem would be read, and which song played during the opening ceremony?

5. Marketing

- How will the museum be funded?
- How would you advertise your site?

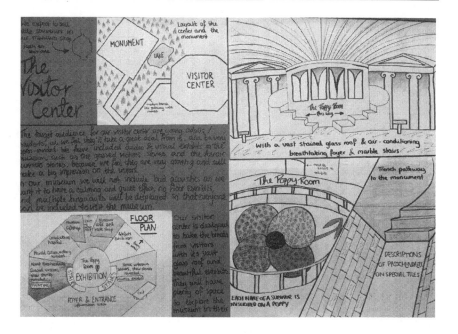

Create a "Fakebook" profile

When researching a key character, students could present their findings in the form of a fake social media profile using www.classtools.net.

Using this tool, students can create a timeline of a person's life, written in the first person and in the present tense (which in itself is an effective way to prevent 'cut and paste' syndrome). They can list 'friends' in blocks on the right-hand side, and create fresh blocks for such things as 'hobbies', 'enemies' and so on. It is even possible to add video clips from YouTube. There is a 'getting started' guide and a suggested mark scheme for Fakebook projects. There is also a large gallery of sample projects to provide inspiration:

Taking it further

Fakebook walls can be created not just for individuals, but for concepts which have changed over time or between cultures (e.g. democracy, communism), to illustrate the changing relationship between countries (e.g. the developing alliance system before World War One).

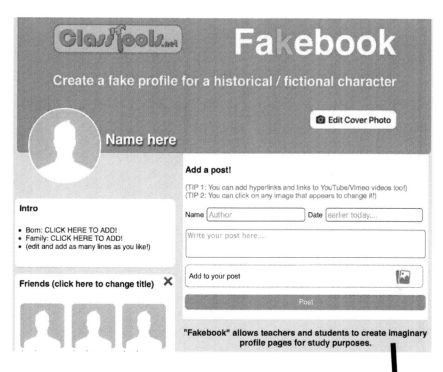

"Fakebook" profile creator at www.classtools.net

Design a propaganda cartoon

Get students to design a propaganda cartoon to illustrate one key aspect of the topic from either a negative or a positive perspective. In a later lesson, the cartoons are swapped and each student answers the question "What is the message of this source?"

Stage 1: Producing the cartoon

In my studies of the Peace Treaties after World War One, I get students to design their own propaganda cartoons. Students first examine a range of famous cartoons from the period. In particular, we focus on the meaning of different symbols (the olive branch, the dove, the crocodile, the sheep) and how metaphors are made literal by cartoonists ('spineless', 'crocodile tears', 'twisting your arm' and so on).

The class is then divided into two teams: one will produce cartoons critical of the Versailles Treaty, the other will produce positive interpretations. Within each team, different students are instructed to focus on a different theme using the TRAWL memory word (Territory, Reparations, Armaments, War Guilt, League of Nations).

A final instruction is that students are not allowed to include any words in their cartoon. This will force them to focus on the visual elements rather than use words as an easy way out.

Stage 2: Analysis and Feedback

In a subsequent lesson, students swap their cartoons with somebody else in the class without any discussion or explanation. They then write an answer to the question "What is the message of this cartoon?" on a piece of paper. It is a good idea to adopt the format "I think a message of this cartoon is...the cartoonist gets this message across by showing....which I think from my background knowledge represents...".

When these answers are finished, the cartoons are put on display with the analysis for each attached underneath. The original cartoonists can then read the interpretation of their cartoon and offer their opinion on how accurately it was interpreted. Discussion can take place about how the message of the cartoons could have been improved further.

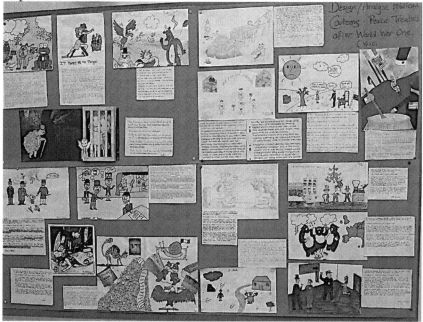

Classroom display of cartoons and their meanings

Treaty of Versailles Cartoon: Writing Frame

I think the message of [name]'s cartoon is that the terms of the Versailles treaty regarding [Territory/Reparations/Armaments / War Guilt / League of Nations] are [fair / unfair].

The cartoonist makes this point in several ways.
• Firstly, the cartoon shows....??? which from my background knowledge I think refers to .... ???
• Secondly, the cartoon shows....??? which most likely means that.... ???
• Finally, the cartoon depicts....??? which makes reference to .... ???

[Your name]

Writing frame template to help students analyse each cartoon

Design PlayMobil™ merchandise

PlayMobil™ recently launched a model of Martin Luther, the German Protestant reformer, complete with quill and vernacular bible. Students could design their own figure of an individual they have studied, complete with accessories.

Students could be asked to consider such things as
- What should the character be wearing?
- What should the character be holding in each hand?
- What additional merchandise could be sold as part of the set?

The first phase of the process could involve getting students to make a list of all the key characters associated with the topic, for example:
- **Origins of World War One**: Kaiser Wilhelm, Tsar Nicholas II, Franz Ferdinand, Sir Edward Grey
- **The Peace Treaties After World War One**: Wilson, Clemenceau Lloyd George and Orlando
- **International relations in the 1930s**: Stalin, Hitler, Mussolini, Chamberlain, Benes

Case Study: The rise of Hitler

When studying the reasons Hitler was appointed as Chancellor of Germany in 1933, get students away from focusing purely on Hitler's own talents and contributions by giving them different members of the Nazi party to consider, and asked them to produce a 'PlayMobil™ concept' highlighting the essential contribution of that individual to Hitler's rise, as show in the example overleaf.

Play Mobil Concept:
How Goering Helped Hitler get into Power

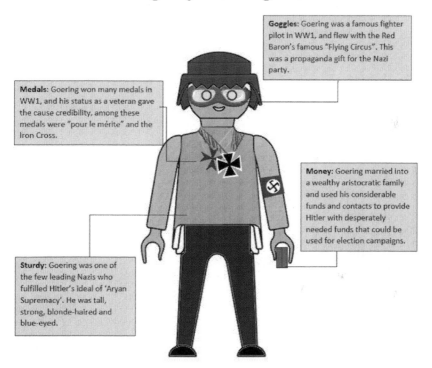

Goggles: Goering was a famous fighter pilot in WW1, and flew with the Red Baron's famous "Flying Circus". This was a propaganda gift for the Nazi party.

Medals: Goering won many medals in WW1, and his status as a veteran gave the cause credibility, among these medals were "pour le mérite" and the Iron Cross.

Money: Goering married into a wealthy aristocratic family and used his considerable funds and contacts to provide Hitler with desperately needed funds that could be used for election campaigns.

Sturdy: Goering was one of the few leading Nazis who fulfilled Hitler's ideal of 'Aryan Supremacy'. He was tall, strong, blonde-haired and blue-eyed.

PlayMobil™ concept designed to highlight individuals within the Nazi party – other than Hitler – who helped the Nazis rise to power. Note how each object is designed to help the student remember a relevant fact about how explicitly the character helped Hitler get into power.

Miming, freeze-framing, body sculptures

With younger students especially, thinking about how to physically represent what has been studied can be a useful learning experience. Thought needs to be given to what character or characters will need to be represented, what their body positions and facial expressions will be, and how they will act out the concept either in motion or as a moment frozen in time.

Freeze framing

This involves getting students, working usually in small groups, to construct a scene which is then photographed and explained. This should represent a key action moment 'frozen in time' to capture energy. It is fun to give each group something different to represent, and to keep this secret until after the scene is created for the rest of the class. In this way the other students can be challenged to guess what is being represented.

Body sculpture

This is similar to freeze framing, except in this case there is a group leader responsible (sometimes silently) for 'moulding' the rest of the group into place. These group members are not allowed to speak or move independently, they can only carry out the instructions of the team leader. This technique can also be based around paired work, with one student the 'sculptor' and another the 'clay'. After a strict time limit, the group of sculptors can then conduct a walking tour of the 'gallery', with each sculptor taking it in turns to explain their 'sculpture'.

Miming / charades

In silence, different students have to act out a key concept, event or scene. Other students gain points if they guess these correctly. For example, when investigating the power of the Medieval church, start by giving the students a list of key ways why the church was so powerful, then inform them that different students will be allocated one of the ideas at random to mime in front of the rest of the class. They then have ten minutes to consider in silence how they would act each one out. It's a great way of providing some focus to the reading.

	A. Power	B. Help	C. Fun
1	**Excommunication** is when the Pope condemns someone's soul to hell	**Confession** of your sins to a priest will help you get into heaven	**Holidays** (holy days) are days when everyone was given the day off work
2	**Courts** exist just for the Church for the trial of "sinners"	**The Mass** (bread and wine ceremony) helps people get into heaven	**Harvest Festival** is a massive party organized by the Church each year
3	**Sloth**: The Church can punish you for being lazy	**Baptism** protects young children from going to hell if they die	**Sports competitions** were organized between local churches
4	**Gluttony**: The Church can punish you for getting drunk	**Relics** (holy objects like the bones of saints) can get people into heaven	**Socialising**: Sunday Church is where people meet up and chat
5	**Envy**: The Church can punish you for being jealous of other people	**Pilgrimages** to holy places will help you get into heaven	**Music**: The choir and the church band is where people enjoy music
6	**Land**: The Church owns almost half of the land in the country	**Flagellants** say that whipping yourself will help you get into heaven	**Drama**: The church organizes plays based on stories from the bible
7	**Tithes**: Everyone has to pay taxes to the Church	**Monasteries** are places where people could devote themselves to God	**Art**: Stained glass windows and wall paintings are in the church
8	**Mortuary Fees**: The Church charges a fee to bury dead people	**Last Rites** (special prayers) are give for dying people by priests	**Reading**: The priest reads out exciting stories from the Bible each week

Miming challenges for a study of the Medieval church

Thereafter, call up a random person in the class, and secretly point out to them just one of the points from the table to mime to the rest of the group.   At the end of the mime (which should take no longer than a few seconds) each member of the class should write down in the space below the point from the table which they think it represented (e.g. "A5", "C2").   The game is repeated using 9 other students miming 9 other points, one after another. The teacher will then reveal the correct answers and the students can add their scores.

'TripAdvisor'™ graphics

To revise the impact of an event or individual upon particular places over time, students could produce mock 'TripAdvisor' reviews, labelled onto a map.

The rating for each place could reflect how successfully the problem in that area was dealt with. This idea was formulated by one of my most creative historians, who was summarising how successfully the League of Nations dealt with the border disputes it faced in the 1920s.

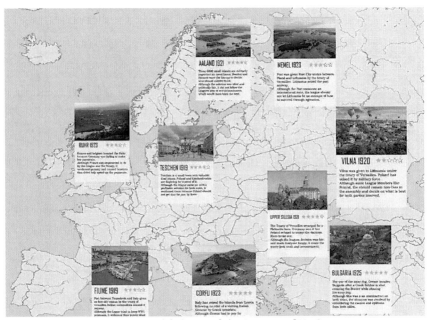

Successes and failures of the League of Nations

Taking it further

Each 'rating' could reflect the degree of responsibility that each country/place held for the outbreak of a particular war. This might be entire countries (for example in the origins of World War One) or particular events within them (for example, the Sudeten crisis / the Anschluss, in the years leading up to World War Two).

Design a theme park for the topic

Given genuine plans to build a theme park centred around Napoleon Bonaparte and the story of Freedom Land theme park in the USA, it is an interesting idea to get students to design a theme park to entertain and educate visitors about a particular topic of study.

Rides, games and facilities should all tie-in with the people, events, themes and concepts associated with the topic. These are then presented to the teacher, in role as a venture capitalist, who then declares an overall winner.

This task could either be tackled at the end of a topic, to consolidate and extend existing knowledge, or right at the start, to provide students with a focused research and transformation task which provides them with an overview of the topic in question.

Case study: Tudor England

Before starting a study of the Tudor period, students are put into groups and asked to discuss any theme parks they have visited, what their favourite rides were, and to identify what the actual 'theme' of each park was. Some of these themes are pretty obvious (Disneyland in the USA), some are more clearly didactic in nature (EuropaPark in Germany) and others have no discernible themes at all (Alton Towers in England).

Next, tell students that a millionaire businessperson is keen to invest a large sum of money with the individual or group that comes up with the theme park which most successfully matches entertainment with educational value. The various zones, rides, facilities, merchandise, logo, mascots and so on will all need to integrate effectively with the topic. The location and name of the park will also need to be considered.

Some Tips	
Shooting gallery	The target being the villains of the period or the enemies of the ruler
Water ride	Tied in with naval battles, famous ships, floods
Costumed employees	who can have their photo taken with visitors (major characters of the period, also highlighting fashions)
Ghost train	People killed / executed during the period
Gift shop	Various trinkets and knick-knacks highlighting key events and individuals, including themed clothing, mugs, soft toys and posters
Restaurant	Popular food and drink of the time
Roller coaster	Particularly tumultuous events or policies
Play area for kids	Toys and games of the period

Taking it further

- Rather than present students with the topic and ask them to design a theme park around it, ask the students themselves to nominate a particular topic, period or theme themselves as part of their revision schedule.

Brochure for the short-lived "Freedomland" in the USA

Convert statistics into infographics

To help students memorise and reflect upon key statistics more effectively, encourage them to represent them visually.

Case study: apartheid South Africa

The impact of apartheid on black South Africans is difficult to comprehend. So I provide students with some essential statistics about apartheid and then challenge them to convert them into an 'infographic' (for example, using an online tool like Piktochart, Canva or Infogr.am).

Some sample statistics

- Blacks were only given 13% of land - designated as "Homelands" – despite being 80% of the population.
- There was very little arable farm land in the Homelands. For example, only 15% of the Ciskei was arable, 89% of Ciskei children suffered from malnutrition.
- None of the Homelands had significant mineral resources.
- A survey by the Lawyers Committee for Human Rights found that 83% of all detainees held by South African government authorities had been physically abused.
- The wages of Whites were 8X that of Blacks.
- According to The Economist, on average 50,000 children died every year during apartheid from the effects of malnutrition, while South Africa exported over $1 billion worth of food annually.
- The major cause of death for black children in South Africa was disease brought on by malnutrition: for white children the major cause of death was swimming pool accidents.
- Only 3% of practicing doctors in South Africa were Bantu (black). Infant mortality among rural blacks was 282 per 1,000 births while among whites 12 per 1,000.
- According to the South African Council of Churches, 3. 5 million Bantu were forcibly removed from "white" South Africa to the Homelands after 1960.
- The government spent over seven times as much to educate a white child as it spent to educate a black child.

- On average, there was one teacher in each white South African school for every 18 students. In black schools the ratio was one teacher for every 43 students.
- If you were white in South Africa, you could expect to live 72.3 years. Bantu could expect to live 58.9 years. Blacks lived an average of 56.1 years and Indians, 63.9 years.

Examples

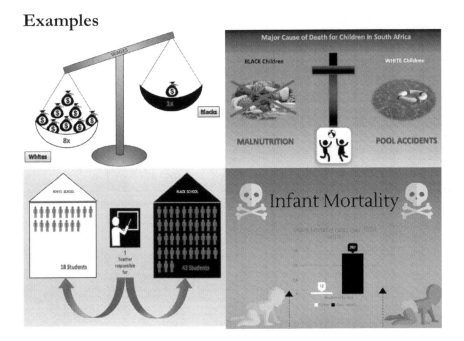

Taking it further

- The completed infographics can form the basis of an excellent classroom display. To make this more interactive, challenge students to match each infographic on display to the key statistic from the list which it represents.
- Rather than simply provide the students with these statistics straight away, engage them further by starting the lesson with a "Guess the statistics" quiz (page 84).
- Challenge students to render some of the statistics using a rice display (page 272).

Design / destroy a banknote

Get students to design their own banknote to commemorate a particular event or individual – and propose too whose face on which current banknote it should replace and why. Coins can be used too.

Whenever a national bank introduces or withdraws a particular historical character from a banknote, it is a matter of keen debate and discussion. For example, in the UK the recent decision to replace Elizabeth Fry on the £5 note with Winston Churchill led to a petition complaining about the lack of women on banknotes that resulted in a commitment that Jane Austen would appear on the £10 note from 2017. There was another petition to depict Aneurin Bevan, architect of the National Health Service, on the £20 note. In the USA There was a similar campaign to replace Andrew Jackson on the American $20 bill.

Case study: Who deserves to be on a banknote?

After introducing the importance of banknotes in the way outlined above, ask students who they think deserves to be commemorated on a banknote, and why. This forms a very neat conclusion to the "Who is your History Hero?" knowledge cube project (page 268), for example. Students could then design the banknote themselves, including:

- A picture of the character
- An image which symbolises their greatest achievement
- An inspiring quote by the character

Taking it further

Idea 1: Denominations to reflect significance
An added dimension to the activity could be to decide as a class upon the most worthy characters to appear on banknotes. Then, different denominations of currency should be designed to reflect the respective importance of the characters: the character chosen for the £50 note, for example, should be considered more significant than that on a £5 note.

Idea 2: Who should be REMOVED from circulation?

The question could be reversed. After asking students who deserves to be introduced onto a banknote, challenge them to decide who therefore needs to be removed from current circulation in order to make way for them.

Idea 4: Coins instead of banknotes
Students could focus on coins instead of banknotes, using the badgemaker at www.classtools.net to design their own coin. This is particularly effective if you have a collection of coins from different countries to show them, as per these World War One commemorative coins:

World War One commemorative coins from various countries

Idea 3: Banknotes around the world
The project could be expanded into an entire unit. The people commemorated on different currencies around the world could be researched, then the overall results contrasted and compared in a variety of ways. Are women commemorated in equal proportion to men in different countries? Is there a focus on literary, or scientific figures, or a balance? What do these analyses tell us about the culture and values of each country?

Create a Google Doodle™

At the close of a topic, ask students to design their own 'Google Doodle' to represent the essence of the subject, a key moment within it or a central individual that they have learned about. What symbols, colours, terms could they use?

A Google Doodle is a temporary alteration of the logo on Google's homepage to commemorate a holiday (such as International Women's Day), event (such as Bastille Day) or individual (such as Alan Turing). As such they provide a rich mine of inspiration for student projects.

Case study: the Black Death

This example from Carol Stobbs shows how a study of the Black Death could be concluded by getting students to create a Google Doodle:

Google Doodle: The Black Death (courtesy of Carol Stobbs)

Produce a board game

Creating an educational board game is an effective method of consolidating knowledge of a topic.

Credit should be given to the students based on the gameplay, the presentation and the simplicity of the rules, but with a large proportion of the total marks being set aside for the educational value of the game. In a subsequent lesson, students play several games over the course of one or two lessons and peer assess each one.

Although there is a temptation to see this approach as being particularly suited to younger year groups, it also works surprisingly well with older students: mine produced games based on Stalin's rule of the USSR with an interesting range of game cards based on positive and negative examples of his economic, political and cultural policies.

Case study: the Black Death

Step 1: Imparting the information

With younger students I adopt this approach when teaching them about the spread, symptoms, cures and consequences of the Black Death. I start by providing all students with a summary sheet of key points under those three headings. As a warm-up exercise, they spend a few minutes reading through the points in the table. For each one, I ask them to consider how they could present this as a "mime" to the class.

	A. Causes (tip: particularly useful for 'factual test' cards)	B. Symptoms (tip: particularly useful for 'bad news' cards)	C. Cures (tip: particularly useful for 'good news' cards)
1	Punishment from God for our sins	Boils ('buboes') appear under the arms and between the legs	March around town whipping yourself asking God's forgiveness
2	Touching someone who already has the plague	The victim starts feeling a bit dizzy and weak	Drink a glass of your own wee twice a day
3	Jews allegedly poisoning the wells	The victim starts to suffer from internal bleeding	Cut a hole into your skull to let out evil spirits

4	Fire from the heavens	Black spots and blue blotches start to spread over the body	Open your veins and let a pint of blood pour out
5	Position of the planets	The tongue turns brown and the breath starts to stink	Hold sweet herbs to your mouth to drive away the bad air
6	Rubbish in the streets	The victim starts to sweat and to develop a fever	Kill all the cats and dogs in the town
7	Bad smells	The boils under the arms and legs grow as large as apples	Slice buboes open, squeeze out poison, seal the wound with poo
8	Bad food, especially meat and fish	The victim starts to vomit and cough up blood	Sit in a sewer. The bad smells will drive away the Black Death smells
9	Evil spirits in the body	The victim starts to from fits and spasms	Shave a chicken's bottom and strap it to your plague sores
10	Too much blood in the body	The victim dies	Swallow the powder of crushed emeralds

I then call up a person in the class and secretly point out to them just one of the points from the table to mime to the rest of the class. At the end of the mime (which should take no longer than a few seconds) each member of the class should write down which they think it represented. The game is repeated using 9 other students miming 9 other points, one after another. I then tell the class the correct answers and ask them how many they get right?

Step 2: Formulate the concept

Next, students are invited to in pairs or in groups of three to come up with their game concept. This phase is particularly important to structure properly, so I provide students with the following questions in the form of a handout which helps them to methodically generate an effective game design:

How do you decide who starts the game?
- Roll of the die?
- Answering a factual knowledge question?
- Will the players take on different roles?

Can they choose these, or will they be allocated?
- Will they have particular advantages or handicaps?
- What is the objective of the game? Is the winner:
  o The last person left alive?

- o The first person to reach a certain place?
- o The first person to have reached several places on the board?
- o The first person to have collected certain objects?
- o The first person to answer a set amount of questions?

Will the players:
- Always head in one direction (around the board – like Monopoly)
- Zig-Zag upwards (like Snakes and Ladders)
- Be able to choose their direction (like in Trivial Pursuit)

How will the cards picked up affect the game?
- Go to "jail" (which would represent what in terms of this topic)?
- Move forward places on the board?
- Miss a turn?
- Demand / perform a forfeit?
- Require the player answer a factual question, then rewarded / punished based on their answer?

What will the board look like?
- A map of key places associated with the topic?
- Will it be on several different levels?

I find it is worthwhile during this brainstorming phase to pause after the first ten minutes, have a discussion about how things are progressing, and then tell the class that after another ten minutes we will discuss ideas they have come up with regarding (for example) the shape of the board. Repeat this process of ten minutes of design work and five minutes of feedback on a particular issue for the duration of the lesson to ensure the class stays focused and productive.

Step 3: Produce the cards

The next lesson should be devoted to producing the cards for the game (these will be picked up by players if they land on particular squares on the board, labelled in this case 'Causes card!', 'Symptoms card!' or 'Consequences card!').

Different students in each group should take charge of producing "good" and "bad" cards for each category using the original prompt sheet to help them. For example, a "Consequences card" might read

"Good news! The shortage of labour following the Black Death so your wages go up – move forward three places!" (the actual 'outcome' of each card, of course, depends of the game concept in question and can be added later if this is still being decided).

As far as possible, aim for an equal number of 'good' and 'bad' cards, and highlight key words in bold.

Step 4: Make the game

Homework time should then be set aside for students to actually make their board games. I make a particular point at this stage of instructing students to ensure that they produce clear instructions about how to play the game as part of this process, because other students will not get a great deal out of the experience if they don't know the rules. They should also ensure that if they need things like counters and dice, they obtain these too.

Sample board game

Step 5: Play the games

When all the work has been collected in, set aside at least one hour for the class to play each other's games. Prior to the lesson, spread the games around the room and identify each one with a number on a slip of paper.   Students should start by sitting down alongside their own game and having five minutes to make any final adjustments. Then, each group proceeds to the next game in the room (for example, if they have produced game 1 they move to game 2; the group with the final game should 'loop round' to game 1). Before they start, instruct them that whilst playing, they should assess the game based on its educational value (most important), creativity, presentation, and gameplay.

Students should then have ten minutes to play the game they have been allocated (it is a good idea to have a classroom timer on prominent display, for example the one I have developed at www.classtools.net/timer).

Step 6: Assessment and feedback

When the ten minutes is up, students should have a further few minutes to give the game a score out of 25, which I divide up by allowing a maximum of 10 points for educational value and 5 each for creativity, presentation, and gameplay. Each group can be given a slip of paper for this purpose, and the teacher can then use these later to inform their own marking and feedback very efficiently.

With these slips completed and handed in to the teacher, students can move to the next game in the classroom and the process can be repeated for as long considered appropriate. Sometimes I take an hour on this, but if the students are clearly getting a great deal from the exercise and are keen to do so then I try to find further time to ensure that all the games are played by as wide a range of people as possible.

Taking it further

- Get students to produce separate 'quiz' cards which simply test factual knowledge as part of the game. For a game based on Trivial Pursuit or similar this is essential anyway, but for other games they provide an excellent additional way of testing factual recall.

- Provide students with a Google Form to record their feedback rather than paper slips. The entire spreadsheet of results can then be exported simply into an Excel spreadsheet by the teacher to make the marking and feedback process easier. The job of the teacher is then to simply export the spreadsheet of results, order them in terms of each game marked, and then work out the average grade for each game. Occasionally adjustments need to be made based on the fact that certain teams may mark themselves or others more harshly or generously than others.

- If the games are going to be played over several lessons rather than one, provide each group with their feedback slips at the end of the first session and give them further homework time to develop their games as appropriate to ensure higher scores in the next round.

- Students could use peer assessment slips (page 222) to express their judgment about how much each team member contributed to the task. This is a very simple and effective way of ensuring that any student who contributed more to the task during the homework phase is given appropriate credit.

Guess who?

This game involves players trying to identify which person's face has been selected by their opponent through a process of elimination by asking a series of closed questions.

This popular game can easily be adopted for the classroom, but the danger is that students merely learn about the facial features of the characters in question ("Is your person male?", "Is your person smiling?" and so on) , which is rather pointless. Instead, demand that students instead ask questions focusing on life, career and significance, using a set of cards to help them.

Case study: the Abolitionists

In this example, produced by one of my students as a 'choose your own homework' outcome on the abolitionist movement, players are provided with a set of cards providing information about the people whose faces are used in the game. They read these carefully and formulate their questions appropriately, so learning about the key characters in the process.

"Guess Who?" game based on the abolition movement

4
ANALYSING, CATEGORISING, COMPARING, LINKING

When analysing the nature of cause, effect and significance, history students need to learn how to compare, contrast and link key factors to work towards an independent conclusion.

Decision trees

Decision trees are a fun and effective way to get students reflecting carefully about the similarities and differences between various factors. They work on the same principle used by questionnaires in time-killing magazines where each yes/no answer takes you down a different branch until you end up with a final answer to the central question.

Example: What is your ideal Medieval job?

When studying Medieval religious beliefs and practices, provide students with a list of activities which people in the Middle Ages thought would help them get to heaven. Explain to students that they will be acting like a careers advisor to help people decide their ideal route to paradise:

Stairway to Heaven **How will YOU get to paradise?**	
Franciscan Friar Do you like the idea of devoting your entire life to God, but still want to be able to travel around and help ordinary people at the same time? Yes?! Then the Franciscans are for you! Your job is to move around from place to place spreading the word of Jesus and helping out in the community however you can. You will have to take a vow of poverty, though, so if you like material things then you may wish to think twice!	**Pilgrim** Do you like the idea of travelling with friends to foreign lands? Have you got a spare bit of money to fund the trip? If so, the job of pilgrim is just for you! You will go to holy places like Lourdes in France, and see relics of holy people – even their mummified hands, and pieces of the cross Jesus was crucified on! By praying at these places and going on these journeys you will please God and get into heaven!
Cistercian lay brother Not too bright, but not afraid of a bit of hard physical work? Then why not become a Cistercian lay brother?! All you have to do is go along to the Cistercian Monastery and work as a gardener, a builder or a plumber. This is a great job if you fancy a quiet life - you will not be allowed to leave the monastery once you have joined up.	**Crusader** Do you like adventure? Is physical activity – even violence – your sort of thing? If so, Crusader could be just the thing for you! You will go to the Holy Land with an army of comrades to fight the Muslims who have taken over Jerusalem. It's dangerous work, and you will need a fair bit of cash to fund the enterprise, but God will be pleased with you!
Augustinian monk Do you like the idea of living in a secluded monastery away from the hustle and bustle of everyday life? Are you not too keen though on being completely out of touch with the real world? Augustinian monk is just the job for you, then! You will spend most of the day at quiet prayer, but you will also be able to provide shelter for travellers and medical care in the local community!	**Flagellant** Not too keen on travelling? Not too scared of a bit of pain? Maybe Flagellant is just the job for you! All you have to do is walk around town whipping yourself for your sins. God will be so pleased that you are punishing yourself on earth that he will let you into heaven as soon as you die.
Cistercian monk Are you bright and ambitious? Do you like the idea of a quiet life? Cistercian monk is the right path for you! You will live your life in quiet devotion to God in a monastery deep in the countryside. You will have to leave all your family and friends behind, but the peace and tranquillity – in fact, you will not be allowed to speak at all because you will take a vow of silence!	**Charity worker** Do you have bit of time and / or money to spare? Do you like the idea of helping others through the Church, without having to give up your ordinary way of life? Yes? Then why not do some "Good Works"? If you help the poor by washing their feet or giving them bread, God will be pleased! If you buy an "indulgence" from a "Pardoner", God will forgive you your sins! If you leave money to the Church when you die, you will get into heaven more quickly!

Students then produce a decision-making tree to help people decide which "stairway to heaven" most closely matches their own personality, interests and abilities. For example, one question might be

"Do you like travel?". Students can draw up their findings as an A3 diagram, a mind map, or even an interactive website if they are so inclined.

The crucial tip to give students is that they should aim to design questions which divide the remaining factors into two roughly balanced "Yes" and "No" categories. This is what really gets them thinking and reading carefully.

The following template, created using the SmartArt > Hierarchy feature in Microsoft Word, gives students a useful starting point. I award extra credit to students who include illustrations and even additional jobs they research themselves to add into the project.

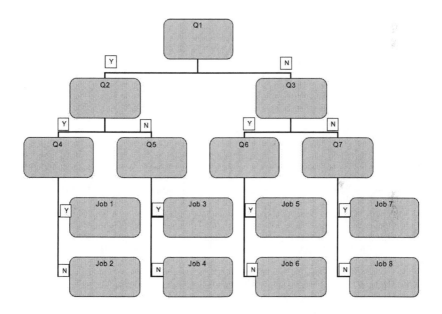

Taking it further

Get students to test their decision trees out on each other in a 'speed-dating' format. They may spot how their original questions need to be amended. Make sure that details about each answer, rather than just (in this case) the job title is included. For display pieces, a particularly effective technique here would be to have each final answer in the format of a gift card or advent calendar, where the viewer has to physically open up the card to learn more.

Linkage bingo

This whole-class game helps students to summarise issues of cause or effect, and then to link them together in a meaningful way prior to producing an essay.

The class should be divided into teams. One person in each team should be the scribe. A version of the template will be on the whiteboard ready for the teacher, as quizmaster, to fill in as the game proceeds.

	> 1. Political	> 2. Religious	> 3. Military	> 4. Regional
1. Political factors >	POLITICAL FACTORS X 3			
2. Religious >		RELIGIOUS FACTORS X 3		
3. Military >			MILITARY FACTORS X 3	
4. Regional >				REGIONAL FACTORS X 3

The template shown above, which I use to investigate the causes of the Spanish Civil War, is merely a suggestion. It can be adjusted by the teacher to list however many factors need to be considered for the issue being considered.

Example questions:

- What were the main causes of the Spanish Civil War?
- Why was Hitler able to become Chancellor of Germany?
- What were the effects of World War One?
- What was the impact of Stalin's rule on the Soviet Union?

Round 1: Revising the factors

In this round, each team will be challenged to contribute factual points to place into one of the darkly shaded cells (randomly chosen by the teacher).

Each team gains one point for each valid, explained point they make, up to a maximum of three points.

Each team will be given five minutes preparation time to decide what they could contribute for all the cells before the round begins.

Round 2: Linking the factors

The teacher should roll the die for each team. The number allocated to each team corresponds to the factor on the left that needs to be connected to one of the blank cells along that row. For example, if the team rolls a 'two' they need to explain how socio-economic factors led to or exacerbated one of the other factors.

The entire class will be given several minutes of team time to prepare their thoughts. Each well explained point will gain two points for the successful team and will be written into the table by the teacher.

Taking it further

- The teacher may initially roll the die twice for each group to provide both a row and a column that the team will need to complete.

- As the game proceeds and fewer cells are left blank, teams may nominate the cell they wish to complete (or nominate one for the next team).

Homework / extension tasks

When the table is complete, the game is over. The teacher will provide students with a completed copy of the record sheet. Students produce their own flowchart of the strongest links as the basis of an essay plan. They write the opening topic sentences as appropriate and discuss these with the teacher before writing the essay in full.

Paper people

To help students connect factors together in a 'chain of causation', take each individual (or personify each factor – for example, Nazi Propaganda could be personified as Goebbels) and connect them together in a paper chain.

The completed diagrams not only form the basis of a classroom display, but can also be used for essay planning: each link explained across the arms forms the 'topic sentence' of each paragraph and the 'body' of the paragraph is the 'body' of the person.

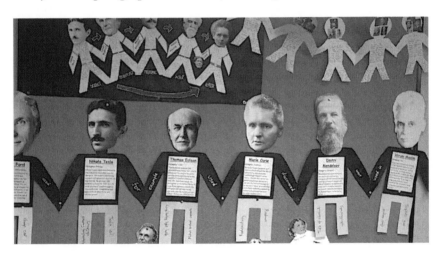

Here are the instructions I gave to my historians after completing their balloon debate (page 58) considering 'Who was the most significant figure of the 19th Century?':

- Highlight five key individuals within different categories
- Include an image of each key character as its face
- Include the name of each key character across the shoulders
- Include detail about achievements. in the body
- Include sentences about qualities of each person on the legs
- Establish connections between people on the arms

Target diagrams for categorisation

Target diagrams enable students to break down a key question into categories and subcategories. Three factors are placed in the centre of the diagram. In the next layer, each factor can then be broken into two examples. In the final layer, each of these examples can then be substantiated with factual detail / illustrative points.

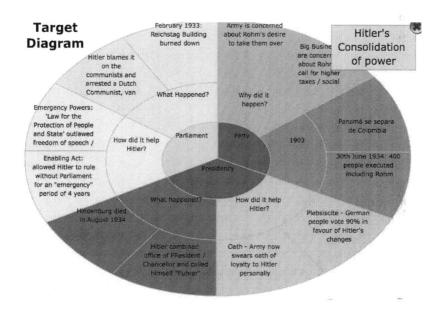

Sample lesson plan

Provide students with a key question, for example "What were the effects of World War One?". Students are asked to come up with three broad categories that could be used as the basis for the investigation, e.g. social / political / economic. These are written into the central area.

Then, students comes up with two examples for each category. This process could be managed as follows:

- Give each student a number (1, 2 or 3) corresponding to one of the three categories.
- Each student has a few minutes to come up with two key examples to illustrate their allocated category of factor.
- All the number "1"s sit together and compare their ideas, as do the "2"s and "3"s.
- Each group decides what the two best points are to keep.

The teacher then asks each group to feedback with their findings. These are recorded in the middle layer of the diagram.

Finally, the students are asked to fill in the final layer of the diagram themselves with substantiating detail for each of the six examples now identified. They could do this in groups and feedback to the class again.

Alternatively, the teacher could save the template onto the network so that students can open it up and work on it individually, or print off copies so that they can be completed by hand.

Taking it further

- The teacher could complete one segment of the diagram (Social, Political or Economic) in advance of the lesson to give students a clearer idea of what needs to be done with the remaining two sections.
- Students could write an essay based around the key question using their template as the basis as their central three paragraphs.

Venn diagrams

A Venn diagram allows students to compare and contrast the similarities and differences between two or three key events, concepts or people.

In a Venn diagram, which usually consists of three overlapping circles, characteristics shared in common go in the central area; those shared by just two factors go in the area where those two circles overlap; characteristics possessed by just one go in the outer area of that circle where it does not overlap the others.

Stage 1: Individual work

To get started with Venn diagrams, ask students to identify three key people, events or factors they have become familiar with. In History, they could compare three different rulers or countries.

Hexagon Venn template available at www.tarrstoolbox.net

Stage 2: Group Quiz

After students have finished their individual Venn diagrams, the teacher could follow this with a team competition. rules are very simple. Once the students have completed their work, they are put into teams and have a few minutes to compare their findings and develop their diagrams.

Then, each team will be given an answer buzzer. The teacher will nominate one "Zone" of the diagram. The first person to press the buzzer can answer by providing a relevant point that fits into that section of the diagram. If they are correct, they win for their team the appropriate amount of points for their team. If they are wrong (or hesitate or repeat an idea already shared), they lose the same amount of points for their team. The quiz can continue over several rounds. The end result is that all the students end up with a detailed resource for revision purposes or for the write-up phase of the project.

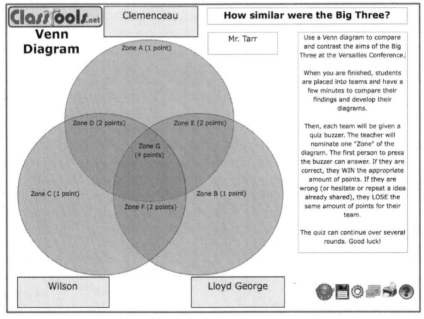

Sample Venn quiz layout

Wedding invitations and bio-poems

Provide students with two characters from their studies, spot connections between them, then design a wedding invite.

Template available at www.tarrstoolbox.net

In the example shown here, note how the students are encouraged to include specific relevant details from their studies in the poem and in the 'further information' at the bottom of the invitation.

Incorporating a bio-poem

The poem provided in the example on the previous page follows no particular format, but this would be a good opportunity to get students to create a "Bio-poem" for each character. The format is as follows:

- Line 1: First Name
- Line 2: Four descriptive traits
- Line 3: Sibling of...(or parent of / child of)
- Line 4: Cares deeply about...
- Line 4: Feels...
- Line 5: Fears...
- Line 6: Needs...
- Line 7: Gives...
- Line 8: Longs to see...
- Line 9: Resident of...
- Line 10: Last Name

Taking it further

The bio-poem format can be adapted. For example, discuss with the class what alternative openings could be used and then decide upon a common format before beginning the task. For example, here are some additional stems:

- Understands that...
- Enemy of...
- Pretends to...
- Whose lasting legacy is...
- Hero to...

The best poems could be illustrated, read out in class or recorded, and used for display purposes.

Sports commentaries

To help students consolidate their understanding of the similarities and differences between key groups (such as parties, countries, ideologies or religions), get them to produce an emotionally-charged sports commentary in the form of a dialogue between two pundits which transforms the 'groups' into 'teams'.

Case study: the European Reformation

After studying the European Reformation with my younger students, I provide them with the following overview of their task:

> "It is 1525. The Reformation is at its height. Against this tense background, Italy (Catholic) and Germany (Protestant) are about to have a celebrity soccer match. Pope Leo X is the inspirational captain of the Italian team, and Martin Luther is leading the Protestant team.
>
> Produce a blow-by-blow account of how the match develops, making sure that their different religious views dictate the "shape of the game". For example, maybe the Pope will insist on the referee speaking in Latin, which leads to an unfortunate "off the ball incident". Maybe Luther has some trouble motivating his team to "play out of their skins" because he has already told them that "Good Works" won't help them into heaven...it's up to you to be as creative (and clichéd) as you can, using as many of the key words provided by your teacher as possible!
>
> By all means change this to a cricket / basketball / other type of sport that you are more interested in".

Step 1: Converting historical knowledge into sporting analogies
We then proceed to review the key points of division between Protestants and Catholics by revisiting the key questions which they asked to "Martin Luther" in one half of the previous lesson, and "Pope Leo X" in the other half (Oscar-winning performances from myself in both instances, obviously). Pairs or groups of students are given a different one of these questions, recall what different answers were given by the Protestant and the Catholic, and then consider how they could turn this into a sporting metaphor.

Key Question	Protestant view	Catholic view	Converted to sports commentary
Who is the head of your church?	Nobody – 'priesthood of all believers'	The Pope	Protestants don't have a manager / established 'formation'; Catholics have a clear "captain" and team formation from Pope > Cardinals > Bishops (etc)
What is purgatory?	A fiction invented by Catholics	A halfway house between heaven and hell	The bench: Catholics can sit on the bench. Not the Lutherans – you're either on the pitch, or on the coach! To represent 'indulgences', the crowd could pray (or pay!) for the man on the bench, who then is able to join his teammates in the match!
What language do you think the bible should be in, and why?	Latin, to ensure consistency and clarity	Vernacular, so people can read it independently	Players could sing their 'national anthems': Catholics will sing in Latin (commentator can't understand it, but at least it's harmonious); Protestants have it in English (all sing something slightly different to each other).

We then continue with this process – considering how to represent Catholic belief in transubstantiation, relics, monasteries, the seven deadly sins and clerical celibacy – until we have a range of ideas ready for the 'game'. By the end of this stage, students are probably becoming clear on how the game might unfold from the moment the teams arrive on the pitch to the awards ceremony at the end.

Step 2: Creating the dialogue

The next task involves writing the actual dialogue. The best of these commentaries will not only make use of clever metaphors converting historical realities into sporting analogies, but also demonstrate a suitably humorous use of heightened emotion and cheesy clichés popular with sports commentators everywhere. Therefore, I like to spend a bit of time firstly discussing the concept of cliché and brainstorming some examples on the board ("sick as a parrot", "game of two halves", "over the moon") that can be sprinkled into the pieces.

Students should then be given, or agree upon after discussion, a list of key words which they will all try to include in their work, before proceeding to write their final commentary. The following is an extract from an example produced by one of my students which gives a flavour of what is might result.

Kevin: Hi, and welcome to the Catholic-Lutheran Celebrity cup final, which promises to be an absolute football classic. It looks like the teams are coming out and just look at those team strips!
Barry: Incredible, Kevin! For the benefit of those of you listening on the radio, the Catholic strip is gorgeous silk, reflecting their belief in praising God with highly decorated churches and images!

Kevin: And look at the Lutherans in contrast – plain whites, showing their belief that the church should be plain and simple so we should focus on the Bible...
Barry: Quite breath-taking...and it appears the Pope and Martin are already arguing with the referee about whether the game should be refereed in Latin or in German – a bit of a replay of their argument about what language the Bible should be in, Kev! This could get really ugly...
Kevin: Well, the referee has blown the whistle and it's 'game on'...straight away the Catholic team are looking on form...the manager, Pope Leo X, has of course banned any of his team from getting married or even having girlfriends because he believes it distracts them from their devotion to God, and that strategy certainly seems to be paying dividends, doesn't it, Barry?
Barry: Absolutely, Kev. The Lutherans do seem a little big sluggish today. Rather than promoting celibacy, Luther has allowed his team to get married and have children to honour God and his creation, but there have been criticisms that this has led them to take their eye off the prize...
Kevin: Yes, Barry. I'm sure that you share my concern about the rather worrying stories of WAGS like Katherine von Bora dragging the name of Lutheranism through the mud...

(continues...)

Taking it further

- Some of the best dialogues should be converted into audio recordings, complete if possible with sound effects.
- *Private Eye*, the UK satirical magazine, has collated hundreds of verbal gaffes by sports commentators that can easily be located with an internet search for "Colemanballs".
- Moreover, I find it is very helpful to show students a few classic spoof comedy sketches of the sports commentary genres to provide some inspiration. My favourites, which can all be found on YouTube easily enough, are:
  - "World Cup 1994" by Alan Partridge ("He's got a foot like a traction engine!")
  - "Staring Final" from Big Train ("live from Wembley Stadium"!)
  - "Sky Football" from Mitchell and Webb ("the football will officially go on forever")
  - "Alan Latchley meets Clive Anderson" by Peter Cook ("Football's a cruel mistress")

Crime boards

When requiring students to spot connections and contrasts between different groups and individuals, challenge them to present their findings in the form of a 'crime board' complete with photographs, written sources, string and annotated sticky notes.

Case study 1: anti-apartheid movements

As part of our investigation into why the anti-apartheid movement failed to achieve its objectives by 1964, one factor we evaluate is the division between and within the various groups involved. The PAC split from the ANC over the issue of how far the movement should co-operate with white activists, and both of these two movements in turn split again over the legitimacy of violent action, with Mandela and the MK adopting a programme of sabotage against property, with Leballo and POQO going even further by sponsoring assassinations of their opponents. The whole picture is made more complex still by the existence of a whole range of other groups based around different races, economic and political interests.

To help students draw things together, I encouraged them to produce a crime board. We established a scenario to start with: it is 1960, Prime Minister Verwoerd has just suffered an assassination attempt, and we as the police are trying to get to the bottom of who might be responsible:

The Scene
On 9th April 1960, Verwoerd opened the Union Exposition in Milner Park, Johannesburg, to mark the jubilee of the Union of South Africa. After Verwoerd delivered his opening address, David Pratt, a rich English businessman and farmer from the Magaliesberg, near Pretoria, attempted to assassinate Verwoerd, firing two shots from a .22 pistol at point-blank range, one bullet perforating Verwoerd's right cheek and the second his right ear.

The regime is determined to hunt down those responsible for the crime, which it regards as a conspiracy rather than the work of a lone gunman.

Your Task
Produce a 'crime board' for the apartheid regime, designed to highlight connections / contrasts between some of the following key figures of the movement. Consider such things as their motives, words, actions and political affiliation, and degree of danger to the regime.

Suspects
Trevor Huddleston | Joe Slovo | Helen Suzman | Bram Fischer | Nelson Mandela | Oliver Tambo | Walter Sisulu | Albert Luthuli | Yusuf Dadoo | Robert Sobukwe | Potlako Leballo | Nelson Mandela | Ruth First | Denis Goldberg | Molly Blackburn | Frederick Harris | Miriam Makeba | Alan Paton

Starting with a range of photographs of key campaigners and primary sources including speeches and pamphlets, students then started organising them into meaningful categories, spotting connections between them using string, then explaining these connections using sticky notes. They then used their completed work as the basis of an answer to the task "Compare and contrast the aims and methods of anti-apartheid campaigners before 1964".

"Crime board" focusing on the assassination of Verwoerd

Case study 2: Jack the Ripper

Here are two crime boards produced by my students to reach conclusions on the identity of Jack the Ripper after considering the evidence:

Crime boards analysing the evidence from the Whitechapel murders

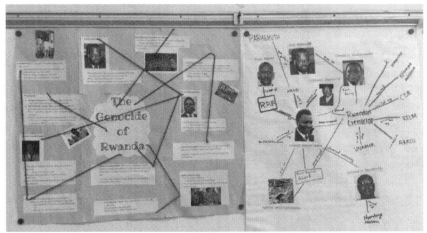

The Rwandan Genocide

Dialogue poems

Dialogue poems are designed to compare and contrast the perspectives of the same event or situation from the point of view of different parties involved. Students can read existing poems, or write their own, to examine the main controversies and viewpoints surrounding particular topics.

Case study: "Two Women" (anonymous author)

The socialist President Salvador Allende of Chile was overthrown in a military coup in 1973. After studying this topic with my students, a pair of the girls read out this anonymously written poem (line by line so they alternate). It represents the differing views of the working class, and the privileged class, about Allende's rule and the Pinochet regime that replaced it. We then discussed its meaning, annotated it with historical details, and discussed how (or indeed if) the two women could resolve their differences.

First student	Second student
I am a woman.	I am a woman.
I am a woman born of a woman whose man owned a factory.	I am a woman born of a woman whose man laboured in a factory.
I am a woman whose man wore silk suits, who constantly watched his weight.	I am a woman whose man wore tattered clothing, who constantly suffered hunger.
I am a woman who watched two babies grow into beautiful children.	I am a woman who watched two babies die because there was no milk.
I am a woman who watched twins grow into popular college students with summers abroad.	I am a woman who watched three children grow, but with bellies stretched from no food.
But then there was a man;	But then there was a man;
And he talked about the peasants getting richer by my family getting poorer.	And he told me of days that would be better, and he made the days better.
We had to eat rice.	We had rice.
We had to eat beans!	We had beans.
My children were no longer given summer visas to Europe.	My children no longer cried themselves to sleep.
And I felt like a peasant.	And I felt like a woman.
A peasant with a dull, hard, unexciting life.	Like a woman with a life that sometimes allowed a song.
And I saw a man.	And I saw a man.

And together we began to plot with the hope of the return to freedom.	I saw his heart begin to beat with hope of freedom, at last.
Someday, the return to freedom.	Someday freedom.
And then, One day,	But then, One day,
Planes were overhead, guns firing close by.	Planes were overhead ,guns firing far away.
I gathered my children and went home.	I gathered my children and ran.
And the guns moved farther and farther away.	But the guns moved closer and closer.
Then they announced freedom was restored!	Then they came, young boys really.
They came into my home along with my man.	They came and found my man.
Those men whose money was almost gone,	Men whose lives were almost their own.
And we all had drinks to celebrate.	And they shot them all.
The most wonderful martinis.	They shot my man.
And then they asked us to dance.	And then they came for me.
Me.	For me, the woman.
And my sisters.	For my sisters.
And then they took us,	Men they took us,
They took us to dinner at a small, private club.	They stripped us of the dignity we had gained.
And they treated us to beef.	And then they raped us.
It was one course after another.	One after another they came after us.
We nearly burst we were so full.	Sisters bleeding, sisters dying.
It was magnificent to be free again!	It was hardly a relief to have survived.
The beans have almost disappeared now.	The beans have disappeared.
The rice – I've replaced it with chicken or steak.	The rice, I cannot find it.
And the parties continue night after night to make up for all the time wasted.	And my silent tears are joined once more by the midnight cries of my children.
And I feel like a woman again.	They say, I am a woman.

Taking it further

Rather than simply locate and read existing dialogue poems, students could write their own at the end of a topic. Examples might include:

- A Muslim and a Christian giving their perspectives on the causes, events and consequences of the Crusades
- King Henry VIII and Thomas More explaining how and why they moved from being friends to enemies (Becket and Henry II would work here too)
- A Hiroshima bomb victim and a U.S. Air Force pilot flying the plane that dropped the bomb
- A German and a British citizen describing the events that led to the outbreak of World War One
- An American and a Soviet observer describing the events that led to the development of the Cold War.

Speed dates / Blind dates

The "dating" format requires students to consider or research one area in depth, and then exchange their knowledge against the clock with classmates. It is an efficient means of sharing ideas and knowledge and helps students spot comparisons and contrasts between different ideas, answers or categories of information.

Method 1: Exchanging factual information

Speed-dating works particularly well for topics where there are lots of key personalities to learn about: for example, a comparison of Roman Emperors, or the attitude of different types of people towards Hitler in Nazi Germany in the 1930s. However, the technique can also be used to compare and contrast factors, objects, themes or events in any field.

Method 2: Exchanging ideas, interpretations, opinions

An effective twist on the speed-dating method is to conduct "Blind Dates" not to exchange factual information, but rather opinions and interpretations. In this format, all students are given an open question or a thesis statement to form a judgment upon. Each student has a short amount of time to formulate their response to the question, and then students are paired up to exchange their ideas. Each student then adjusts their original answer to accommodate any fresh ideas from the discussion, then moves to a fresh partner.

This process can be repeated over several rounds, and then a fresh question can be posed once all perspectives on the first one appear to have been absorbed. In this second round, the question can be considered in pairs before all students then move to a fresh partner for the first round of the new speed-dating activity.

Stage 1: decide on the criteria and conduct the research

The first step is to settle upon the most important areas of comparison and contrast. Some of these are transferable whoever is being studied: "Early life / upbringing", "Greatest successes", "Biggest mistake", and so on. Others though need to be tailored to the particular topic: for example, when studying civil rights campaigners, sensible headings might also be "Attitude to nonviolence" and "Contributions to particular campaigns"; in contrast, a study of Roman Emperors might use "Domestic achievements" and "Military prowess". Once these have been decided, the next step is for each student to research one key individual in order to make notes under the chosen headings.

Stage 2: speed-dating
Prior to the lesson, the classroom should ideally be arranged for paired work. Best of all is to arrange the chairs in the room in two rows, facing each other, ready for the conversations to take place. Once the students are in the room, divide the class into two groups. Members of the first team should be given a number (e.g. 1-12), whilst the members of the second should be given a letter (e.g. A-L). Pair the students in the format A-1, B-2, C-3 and so on, then give each pair a strictly limited amount of time to judge the degree of similarity for each category (making brief notes and awarding a score from -2 to +2, for example) – my ClassTools.net countdown timer is ideal in this way for setting up a series of countdown clocks that can run in sequence:

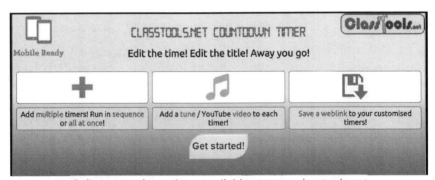

Online countdown timer available at www.classtools.net

When the time is up, all of the 'numbered' students should move around so that we end up with new pairings (A-2, B-3 and so on, all the way up to L-1). The process then repeats for as long as the teacher feels appropriate.

Stage 3: reaching conclusions
At the end of the exercise, each student should be asked who they felt they were best matched with. These results should recorded on the board. Any character who has more than one person choosing them as their 'top date' should then be given the opportunity to hear from each one of these 'suitors' about why they are better matched than their rivals. The individual can then choose a winner, or the class could vote instead.

Taking it further

- Instead of students interviewing each other, they could instead conduct 'speed dating' with particular sources set up around the room.

- Students could make a mask of their character and wear an appropriate costume / carry appropriate props. Acting in role adds an extra layer of interest to the proceedings.

- The matching process could take place over several rounds, so that each category can be considered separately, before a final judgment is given by each student regarding their overall 'best match'.

- Students could follow up the speed-dating exercise by creating a diagram highlighting the connections between key characters.

- The speed-dating research could be consolidated by turning the information learned into Top Trumps cards (page 152).

Top trumps

Because "Top trumps" is a simple game to play, this does not automatically translate into an educationally worthwhile exercise. It must be converted into a game based historical facts and reasoned explanation rather than a mindless card-swapping exercise.

Example 1: the Russian Revolution

The "Top trumps" format lends itself particularly well to topics which require learning about the role and significance of a range of individuals. In this sense, the Russian Revolution provides an excellent example.

Step 1: Producing the cards

I start by providing students with a list of key characters, and get them to design a series of "Top trumps" cards for as many of these as possible using a template I've put together in a word processor.

The categories decided upon by students should be as useful as possible and can either be decided upon in advance by the teacher, or settled upon after discussion with the class. For example, if the focus is on 'significance' the categories might be:

- **When?** (long term, short term)
- **Where?** (local, national, international)
- **What?** (political, socio-economic, military)
- **Who?** (different classes / races, men / women / children)

Step 2: Playing the game focusing on the text, not the ratings

So far, so good. Students have spent time usefully researching or revising key characters, summarising their findings, and using these to make simple judgments in the form of percentage ratings. At this point, though, the rules of the game need to change to ensure that students at all times are discussing and debating the text in their respective cards rather than simply comparing the numbers and swapping the cards without further thought.

To achieve this objective, put students into groups of three and give each player in each group a letter (A, B, C). All players should shuffle their cards. In the first round, player "A" will act as the judge. Player "B" will take the first card from the top of their deck, and decide upon the strongest category for that character. They then name the character, nominate the category and explain why the character should score strongly in this regard (note: they do not need to read out the rating they gave and should be penalised for doing so). Player "C" responds by repeating this pattern for their own character. It is then up to the judge (Player "A") to announce the winner, who takes the card from their opponent in the normal way. Player "C" then takes the lead by repeating the process with the first card from their stack.

Once these two players have had their chance to play one card each, it is time for the next round: player "B" becomes the judge, and the other two take it in turns to play cards against each other. Then in the final round player "C" becomes the judge in the same way. This process can be repeated over several rounds.

Vladimir Lenin Born 1870 Died 1924	
Importance in 1917 The leader of the Bolshevik Party in 1917. Established first communist state, the USSR.	100
Mental Intelligence / Charisma Author of "State and Revolution" (for intellectuals) and "April Theses" (for proletariat). Highly charismatic	100
Physical Bravery Tended to flee away on his train whenever he got the chance, but risked his life through revolutionary action.	50
Gruesome Death Rating Survived an assassination attempt but then suffered three horrendous strokes which left him immobile and speechless	75

Leon Trotsky Born 1870 Died 1940	
Historical Significance Orchestrated the Bolshevik Revolution in 1917 through MRC. Created the Red Army and led it to victory during the Civil War.	90
Mental Intelligence / Charisma Notoriously arrogant and intelligent. Inspiring speaker.	90
Physical Bravery Gave little thought to his own personal safety. Relished being imprisoned. Risked his life on his train during the Civil War	90
Gruesome Death Rating Assassinated on Stalin's orders. An ice pick went through the front of his head. He died in agony days later.	100

Taking it further

• Students can be instructed at particular points) that "lowest rating wins" in certain rounds. In other words, they have to choose the weakest suit for a particular character to ensure they are building up a rounded picture of each person rather than a one-sided and purely positive interpretation.

Which one doesn't belong?

As an engaging starter or plenary exercise, present students with four simple images (or statements) and challenge them to give a reasoned answer to the question "Which one doesn't belong?". Students gain points for any valid reason given.

From obvious surface differences, students should be encouraged to draw out their existing knowledge to keep on spotting increasingly sophisticated connections, contrasts and comparisons.

Case study: Tudor England

Stage 1
Students could be presented with faces of four people they have studied:

In the first round it is likely that the points made will be based on surface appearances ("only one of them is clearly a child", "Only one has a beard") and these points could either be given less credit or discounted altogether. Better students will make more meaningful points demonstrating contextual knowledge ("The second one was the only monarch to rule England for more than 40 years", "The first one was the only one to have any children of his own").

Stage 2
Once these ideas run out, display the names of the individuals to hopefully provoke another round of ideas:

| Henry VIII (1590-47) | Elizabeth I (1558-1603) | Edward VI (1547-1553) | Mary I (1553-1558) |

Stage 3

At the end of the exercise, various points should have been identified that could then be shared with the class:

| Henry VIII (1590-47) | Elizabeth I (1558-1603) | Edward VI (1547-1553) | Mary I (1553-1558) |

None of the others...	None of the others...	None of the others...	None of the others...
Married more than once.	Ruled more than 40 years.	Failed to reach adulthood.	Married Philip II.
Dissolved monasteries.	Had black teeth.	Dissolved chantries.	Was nicknamed "Bloody".
Executed Thomas More.	Defeated the Armada.	Was a firm Protestant.	Was a firm Catholic.

Taking it further

- The "Which One Doesn't Belong?" approach is clearly applicable to any topic, and does not need to be limited to images. Quotes, diagrams, keywords, dates, places, names of books and objects can also be used.
- Students could design their own "Which one doesn't belong?" challenge that could be used in subsequent lessons.

Five techniques to analyse cartoons

Visual sources such as cartoons, portraits, photographs are a mainstay of the history classroom and provide a wonderful tool not only for starter and plenary activities, but invaluable raw material for helping students draw deductions, compare interpretations and substantiate their own judgements by bringing in additional background knowledge.

They also provide an accessible way into the historical debate for students who are less able readers. What follows here are several ideas about how to help students interpret cartoons and use them to deepen their historical understanding.

Case studies

1. Idioms – how do cartoonists use them literally?

Political cartoons frequently make use of idiomatic expressions, represented in literal form. To help students spot when this is happening, present them with a list of idiomatic expressions and determine how many students can correctly identify the meaning of each. Some of the most popular with cartoonists (such as my all-time favourite, David Low) include:

- crocodile tears
- caught between a rock and a hard place
- look a gift horse in the mouth
- put all your eggs in one basket
- let the cat out of the bag

- burn your bridges
- treated like a doormat
- bury your head in the sand
- have a taste of your own medicine
- a wolf in sheep's clothing

After the class takes notes on the meaning of each, ask them to consider how these could be represented visually, then challenge them to use the internet to locate a political cartoon making use of some of these idioms.

2. Details – can you fill the missing gaps?

The title or caption of the cartoon (e.g. "The Spineless Leaders of Democracy", "They Salute with Both Hands Now") can be hidden and students challenged to provide their own before revealing the correct answer. Another idea is to cover up parts of an image and challenge students to guess what's behind the gaps. To help with this exercise I created an online tool (https://www.classtools.net/reveal) which allows you to quickly upload an image and convert it into as many "tiles" as you wish for this purpose:

3. Interpretations – Can you reverse the message?

Following on from the previous example, students could interpret the meaning of the cartoon - elaborating with background knowledge of course – and then be challenged to reverse the message by changing as few details as possible. In this way they will have to identify the most salient features of the cartoon and consider what would need to be done to reverse its message. Do certain symbols, expressions or words need to be altered, removed, or added? The amended cartoons could be placed alongside the originals with an explanation from the student to create an effective piece of display work.

4. Deductions – Can you use this transparent overlay to highlight the key features of the cartoon?
I have designed a template (freely downloadable from www.tarrstoolbox.net) which can be placed over a written or visual source to provide a scaffolding framework to help students develop cartoon evaluations skills. Ask students to focus on the issues highlighted in the left-hand column first and make annotations as appropriate. Then they swap with a partner, read the work done so far, and focus on the issues covered in the top row. Display the work when it's finished. Ensure each student has a different source. When the work is finished, remove the sources from the templates. Different students must match the overlay to the source it evaluated.

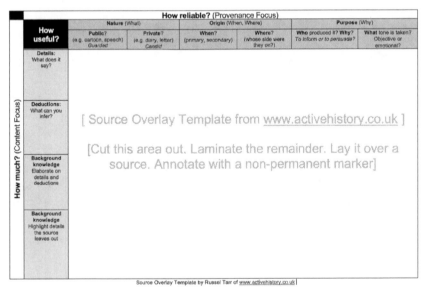

5. Bringing it all together – Annotate the image online
To help students record and share their findings more effectively, and to help teachers produce sample analyses of picture sources, I have

produced a simple online tool which allows you to upload an image, annotate it and share it (www.classtools.net/hotspot):

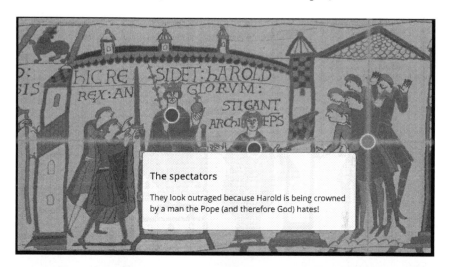

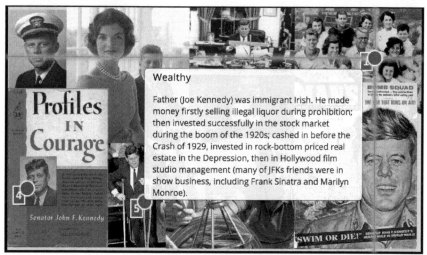

Taking it further

- Students can develop their cartoon analysis skills by designing their own political cartoon (page 107).
- They could also construct an entire essay from first principles using a collection of cartoons using the "Visual Essay Writing" technique (page 293).

Connection webs

One of the most important skills for students to develop is the ability to make connections between factors to reach a sustained, sophisticated judgement.

The following template structure is a useful way to help students to develop skills of selection and linkage.

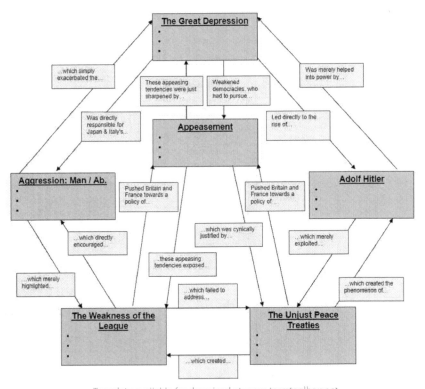

Template available for download at www.tarrstoolbox.net

Students start by charting the "path" through this diagram which they think makes the most sense, and delete any unnecessary links. At this stage they will be left with only five of the 'yellow box' links, as per this example:

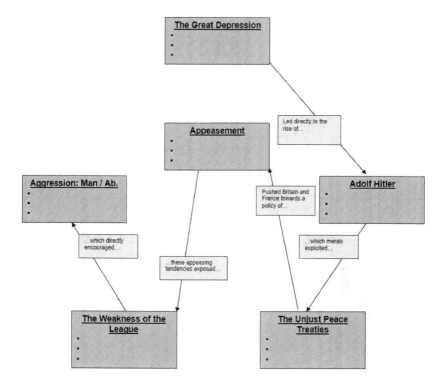

In the next stage, students use the completed 'path' to produce the opening topic sentence of each paragraph of the essay. In the above example, this might be:

- The cause of World War Two was the Great Depression.
- The Great Depression led directly to the rise of Hitler.
- Upon coming to power, Hitler destabilised the international situation by exploiting the unjust peace treaties.

With the topic sentences written, the next stage is to add three points of substantiating evidence in each of the orange boxes. These are then used to develop each topic sentence into a full paragraph.

Taking it further

Students should identify the six initial factors themselves. This could be achieved by giving students a hexagons exercise (page 24) with the objective of arranging them in six logical groupings. The groupings could be listed on the board after different students have come up with different ideas, and these could become a factor auction (page 189).

Six degrees of separation

The six degrees of separation game aims to prove that all people are no more than six social or professional connections away from each other.

As a result, a chain of "friend of a friend" statements can be used to connect any two people in a maximum of six steps. It can easily be used to help students identify connections between the key individuals involved in any topic of study.

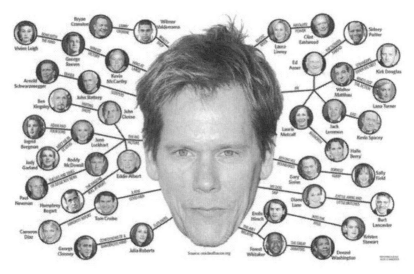

Kevin Bacon is a popular subject for the "six degrees of separation" game

Case study

- Divide the class into teams. Each team takes it in turn to name one key individual related to the topic of study and to state their role / significance. Each team writes this onto a sticky note. Give a point for each name mentioned. Continue until they run out of ideas.
- Each team is challenged to create a diagram out their sticky notes connecting as many of the characters as possible.
- The first group that finishes their diagram wins the game, but only after the teacher has confirmed that all the links are valid.

5
JUDGMENTS &
INTERPRETATIONS

Through the process of linking, comparing and contrasting key factors, students are working towards an overall judgment and interpretation on the historical questions being investigated. This chapter considers methods for helping students reach and share their conclusions with their peers.

Counterfactual history

To help students decide how important a factor was in causing a particular event, ask them to consider whether events would have turned out differently without it.

To have validity, this 'counterfactual' approach should not descend into mere speculation. Instead, students should be prepared and trained to substantiate their assertions with evidence to help build a case for a given factor being a genuine cause, a mere catalyst, or downright irrelevant. It also gets students thinking about some deep questions about causation such as the intentionalist view of history (which places an emphasis on the actions of individuals) as opposed to the more deterministic structuralist interpretation (which focuses instead on the role of institutions and deep-seated conditions). From there, it is a short step to the philosophical discussion about free will versus determinism. It is also an approach which has been pursued by major historians such as Sir Richard Evans and Niall Fergusson.

Example: Why did Hitler become Chancellor of Germany?

Step 1: Review the narrative
At the end of a detailed study of the causes why Hitler became chancellor of Germany in 1933, start by presenting students with a summary of what they have learned so far as a summary digest:

"In 1921, a final reparations sum of £6.6 billion was imposed upon the Germans. Claiming that their economy was already severely damaged by territorial losses under the Treaty of Versailles, they claimed they were unable to pay. So in early 1923 the French and the Belgians invaded the Ruhr. Strikes and demonstrations led to complete economic collapse, and the government made things worse by simply printing off more paper money to 'inflate' the economy again. The result was hyperinflation, which wiped out life savings overnight and led to a surge of support for Hitler's Nazi party. At this point, Hitler sensed an opportunity and launched his Munich Beer Hall Putsch. This was easily crushed by the police in clashes which led to the deaths of several Nazis. However, Hitler used his subsequent trial to promote his ideas and used his prison sentence to write *Mein Kampf* and to change his strategy ("We must hold our noses and enter the Reichstag). Meanwhile, Germany superficially recovered: the USA gave Germany a series of massive loans in the Dawes Plan (1924). However, in 1929 the Wall Street Crash sent the American economy into a sharp Depression. The USA called in its loans from Germany, which threw the German economy into another crisis and which once again led to a surge in support for the Nazi party. By the end of 1932 the Nazi party was easily the largest party in Parliament (although its support was already beginning to decline as the Depression started to fade away), and President Hindenburg was persuaded by his advisors to appoint Hitler as Chancellor in a coalition government in January 1933. Hitler rapidly manipulated the situation to turn himself into a dictator. Within ten years he had unleashed World War Two, which not only destroyed Germany but which also accelerated the collapse of the British Empire, the emergence of the USSR and the USA as world superpowers, and the declaration of Israel as a safe home for the Jews following the horrors of the Holocaust."

Step 2: From narrative to analysis: identify the key factors

The next stage is to discuss with the students what appear to be the most important factors explaining Hitler's rise to power. To help with this process, different students could be encouraged to identify short-term, mid-term, and long-term factors; others might be asked to identify political, economic, or diplomatic factors. List these on the board and, if there are too many, reduce them down to the most popular (for example, by using the 'factor auction' approach).

Step 3: Construct the counterfactual

This important stage involves constructing a feasible alternative scenario to what actually occurred in relation to the each given factor. These can be provided by the teacher, or formulated in groups. For example:

- **Factor**: The 'Backstairs Intrigue' of von Papen and Hindenburg.

- **Counterfactual**: "In 1933, Hindenburg refused to appoint Hitler as Chancellor"
- **Factor**: Hitler's personal charisma.
- **Counterfactual**: "In 1923, Hitler was killed during the Munich Putsch"

Step 4: Frame the question for consideration

Next, explicitly guide the students to consider what might have happened in these counterfactual scenarios by framing a clear question for consideration ("Will the party still get into power under someone else's leadership after Hitler's death?", "Will the Nazis find it increasingly difficult to get into power due to Hindenburg's intransigence?"). These can be accompanied by more open-ended questions that can apply to all the scenarios (e.g. Does the Weimar Republic become more, or less, stable? Does the leadership and / or strategy of the Nazi Party change? Does support for the Nazis increase or decrease? Does the Nazi party take power sooner, later or not at all?).

Step 5: Reflection and feedback

Students should then be given time to consider one or more of the counterfactuals, either alone or in small groups, before sharing their findings through jigsaw groups and/or a teacher-led discussion. They could then prioritise their factors overall using a tool such as a Triangle 9 (page 167), a matrix grid (page 172) or similar.

Taking it further

When students have finished their reflections, they could rewrite and develop the original account of events provided at the start of the exercise to reflect how things would have turned out had certain "What if...?" events had really happened.

Diamond diagrams for prioritisation

Students are given (or produce) essential pieces of information which they arrange in order or significance, success or status in a diamond diagram.

Most commonly the diamond is arranged for nine factors, but they can also be for sixteen or twenty-five. In my history classroom I have used them to arrange the outcomes of the Treaty of Versailles from most successful to least successful; evidence that a particular individual deserves to be regarded as a hero or a villain; most important to least important reasons why the slave trade was abolished.

Group / display work: image-based diamond diagrams
Students can order pictures instead of text statements – for example, images which create a positive impression of a figure or period go towards the top. Each factor could be printed off on a separate sheet of A4 paper and then arranged as a group exercise. In the picture above, students researched the origins of surnames of people in the class. The ones that corresponded to jobs – e.g. Baker, Tarr, Butcher – were then arranged in a Diamond 16 diagram from highest status to

lowest status. Different pairs of students came out of class to adjust the diagram after discussion until everyone had their input. We then transferred the diagram onto a display board.

The "Triangle 9" template

Diamond templates have a lot of wasted space which could be much better deployed for including explanations and illustrations of student reasoning. With this in mind I have created a 'Triangle 9' template: it works exactly the same as a Diamond 9, but with specific areas created for students to explain clearly why they have decided to place some factors nearer the top or the bottom. You can download the Triangle 9 Template, along with Diamond 9, 16 and 25 templates, from www.tarrstoolbox.net.

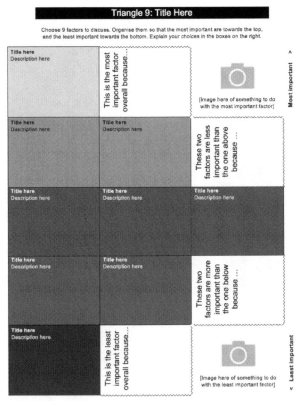

Triangle 9 template available at www.tarrstoolbox.net

Continuum lines: measure opinions on one issue

Continuum lines are a simple and effective technique for providing a breakdown of a complex question.

For example, when considering the question "Did Napoleon betray the spirit of the French Revolution?", debate each key policy area using a "Teacher on Trial" format (page 70) and then conclude by organising the policies along a continuum line containing a number of gradated possibilities to end up with something like this:

Did Napoleon betray the spirit of the French Revolution?

Legal Reforms	Church	Finance/Economy	Local Gov't	Education	Propganda	Censorship	Slavery
Revolutionary?		**Reformer?**	**Consolidator?**		**Underminer?**		**Reactionary?**

The completed diagram can then be used as the basis of an essay plan, with each of the policies being dealt with from left to right.

Taking it further

- Continuum lines can be combined effectively with the 'Wheel of Life' template (page 170). The policies listen in the example above (for example, education, propaganda and slavery) could form some of the main spokes of the wheel, and students can then rate each one in terms of its success.
- A second issue of debate can be added to create a matrix grid (page 172) or an interpretation battleships exercise (page 173).

Wheel of life

This is a simple, visual way to evaluate historical characters and events from more than one perspective.

At the end of the study, students are given a historical character to evaluate and write their name into the template.

They then decide on at least four, but up to eight, ways to rate this character (e.g. loyalty, friendliness, intelligence, determination, tolerance – this can form the basis of an interesting classroom discussion in itself).

Next, students place a dot on each line to rate the character for each of the categories (with ten being the best score).

The dots are then joined up, and the area within shaded in a bold colour, to produce the completed wheel of life.

To round off, students should provide an explanation for their diagram underneath or overleaf.

Taking it further:

- Arrange students into a continuum line (page 169), with the most positive interpretations at one end, and the most negative at the other. Ask the student at each end of the line to justify their opinion and then ask the rest of the class to swap positions if they have been persuaded that their original judgment was too harsh or lenient.
- Create an interactive Wheel of Life using the dedicated template at www.classtools.net/lifewheel.
- Print off the wheels of different students and arrange them in a Diamond 9 diagram (page 167) as a classroom display piece.
- Create a 'physical' wheel of life by arranging eight students on the playground – each step outwards from the centre of the circle (up to a maximum of ten) for each of the categories of analysis.

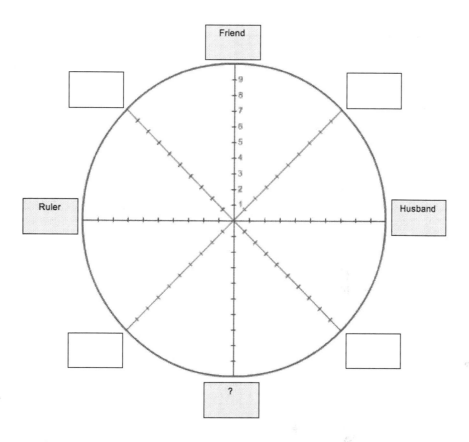

The wheel of life template can be downloaded at www.tarrstoolbox.net. Although it most obviously lends itself to assessing key individuals, it could also be used to assess the success and failure of a regime such as the German Weimar Republic or similar.

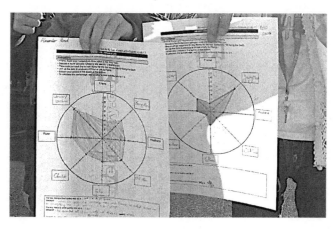

Matrix grids: judge two issues at once

It is often necessary to form a judgment on two separate but related issues. Matrix grids do this in a visually engaging way.

For example, "How successfully did Lenin rule Russia?" and "How Marxist was Lenin's regime?" are connected, but subtly different (for example, his greatest practical successes in economic terms came when he departed from strictly Marxist principles).

To highlight these differences, and to get students thinking about each one more deeply, conclude the study by dividing the board with a horizontal and a vertical line to create four squares. The vertical line represents one issue (e.g. "Success / Failure") and the horizontal the other (e.g. "Marxist / Not Marxist").

Next, consider different dimensions of the topic that can be used to reach a judgment. In the example outlined above, these would be key policy areas: the Treaty of Brest Litovsk, the Civil War, The NEP, the handling of national minorities and so on. For each one, discuss where it belongs in the diagram and then write it into that spot.

Finally, ask each student to write their own name (in a different colour) to represent their overall judgment.

The completed diagram can form the basis of an essay consisting of four main sections corresponding to the zones of the diagram.

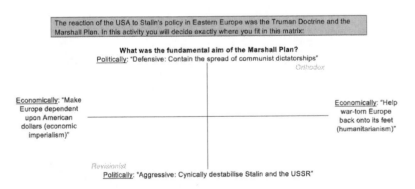

Example matrix grid: What was the aim of the Marshall Plan?

Interpretations battleships

This activity is a development of the matrix exercise, making it more sophisticated and engaging. It is a particularly effective way to get students analysing lots of information for a fresh topic.

I use this approach very effectively to teach Eisenhower's foreign policy without any prior knowledge or preparatory study.

As per the matrix format (page 172), students are given two key questions to consider (e.g. "How successful...?" and "How innovative...?") and then place particular pieces of evidence along the horizontal and vertical axes to reflect what is suggests is the correct spot with regard to each question. In the following example, students considered the two questions "How successful was Eisenhower's foreign policy?" and "How new was Eisenhower's 'New Look' foreign policy?".

However, the twist is to turn the whole process into a team competition called 'interpretation battleships'. This involves subdividing each quadrant of the matrix into four boxes (thereby creating 16 boxes in total). These are then individually referenced using a simple key (horizontal = letters, vertical = numbers), creating a grid of 16 squares:

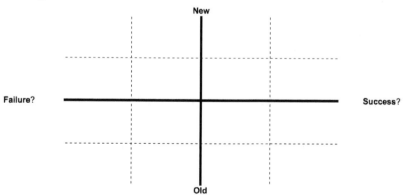

Sample grid for analysing Eisenhower's foreign policy

Phase 1: Individual research / group discussion

Each member of the class is provided with the pieces of evidence that will be considered. In the case of my lesson, this consisted of a very detailed article covering nine different policy areas, each considered under a different subheading. These policy areas are divided between three different teams. Working individually at first, then comparing their ideas with the rest of their team to reach a group agreement, students decide where their allocated policy areas and pieces of evidence belong in the matrix, and write a sentence of explanation on scrap paper ready for the game.

When they are finished with these allocated areas, they should repeat the process a second time for the remaining factors so that they have had change to consider them all. At the end of the process, each team will end up with their own version of a matrix which might look something like this:

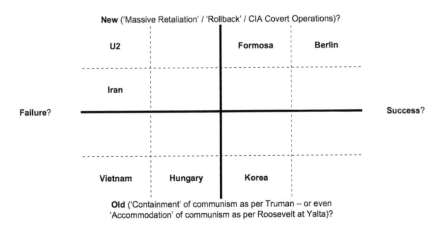

Phase 2: playing interpretation battleships

When everyone is ready, the first policy area and piece of evidence is introduced. The group who was allocated this piece of evidence (the "Quizmaster" team) stays quiet whilst the other two teams nominate the cell of the table that they think it should belong in and explain why. They should try to persuade the Quizmaster team with their reasoning.

The Quizmaster team listens carefully and then confers to decide whether they want to keep this factor in the cell they originally decided, or whether they want to adjust their decision based on the ideas they have heard.

The Quizmaster team then announces where, after full consideration, the factor belongs in the grid, and explains their choice. The teacher should record this decision in a 'class' version of the matrix. A competing team gets one point if it placed the factor in the same quadrant as the Quizmaster team, and a further point if they placed it in exactly the same cell.

All students take notes to make sure they are clear for the reasoning behind this, and then the process is then repeated for the remaining cells of the table.

Taking it further

This approach is a really efficient way of getting through a big topic very efficiently and analytically which might otherwise involve inordinate amounts of classroom reading and teacher-led discussions.

It could be followed with a source-work exercise, where the views of key historians on the issues covered have to be organised in the matrix. This would be a very good extension or homework task for individual students to ensure that historiography was incorporated.

Each quadrant of the completed diagram can form the basis of a four-paragraph essay addressing both of the key questions covered at the start of the activity.

Another example of 'interpretation battleships'

Write a school report on a historical character

When assessing the successes and failures of a particular historical figure, consider approaching the task in the form of a school report. This can be the basis of a consolidation exercise at the end of a topic, or an efficient way of covering fresh material.

Start by identifying the main 'subjects' that reports will be required for (e.g. economics, law, politics...) and write these down.

Discuss the successes and failures relating to the first subject. Consider how this could be written in the form of a school report ("Tsar Alexander II has had a mixed term in terms of his legal reforms...", "Adolf has been rather disruptive in his attitude to group work in recent weeks..."). Students tend to have a bit of fun recycling teacher platitudes and getting in the habit of writing a 'compliment sandwich' that starts with something positive, then makes a criticism, then closes with another positive point.

Next, provide students with an A3 version of a school report template. They then write the first report in strict timed conditions, using key words. When the time is up, repeat the process for the remaining subjects.

Taking it further
- Students should provide an effort and attainment grade for each subject as well as a written comment. This could provide the basis of an interesting discussion.
- After completing each subject report, students should swap their sheets with another member of the class. In this way, each subject report is written by a different person and looks more authentic when it returns to the original owner.
- After the exercise is completed, students should underline clear evidence of success in one colour, failure in another.

| BERLIN NAPOLA: SUMMER REPORT 1939 |
NAME OF STUDENT:

SUBJECT	GRADES		Comments
	Attainment (A-E)	Effort (1-5)	
Maths			
			Key term: Aliens; Untermenschen; Stab in the Back
History			
			Key term: Subhumans; Reichstag Fire; Treaty of Versailles; Polish Corridor
Biology			
			Key term: Aryans; Social Darwinism; Euthanasia; Sterilisation
Geography			
			Key term: Lebensraum; Alsace Lorraine
Physical Education			
			Key term: Master Race; Hitler Youth; League of German Maidens
Religious Education			
			Key Terms: Führer; German Faith Movement; Reich Church

Form Tutor's comments:

Sample report template available at www.activehistory.co.uk. Note how it is helpful to provide students with key words within the template to help them frame their report. I get the students to pass their report sheet on to a fresh partner after each subject has been presented by the teacher and summarised by the students.

Triangulation: judge three factors at once

This method allows for three related interpretations to be compared visually. Write the three factors, options or interpretations on different points of a triangle. Students have to then write their initials in the appropriate spot to indicate their position.

Next, get students who are most clearly in disagreement to explain their choices to the class. Allow other members of the class to adjust their position in the triangle based on what they hear.

It is a good idea to blank out the central part of the triangle. This prevents students from defaulting at the 'fence-sitting' option of placing themselves in the middle of the triangle:

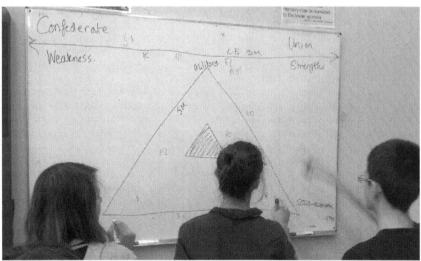

Was the Union victory in the American Civil War due to political, military or economic factors? This particular example is being combined with a continuum line (page 169) to help students decide whether Confederate weakness, or Union strength, was the main cause of the war's outcome.

Relationship webs

A relationship web is a visually engaging way of charting the changing relationship between nations and individuals over time, helping to identify key turning points and essential continuities.

Case study: the causes of World War One

Understanding the complexity of international relations, and the development of the alliance system, is central to a study of the origins of World War One. Provide students with a detailed timeline of key events focusing on essential turning points in the relationships between the major powers of Europe. To the right of each event is a simple summary of the six main countries under consideration: (B)ritain, (R)ussia, (F)rance, (G)ermany, (I)taly and (A)ustria-Hungary.

The students then use dotted black lines to represent friendships ("ententes"); solid black lines to represent firm military agreements ("alliances"); dotted red lines to represent tension; solid red lines to represent clear enmity. The first event in the timeline looks like this: how would you convert each into a diagram in the manner described?

1871: The Franco-Prussian War The new state of Germany defeated France and took Alsace-Lorraine from her. France was isolated in Europe as the only Republic among the major powers. The royal families of Germany, Britain and Russia were linked by marriage.	B F I	R G A

Students should then move on to the next event in the timeline and consider what needs to be adjusted in the new diagram to take account of what has changed. This is an important point: the new diagram should represent an evolution of the previous one, and not merely the particular event described in the new timeline entry, as indicated here:

1873: The Dreikaiserbund Germany, Russia and Austria joined together in a "Dreikaiserbund" to limit the influence of France. Britain preferred to remain aloof in what she called "splendid isolation".	B R F G I A
1878: Treaty of Berlin Russia defeated the Ottoman Empire, but Germany refused to support Russia's attempt to get control of the Dardanelle sea route. This pleased Austria but weakened the Dreikaiserbund.	B R F G I A
1879: The Dual Alliance Germany and Austria-Hungary made a formal military alliance to protect themselves from Russia.	B R F G I A
1882: Triple Alliance Italy joined Germany and Austria in their new alliance. Russia is left more isolated, but Germany is convinced that she cannot form an alliance with Republican France.	B R F G I A
1894: Franco-Russian Alliance Russia formed a military alliance with France to protect herself against the Triple Alliance. Germany is shocked and surprised, but at least Britain and France remain colonial rivals.	B R F G I A

This process continues for the remaining events up to 1914, thereby showing the changing pattern of friendships and enmities in the diagram to the right of each part of the story. At the end of the process, students can be invited to consider the most important turning points in the story and who or what was most responsible for Germany's feeling of 'encirclement' by 1914.

Taking it further

- Students could take their completed work and convert it into a map-based version, which would highlight still more clearly Germany's anxiety about 'encirclement' by 1914 – perhaps in the form of a Tripadvisor graphic (page 113). Some students might even want to convert their work into an animation.

- The relationship web approach can be used to chart changing relationships between countries in any tumultuous period of history: from sixteenth-century Reformation Europe to international relations between the two World Wars. However, it can also be used in different contexts – for example topics dealing with the rise and decline of Empires, or the development of the European integration movement.

- The method can also be used to chart relationships between individuals as well as countries. To develop the case study provided here, students could look at how the run-up and events of the First World War created tensions within the British government (between figures like Grey, Asquith, Lloyd George and Churchill). Similarly, factions in the Tudor court, power struggles within Nazi Germany and the machinations of Stalin during his rise to power could be powerfully illustrated through the approach.

What 'dream sources' would answer this question?

Instead of using books, articles, worksheets and pre-selected sources to build up the initial bedrock of knowledge, simply present students with the "big question" for investigation and ask them "What hard data would help us to answer this question?".

Thereafter, students need to locate this specific data and then frame their arguments based directly on its findings: in other words, they are doing 'real' history from first principles rather than rehearsing and re-hashing the ideas of other people. Then, and only then, should students proceed to consider what other historians have said on the issue in question: and so they are much more likely to be engaged in this process.

Case study: the rule of Fidel Castro

At the start of our unit on the domestic successes and failures of Fidel Castro, I started by asking students to consider how a government aiming for re-election might seek to 'prove' to the electorate that it had been a success in economic, social, cultural and political terms. Through discussion we came up with the following sorts of ideas:

Some ideas about how we can measure 'success':
Economy : Low unemployment | Few strikes | Low inflation | Good balance of trade | Growth in real wages | Low emigration/High immigration
Society: High birth rate | Increasing life expectancy | Increasing literacy rates | Civil rights promoted (how?) | Sexual equality promoted (how?) | Forges a strong national identity
Culture: Free press | Regime works constructively with the church(es) | Propaganda highlights positive achievements rather than demonises perceived opponents | More museums, galleries

Politics: No mass demonstrations against the regime | No political trials / prisoners | Free, fair, regular elections | Universal suffrage | Parliament has real power to hold government to account

We then took the opportunity to bring the Geography students in from next door, as conveniently they are timetabled against the historians, and they gave us a few extra helpful ideas (although Geographers and Historians both belong to the humanities, History arguably leans traditionally a bit more towards the arts, and Geographers lean a bit more towards the sciences, so they had a lot to offer us for this data-driven approach).

In particular, they threw in references to such things as GDP per capita, the importance of the growth of tertiary industries as a measure of a healthy system, and the "Happiness Index".

Next, we proceeded to consider how we could frame questions which would allow us to empirically measure these various indicators. Some speak for themselves ("Low unemployment" = "Did Castro reduce unemployment in Cuba?") whereas others required a bit more thought ("Sexual equality promoted" = "Did Castro's rule see more women going into higher education?" plus others).

Finally, the class was divided into four groups to try to find answers to each of the questions they identified, then reported back to the class with their findings. The job of the teacher during this research phase is to encourage students to consider as they proceed such issues as whether an answer to the question changes over time (long term v. short term), for different types of people, or how far these successes were because of, rather than in spite of, Castro's policies.

Taking it further

- Students could test their conclusions using the "Brilliance or baloney?" format (page 82).
- After the feedback phase, students should convert their findings into infographics (page 117).

The big picture

When beginning a new topic, challenge each student to interpret the meaning of a different image from a collection shared amongst the class (paintings, cartoons, photographs of buildings / artefacts / individuals). Then, working in groups and then as a class, the students decide upon the best ways of categorising the images. Finally, each student conducts independent research to produce a panel of information to put alongside their own image before putting them all up to create a classroom display.

This is a great way of providing students with the 'big picture' that comes from standing back and looking at the period from a fresh angle of open curiosity: too often, in contrast, teachers simply plunge into providing students with a question for investigation and then focusing on the relevant parts of the story through pre-selected source material.

Case study: The Victorians

As a prelude to our detailed studies into such topics as the Industrial Revolution, the abolition of the slave and the Whitechapel murders, I decided to provide students with a "Big Picture" activity to familiarise them with Victorian Britain. A range of Victorian paintings, photographs and advertisements were placed around the room in advance of the lesson.

The students then had a few minutes to wander around the room in silence looking at the images and thinking about which of these they would like to research further.

Next, with the students standing around the edges of the room, I used the random name picker at www.classtools.net (page 213) to select one student, who sat down at the chair in front of her favoured image. I then repeated this process until all students were seated alongside one image.

All the students were then asked to consider what title they would give to the image, how they would describe it to someone else, and what deductions they could draw from it. These findings were exchanged in small groups, with other members of the team encouraged to offer further ideas to note down so that each student ended up with plenty of thoughts.

Students discussing the deductions drawn from their allocated images

At this stage, students stood around the edges of the classroom to form something approaching a circle so that they could all see everyone else's images. I then explained that the next challenge was to decide upon the most obvious categories to organise these images into. I stipulated that no less than three and no more than five images could be included in each category. Beyond that, it was simply up to each student to try to spot how their image might have something in common with at least one of the others.

Each student then took it in turns to briefly explain the title they had chosen to give their image, what it depicted and what they deduced from it. Thereafter the class was left to its own devices to form appropriate huddles in places around the classroom representing different categories. Once this process appeared complete, each team discussed what their images had in common and therefore what title they would give to their 'section' of the gallery exhibition we were working towards ("work", "leisure", "children" being popular choices).

The final stage of the exhibition task was for each student to research their image further and complete a writing frame to summarise their key findings:

The Last of England
Ford Madox Brown (1855)

This painting shows a family on what looks like a very crowded ship. The woman has a child under her cloak; all you can see of it is the child's hand. The man looks angry and the woman looks unhappy. In the background, you can see some cliffs, possibly the white cliffs of Dover. In front of them and in the background you can see vegetables; so they might be gone a long time. I think they are leaving, or even escaping the country.

From this painting, we can dedcuce that life cannot have been good for everyone, we can tell this because they are willing to risk a long, wet and dangerous journey with a young child. They wouldn't do that unless they had a good reason to leave. We can also work out that they didn't want to leave, but they have had to, from the angry look on the man's face.

From my own research, I have discovered that during the second half of the 19th century, over 5 million people had no choice but to leave Britain. About 3 million of these people went to Australia; all of the others went to other parts of the British empire. Most of them were farmers, without work because of cheaper produce coming into the country from other countries. This painting was mostly inspired by Thomas Woolner, a sculptor and Madox Brown's friend, who left for Australia in 1852.

Farmers losing their jobs to imported goods was only one of the reasons for the people of Britain. The British population doubled from 1800 to 1850 and as the cities grew in size and population, living space got more crowded and families would often find it hard to buy an affordable house. The poor had to live in parts of the city called the slums. Here, large families lived together in a few small rooms; children would not be able to go to school and would have to work just to get enough money to buy food. In this area, there was a lot of death, mostly from fast spreading diseases and malnutrition. Children would often die young or were orphaned when their parents died or couldn't support them anymore. People wanted to escape this with their families for a better and safer life, which was promised in Australia.

This image connects closely to another in the exhibition: *Seven Dials*, an engraving by Gustave Dore an engraving from 1872. Seven Dials shows one of the streets in the slums.

Maddy

Completed individual writing frame

Students then collaborated on a major display piece covering one wall of the corridor outside the classroom. This in turn fed into a comprehensive debate on the subject of "Was Victorian Life Good or Bad?", which we broke down into key categories based around the main themes covered in the exhibition.

The completed display

Taking it further: converting a timeline into pictures

The activity with older students on the theme of the Victorians led me to consider how a similar approach could be adopted for other periods and topics which were not so obviously visual in nature. The concept I formulated was to provide younger students with an overarching timeline of events entitled "The Medieval World" covering a wide range of themes and countries between 1000-1450. Each student chose one event (rather than one) to research further and they – rather than the teacher – has to locate one image associated with it. Once these were printed off, then the process could proceed in the same way as the other exercise – although the themes were rather different ("War", "Religion", "Rebellions", "Inventions", "Voyages", for example).

Living graph

A "Living graph" gets students to select the most important events within a topic, then to rate them (over time) against criteria such as success and failure, significance and insignificance.

Stage 1: Brainstorm
Ask students, working individually or in small groups, to identify what they consider to be the 10 most significant events within the topic of study. The teacher asks students to share their ideas.

Stage 2: Depiction
Students then produce their own living graph and plot their chosen events into it. They should aim not simply to describe "what happens" but also "why it is significant".

Stage 3: Categorisation
Finally, the students have to drag and drop the events high or low on the graph to indicate something of relevance (e.g. success or failure).

In this example, the student has used the y-axis to chart evidence of good / bad relations between East and West to determine the origins of the Cold War.

Factor budget

To help students reflect more carefully about which factors are the most important to cover in their written work, give each factor a 'price' to reflect its perceived importance. Students are then given a strictly limited 'budget' to 'purchase' the factors they are allowed to include in their essays.

Case study: the rise of Hitler

At the end of the study, provide students with a list of essential factors to explain the rise of Hitler (even better, students could brainstorm these as a class). Write these on the board and then invite students to vote for the three they each consider most important, resulting in something like this:

1923 Trial Speech - 1	Hyperinflation - 1
25 Point Programme - 5	November Criminals - 3
Arbeit, Freiheit, Brot - 1	Nuremberg Rallies - 2
Backstairs Intrigue - 3	Propaganda - 5
Beer Hall Putsch - 0	Schleicher - 3
Goebbels - 2	Unsere Letzte Hoffnung – 2
Great Depression - 5	Von Papen - 1
Hitler Youth - 3	Work, - Freedom, Bread - 1

Then, students have a limited 'budget' to purchase five factors they are going to cover in their written piece. In other words, a factor which gained votes from 10 people might 'cost' 10 coins, whereas a factor which gained only a couple of votes 'costs' 2 coins.

The result is that students are forced to cover a wider range of factors rather than simply cover the most popular and the most obvious. If you make the 'budget' correspond to the 'price' of the most popular three items in the list, this will mean students will not be able to use more than two of the most popular factors and will then have to consider using some of the more obscure factors.

Time travel agent: complaint letters v. advertising blurb

When introducing students to a particular historical time and place, get them to research different geographical locations associated with it. Some students should produce a travel brochure focusing on the positives, and others should produce a complaint letter bemoaning all the negatives.

Case study: Ancient Rome

Arrange the class into teams and outline the essential task, which will be to market an appealing "time travel" holiday to the place and period we are studying. They will need to make the holiday as appealing as possible to different target audiences, which I summarise as follows:

1. A **"Fun"** holiday for teenagers on a summer break before starting university;
2. A **"Relaxing"** holiday for a group of working mothers eager for quality time with friends;
3. An **"Interesting"** holiday for a group of retired teachers eager for a cultural experience.

Next, provide the class with a list of places associated with the topic:

Roman Forums	• Forum of Trajan	Arches	• Arch of Severus
	• Forum of Caesar		• Arch of Titus
	• Forum of Augustus		• Arch of Constantine
	• Forum of Peace		• Arch of Tiberius
Shrines and Temples	• The Pantheon	Sports and Leisure	• Theatre of Pompey
	• Shrine of Cloacina		• Stadium of Domitian
	• Temple of Romulus Divisus		• Theatre of Marcellus
	• Temple of Saturn		• Circus Maximus
	• Temple of Vesta		• Colosseum
	• Temple of Concord		• Baths of Diocletian

If there is sufficient time, each team should be given the opportunity to conduct some initial research to determine which sites would be particularly appealing to the different target markets, as the ultimate objective is to produce a package which has elements of 'fun', 'relaxation' and 'interest' within it.

Each member of each team should then choose, or be allocated, one or two sites from different categories in this list to research further (depending on the size of the class, the time available and the amount of sites available to research). As far as possible, each site should be chosen by only one person in the class if this the size of the class makes this possible. In this way, each team will propose a completely different holiday package and the whole class will get to hear about as many sites as possible without undue repetition.

Next, each student investigates their chosen sites using sources available to them and use this research to complete a template like this:

ROMAN HOLIDAY			
Your name	???		
Name of Place	???		
This place is … (shade one, two or all three in yellow)	Interesting	Fun	Relaxing
Because… (explain clearly)	???	???	???

When the students have finished their research, they should use this to produce a group presentation piece on a large sheet of sugar paper. They should include images of the sites, and organise them under the three key headings of "Interesting!", "Fun!" and "Relaxing!". This could even be arranged in the format of a Venn diagram of three overlapping circles.

The teacher should then take the role of a representative for the first group of prospective customers – for example, the teenagers looking for a 'fun' holiday. Each team should have a strictly limited amount of time to explain how their holiday package is clearly 'fun'. The teacher then declares an overall winning team, and perhaps awards each member a couple of sweets (with members of the runner-up team getting one sweet each). The process should then be repeated for the 'interesting' and 'relaxing' holiday.

Whilst the presentations are taking place, each group needs to be taking notes on the various sites. After the exercise is completed,

Students could then individually produce a piece of work selecting the best sites. For example, they could choose three sites for each of the three categories, then rank these in the form of a Diamond 9 diagram.

Taking it further

- Instead of the same teacher acting as the representative for the three different groups, use an older student who has a free period to judge the 'teenager' round, and colleagues to represent the other two groups.

- As a follow-up exercise, get students to consider all of the negatives rather than the positives. Do this by asking them to produce letters of complaint as if they have already been on the trip and it was a "holiday from hell". The class could be organised into three teams for this to represent each of the three groups as identified in the earlier activity. Students could also be paired together to produce a dramatized dialogue – the holidaymaker could storm into the travel agent demanding a refund by explaining the things which had gone wrong, whilst the travel agent would stress all the positive experiences.

Sample student video project viewable at www.tarrstoolbox.net

SMS dialogues

In order to highlight the differing viewpoints of two historical characters, or to consider more closely the relationship between them, produce an imaginary dialogue between them in the form of a text-message conversation.

Start by asking students to identity some of the central dramatic moments within the topic of study, and to identify the two characters most closely associated with opposing viewpoints on this issue (for example, Bukharin and Trotsky could debate the relative merits of the New Economic Policy and War Communism; Lloyd George and Churchill could debate whether Britain should go to war with Germany in 1914). Next, agree upon the key terms, words and events that will need to be included. Students can then proceed to write their dialogue, making sure to include the important historical knowledge as decided. To help facilitate this approach I have produced a freely accessible web tool (www.classtools.net/SMS) through which students can input their completed dialogue: they simply click on the left or the right of the "phone" on the screen to input a line of dialogue. The computer automatically animates the text and adds sound effects to bring the dialogue alive. The completed conversation can then be saved for future editing, or can be embedded into a website or blog.

Taking it further

- This approach works particularly well as a revision exercise, where different students can be allocated different central debates to turn into SMS conversations. These can then be shared with the rest of the class either in paper form or, if produced digitally, as weblinks or QR codes.

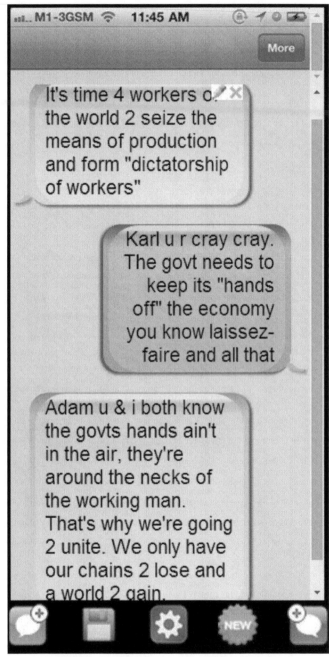

SMS Generator from www.classtools.net

6

GROUP WORK APPROACHES

Many of the ideas discussed so far have a strong element of collaboration within them. Formalised group work strategies are nevertheless an important feature of the history classroom. This chapter proposes a range of particularly effective methods of getting students working together to investigate historical issues.

The Apprentice

Adapting the format of the TV show "The Apprentice" can foster group work, research and presentational abilities.

In my classroom, I use the format of the TV show "The Apprentice" to help students research and prioritise the methods used by the 19th Century Abolition Movement to outlaw the slave trade. Students are organised into teams, each one of which needs to produce a 'joined-up' campaign to abolish the slave trade. This includes choosing a target audience, a celebrity sponsor, merchandise and a publicity stunt. During the feedback phase their methods will be compared and contrasted with the actual techniques used at the time. The most impressive contributors go through to a grand final where they work with the other students to demonstrate their skills of research and presentation. After an overall winner is declared, all students are required to produce an individual project reflecting on why the slave trade was actually abolished.

Stage 1: Introduction to the task

The class is introduced to the task and is arranged into teams of 4-5 people.
For the remainder of the lesson (and ideally for homework) each team has to come up with: (a) The name of their pressure group; (b) A logo and (c) A slogan.

Stage 2: Research and preparation

Lesson time is now set aside for teams to get to work on their campaign.
All teams should start by deciding upon a target market for their campaign and be prepared to explain why they think this group will be

able to help abolish the slave trade. The teacher should ensure as far as possible that each team has a different target market.

Once each team has identified its target market, they will need to decide how to organise the team to decide upon the remaining aspects of the presentation:

- Location for the campaign
- Merchandise
- Celebrity sponsor (based on a real-life personality from the period)
- Publicity stunt

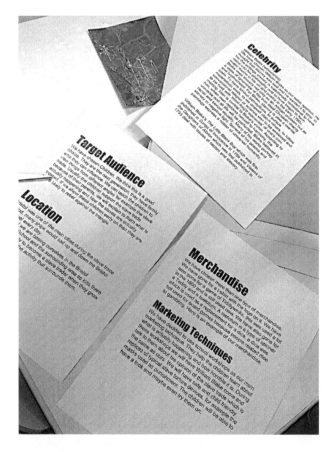

At the end of this preparation period, each team should have arranged their ideas and images onto a large piece of coloured card ready for the boardroom meeting with "Lord Sugartrader".

Taking it further

The teacher could show the teams the series of images relating to life on the plantations (complete with captions). Each team should be allowed to nominate three of these images which they want to add into their campaign. The teacher should then print these off and give them to each team to develop their presentations further (they will be required to justify their choices during the boardroom meeting).

The teacher could also show each team different arguments provided by pro-slavery campaigners in favour of the slave trade. For each one, the team should be challenged to reflect on how they would respond to these arguments.

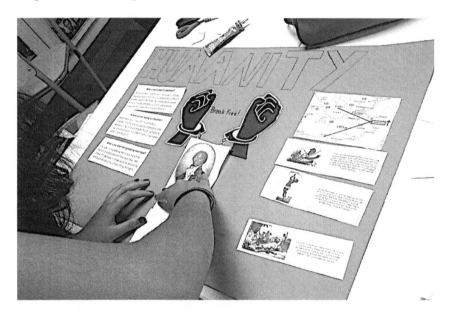

Stage 3: The boardroom meeting

The teacher, in role as 'Lord Sugartrader' now proceeds to interview each team about their campaign. He starts by asking each team in turn about their pressure group name / logo / slogan and why they think it is effective. Other teams might be encouraged or instructed to make constructive criticisms about the work of other teams (to keep this positive, the question might be phrased as 'What do you think is the most effective aspect of the logo/slogan designed by Team X?'").

At the end of this first round of questioning, the class should be shown some actual Abolitionist methods from the period and be invited to comment upon them in terms of their strengths and weaknesses.

This format is then repeated for the remaining aspects of the campaign (location, celebrity sponsor, merchandise, publicity stunt - using the appropriate parts from the presentation).

Taking it further

As part of the feedback process at this stage, the teacher could ask each team leader to answer the question "If each member of the team could be described as a body part, how would you do this?" (page 218).

At a relatively early stage, Lord Sugartrader may wish to 'fire' two people (either on the basis that they have not contributed much, or alternatively because they are clearly 'carrying' the team too heavily and the other members need to be pushed out of their comfort zone). These two people can become Lord Sugartrader's "eyes and ears" for the rest of the session and provide him with useful insights into how the teams are operating.

Stage 4: Deciding upon the finalists

At the end of this session, Lord Sugartrader will need to decide on the finalists. As far as possible, the teacher should aim to keep one person from each team to go through to the final (although this might not be appropriate and it may be that two people from one team become finalists, and none from another).

To keep the process good-humoured the teacher should start by stressing the positive aspects of the whole team before picking one person out for particular praise and announcing that they are through to the final. It is up to the individual teacher to decide whether it is appropriate to explain why the remaining people are "Fired!".

Make it clear that the 'Grand Final' will take place next lesson.

Stage 5: The final

At the start of the lesson, the finalists should stand up. They are then invited to nominate one person each in the class to form part of their new team. They then choose a second person, and so on, until there are just two people left in the class who have not been selected.

These two people become Lord Sugartrader's assistants: they are given a clipboard each and asked to come to the front of the class to await further instructions.

Part 1: Researching how the slave trade was actually abolished

Each finalist is told what the next last task consists of: namely, they will be directed to two websites which provide a varied list of ways in which the slave trade was actually abolished.

They will have 20 minutes to choose two of these which they think were overall the most effective. Lord Sugartrader's assistants will be taking notes on how effectively each finalist approaches this time-restricted task.

At the end of the allotted time, each finalist should nominate the two methods they have decided to research further and deliver their presentation on. They are then given a further 10 minutes to prepare their brief talk to the class about how and why this particular method was effective.

Part 2: Writing an anti-slavery poem

In the next part of the final, the students are given the first few lines of the anti-slavery poem 'The Anti-Slavery Alphabet'. This is a poem in which each letter of the alphabet refers to a different feature of the slave trade.

Each finalist is then given another batch of the letters (e.g. G-K, L-P, Q-U, V-Z) and then has to produce the next part of the poem in this same format, using their knowledge from previous lessons to help them. These are then read out to the class, and compared to the real poem.

In both stages of the feedback process in this session, it is the teacher's role to ensure that the 'assistants' are encouraged to provide feedback about the quality of teamwork that took place.

It is at the end of this process that Lord Sugartrader announces which student has been "hired" as the successful "Apprentice".

Stage 6: Individual outcomes

It is important at the end of this process that all students produce an individual outcome to consolidate their knowledge. They can do this in one of two ways:

- **Option 1:** Produce a Diamond 9 diagram (page 167) outlining the most important methods by which the slave trade was abolished.

- **Option 2:** Students convert a timeline outlining the process by which the slave trade was abolished into an infographic focusing on one theme, event or individual described within it.

Jigsaw groups

The Jigsaw group technique mixes teams on several occasions during an activity to ensure that students speak to as many people as possible. There are three particularly effective ways of using the method.

Method 1: Each group researches the same narrow question using the same particular case study

The simplest way of organising 'jigsaw' groups is to divide the class into teams, then to give each group the same task, divided between the team members in the same way. For example, each group might be researching the impact of World War Two on the Home Front, and each of the four members in each team looks at this from one angle: economic, political, social and military. Each student researches their area alone for a certain period, then the groups are 'jigsawed' by each person moving to sit with other people in the class who have researched the same theme. After exchanging findings in their 'expert' groups, students return to their original 'home' groups and teach each other about what they have learned.

Method 2: Each group researches the same broad question using different case studies

A slightly more sophisticated approach is to provide each group with the same broad question, and to give each member within it the same angle to look at, but to give each team a different case study to research. For example, the class might be investigating "What are the most common causes of war?". Within each team, different students could be required to research military, social, economic and political causes. However, the crucial difference is that each team will consider a completely different war. In this way, the 'expert group' phase can be much more engaging in terms of spotting comparisons and contrasts and thinking about how best to present these to the 'home' groups later on.

Method 3: Each member of each group researches the same broad question using different case studies

I used this approach to when my students each investigated a different 'historical hero'. For the feedback phase in class, students were organised into groups, and each student in each group was given a number (1-5). The first person in each group was given two minutes to explain to the other members of their group what was so heroic about the individual they researched. When the two minutes are up, the second person takes over and so on until everyone has had a chance to speak.

The members of each group then have to consider for a few minutes whether they wish to 'stick' with their original character, or 'swap' to one of the others they have heard about. The teacher might even insist that the group has to reach a majority agreement on which character they will all be 'taking forward' into the jigsaw group phase that is due to follow.

The students are then moved into their fresh jigsaw groups in the normal manner, and the process is repeated so that all students can get to hear about a fresh batch of characters. Thereafter they selected a range of characters they have heard about to arrange into a Diamond 9 diagram (page 167).

Taking it further

The jigsaw group approach works most simply in the way described above: home group, expert group, then return to home group for feedback.   However, it is possible to arrange things so that a third round of discussion can take place in fresh groups consisting of students who have not yet talked to each other already. To do this, don't just give students in each original group a number to represent their (second) jigsaw group; instead, give them a letter as well to represent a final (third) jigsaw group:

- Group 1: 1a, 2b, 3c, 4d, 5e
- Group 2: 1b, 2c, 3d, 4e, 5a
- Group 3: 1c, 2d, 3e, 4a, 5b (and so on)

In this way, when the jigsaw phase takes place, all the students with the same number sit together as before. But at the end of this phase, another jigsaw phase can take place by asking all the people with the same letter to sit together.

Collaborative essay planning using sticky-notes

In this activity, students summarise their arguments and evidence from research onto sticky notes, put them up on the wall, then categorising and link them meaningfully to work towards an overall synthesis and plan of action.

Example: Why do countries turn towards dictators?

Imagine a group of twelve students investigating the most common causes for the rise of 20th-century dictatorships. Each student researches two dictators from different continents. We therefore end up with plenty of data on 24 dictators from all over the world.

Step 1: Give each student a block of sticky notes. For each of their two dictators, they write three sticky notes explaining the methods they used to get into power. These are then stuck up all over the wall:

Step 2: The class gathers around the board, and are asked to read the ideas that have been shared. Ask them to do this individually and in silence for a few minutes, and to reflect as they do so about which factors are coming up most frequently or which are closely related.

Step 3: Students are asked to start organising the sticky notes into definable categories. The teachers should monitor this process to ensure that each students has a chance to get involved.

Step 4: Once everyone seems happy with the arrangement, and 'rogue' factors that clearly only applied to individual dictators have been discarded, talked through each category in turn. What do these factors have in common? So what should be the 'title' for each category? Write these titles on differently coloured sticky notes and add them over each category.

Step 5: Discuss how these categories overlap or are connected. 'Psychopathic Tendencies' might be connected to a 'Willingness to use Violence', whilst 'Pragmatic Opportunism' connects to 'Nationalistic Ideology'. These links should explained with annotated arrows.

Step 6: Talk through the clearest 'path' through the completed diagram and discuss how this is effectively a thesis that can be turned into an examination-style essay.

Talkers and listeners

An effective way of encouraging close examination of image sources, or close reading of text extracts.

Provide one student (the 'talker') with a source, then another student or small group of students with a series of questions to ask about it (the 'listeners'). The talker is not allowed to show the source to the rest of the group, but must instead simply answer the questions they are asked. When the interrogation is finished, the source should be returned to the teacher. Another member of the group then takes over as the 'talker' by collecting a fresh source from the teacher and the process is repeated.

Example: What was the Medieval conception of Hell?
I use this approach as part of my classroom studies on "Was the Medieval Church loved or feared?". The teacher prints off a pile of Medieval images of hell. The class is divided into groups and each person in each group is given a number. The first person in each group should take one of the images from the teacher, look at it carefully, and take it back to their group.

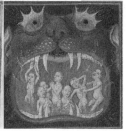

By looking closely at the image themselves, but without showing it to their teammates, they answer a series of questions about it ("What can you *see* in hell? What can you *hear*? What can you *smell*?"). When the discussion is over (each group can take as much or as little time as they think necessary to take notes), the next 'talker' returns the original picture to the teacher (who scribbles the group name on the back of it to ensure that they are not given it a second time during the exercise), and exchanges it for a fresh picture. The process repeats for as long as the teacher wishes.

After completing the exercise, move to a jigsaw group activity (page 202). Give each student in each group a number (e.g. 1–5). Then instruct all students with the same number to sit at the same table. In this way every group now consists of students who used completely different sources of information to their classmates. Give the members of each group a couple of minutes to exchange their findings for each of the key questions and develop their notes with fresh ideas. In this way, everybody in the class will have the opportunity to exchange their ideas with everybody else, either directly in their original groups or by proxy in the jigsaw groups.

Finally, provide each group with a selection of the original images. By this stage they are usually very intrigued to compare and contrast the pictures, to confirm that their interpretations were correct, and to draw out some final observations and deductions.

As a homework exercise, students should use their notes to produce a blood-curdling medieval sermon about the horrors that await sinners in hell!

Students comparing medieval images of hell

Discussion group role cards

To ensure that each student is able to contribute effectively and independently during a group task, consider giving each person a different role card:

Creative Risk-taker*

*Everybody should take this role in the first stage of the task to ensure plenty of ideas

You think about the problem critically and rigorously

You think of creative approaches to the task

You share these ideas with enthusiasm

Co-Ordinator (Caring, Principled)

You allocate roles to group members who are unsure what their role should be

You invite each person to contribute their ideas and ensures they are listened to

You pull ideas together at the end in an overall plan everyone is happy with

---

Elaborator (Inquirer, reflective)

You encourage each speaker to explain their ideas fully

You remind people to provide evidence for their arguments

You help people do these things if they struggle to do so themselves

---

Researcher (thinker, knowledgeable)

You identify where the group's ideas require more detail and explanation

You are the only person allowed to ask the teacher for information

You conduct the research and provide it to the group

Secretary (open-minded)

You write down the group's findings and decisions without judgement

You ask for clarification and detail from the group if necessary

You make sure the secretary understands your findings

Timekeeper (balanced)

You make sure the group is using the time well

You tell the group when it is time to move on to the next job

You tell the group when it is time to start rounding off

Presenter (communicator)

You ensure you understand what the secretary has written

You present what the group has done to the class and the teacher

You are prepared to answer questions

Template available for download from www.tarrstoolbox.net

Stage 1: individual reflection

Everybody in each team should be a 'creative risk-taker' and have some time to reflect individually on a suggested approach to the task.

Stage 2 : choosing roles

Each member of the group takes at least one of the remaining roles after taking the time to read them (they may choose more than one role). The group will need at least one co-ordinator, who can help the other members decide what roles are important for the success of the task and which are be suited to different members of the team.

Stage 3: group discussion

The co-ordinator(s) chairs the discussion. The elaborator(s) makes sure ideas are being explained fully at each stage. The researcher(s) identify where further research is needed and should conduct this. The timekeeper ensures that the pace of the task is maintained. The secretary keeps a record of the ideas decisions. The presenter(s) are responsible for converting the work of the secretary into a class presentation.

Taking it further

This approach works particularly well when combined with peer assessment slips (page 222).

Destroy or deploy?

When preparing students for a debate, spread a variety of relevant sources around the classroom. After giving students time to move around the room examining the sources, invite different teams not only to nominate sources they wish to "deploy" in the debate to support their case, but also other sources they wish to "destroy" because they might be used by their opponents.

Case study: the origins of World War One

Background to the debate

At the end of a detailed thematic investigation of the causes of World War One, focusing largely on the main themes (alliance system, colonial rivalry, arms race, nationalism and imperialism…) I always conclude by getting students to debate "who" rather than "what" was responsible in the form of a courtroom trial.

First of all, each member of the class is given a number between one and six – corresponding to Russia, France, Germany, Serbia, Britain and Austro-Hungary – and challenged to produce two prosecution questions blaming that country for World War One ("Is it not true that…which is demonstrated by the fact that…?"). They then get into their teams to compare the questions and decide overall upon their best two.

Next, each team is told which country they will be defending (i.e. the country which followed them in the original list, with the team prosecuting the Austro-Hungarians at the end of the list now defending the Russians at the start of it).

At this stage, everyone should now be clear who they are prosecuting and who they are defending. Each team is finally given the prosecution questions they will need to answer, and use the remaining time, plus homework as necessary, to frame their responses.

	A. "Guilty!": Questions	B. "Not Guilty!": Responses
A. Russia *Tsar Nicholas II*	1. Is it not true that your autocracy formed a military alliance with Republican France, thereby encircling Germany and provoking a reaction from her?	
	2. Is it not true that you deliberately ignored Germany's request to demobilise in Summer 1914, thereby escalating the Austro-Serbian war into a more general European conflict?	
B. France *Rene Viviani*	3. Is it not true that France was desperate for revenge ("Revanchisme") against Germany after the loss of Alsace Lorraine thereby poisoning international relations?	
	4. Is it not true that you reached a cynical deal with Britain to take control of Morocco, and then both of you humiliated the Germans in the two crises over the country that followed?	

Sample questions for the debate relating to World War One

Destroy or Deploy?

In the following lesson, I decided that I wanted students to integrate some fresh primary sources rather than simply rely on their existing classroom notes. This would hopefully get them thinking about the issues from a fresh angle, keep the rest of the class interested during the debate by presenting them with genuinely novel historiographical perspectives, and help bring in some evaluation skills as the reliability and utility of the sources was interrogated. So prior to the lesson I printed off a wide range of visual and written sources from past examination papers relating to the origins of World War One. I cut them out and spread these all around the room. When the class entered, they were then given the following instructions:

Surprise witnesses: DESTROY or DEPLOY?

1. You will be given 10 minutes to examine the numbered sources around the room. As you examine the sources, try to decide:
• Which sources support your defence case
• Which source supports your prosecution case
• Which source undermines your defence case
• Which source undermines your prosecution case

> **2. When the ten minutes are up, each team will take it in turns to nominate one source to "Destroy" or "Deploy"**
> • **DEPLOY** means you want to use it in the debate: in other words, it helps support the points made by your prosecution questions, or your defence responses.
> • **DESTROY** means you want to remove it from the debate altogether: in other words, it supports your opponents or undermines your defence case.
> **3. The process will repeat until all groups have made all the choices they wish.**

As outlined above, the main part of the process involves teams taking turns to announce which (numbered) source they wish to "Deploy" (at which point they should be handed their chosen source to keep safe) or to "Destroy" (such sources should ostentatiously be placed into a brown envelope marked "Top Secret" or similar). Expect some howls of protest from groups who were desperately keen to "Deploy" these as part of their own case!

Thereafter, each team should develop their prosecution questions and defence responses as appropriate with the sources they have identified.

Taking it further: what to do with 'destroyed' sources?

The key thing to decide is what use to make of the "destroyed" sources. After all, these are likely to be some of the most interesting and compelling witnesses in the entire debate. There are several options:

- Tear them into little pieces and throw them away in front of the class. Brutal, but suitably dramatic and might be useful for making a point about gaps in the historical record being something that historians continually have to grapple with!

- Provide them to a series of 'judges' in the class (e.g. absentees from the first lesson) to frame their own questions based upon to give them an active role during the debate.

- Use them to produce an examination-style source work exercise so that students are presented with a fresh layer of knowledge and interpretation.

- Use them as the basis for a display ("CENSORED! The hidden story behind the outbreak of World War One!") whereby each team has to provide an explanation about why they 'destroyed' the sources on display.

Random name picker

When arranging groups for team tasks, remove any arguments about who should belong in each group by using the random name picker at classtools.net.

Names can simply be cut and paste from a word processor, mark book or register, then you are presented with a 'roulette wheel' which spins round for a few seconds upon the click of a button before settling upon a random student. Student names can automatically be removed after they are chosen and you can save each generator as a URL or embed it in your website, blog or virtual learning environment.

Random name picker from www.classtools.net

Taking it further

- For added atmosphere in the ensuing group discussions / presentations, make use of the 'audience soundboard' freely available at www.classtools.net.

Re-enact a conference

When studying how successfully different countries achieved their aims in an international conference, conduct a re-enactment where students score points for achieving their national objectives. Then study the terms of the real agreements that were reached to determine who gained the most and how creatively they solved the problems they faced.

The example I give here relates to the Versailles Conference held after World War One, but the format is one which I use when studying other international conferences – for example, the Yalta and Potsdam Conferences which followed World War Two.

Case study: the Versailles conference of 1919

Stage 1: Individual work – working out the objectives

After studying the general aims and motives of the Big Three (Clemenceau of France, Lloyd George of Britain and Wilson of the USA) give each student in the class a number: [1] Britain; [2] France and [3] USA.

Working individually, each student decides what their national objective probably is for each of the following five issues:

Saar **Rich iron-** **producing area,** **the industrial** **heartland of** **Germany.**	A. Have a *plebiscite* to allow the inhabitants self-determination.	B. Give it to France for 15 years, then have a *plebiscite*	C. Give it to France. This will strengthen France and weaken Germany.
Colonies **Mainly in Africa,** **cause of great** **rivalry with GB.**	A. Share them out between the Empires of Britain and France.	B. Make them "*Mandates*" – divide them between the winners, who rule them under supervision of the League.	

Rhineland The border area between Germany and France, heavily defended.	A. *Demilitarise* it permanently, but leave it as part of Germany so she is not too weakened.	B. *Demilitarise* it for 15 years, leaving it as part of Germany so that Germany is not too weakened.	C. Turn it into an independent state to severely weaken Germany.
Alsace-Lorraine Taken from France in 1870	A. Have a *plebiscite* to see if its inhabitants want to be French or German	B. Give it to France. It was seized by the Germans in 1870 and should be returned.	
Polish Corridor A strip of land which would give Poland access to the sea, but split Germany into two sections.	A. Give it to Poland to allow the country access to the sea, in such a way to weaken Germany	B. Give it to Poland to allow the country access to the sea, but causing minimum damage to Germany	C. Have a *plebiscite* to see if the people there want to be German or Polish before deciding anything

The "SCRAP" over territory
(**S**aar, **C**olonies, **R**hineland, **A**lsace-Lorraine, **P**olish Corridor)

Stage 2: Group work – agreeing upon and ranking the objectives

Next, students sit together with other people who are in the same national group to compare their findings and reach an overall agreement on their objectives (from their prior learning they will know that Wilson was the most idealistic, Clemenceau the most vengeful and Lloyd George the most pragmatic). Encourage students to discuss quietly – they don't want to give away their objectives to the other teams!

Once each group is in agreement about what they aim to achieve, the next step is to prioritise these objectives. Each team needs to write '50 points' in the cell of the table corresponding to the objective which is most important to them, indicating how many points they will win if they succeed in securing this objective at the conference. They then write '40 points' in the next most important objective, and so on until they have put '10 points' into the objective they are most likely to compromise on.

Stage 3: Role play – re-enacting the conference

The next stage is to arrange the class into teams of three, with one British, one American, and one French representative in each team.

Starting with the first issue (the Saar, in this instance), France should outline what she wants. Britain can reject this proposal, or agree to support France in return for France's vote on another issue. The US can do the same. France can choose to accept or reject any deal "on the table". If a deal takes place, then France's proposal for the Saar should be highlighted as being "agreed". In addition, the issue that France "traded" on is highlighted as "agreed" too.

Once agreement (or a stalemate) has been reached on the first issue, the team moves on to the next unsolved issue. This time, Britain should open the negotiations. This process of trading and negotiating should continue until all of the issues have been resolved or until the teacher declares that no further time is left available.

At the end of the allocated time – maybe 20 minutes – each player can then add up their scores based on the objectives they successfully achieved. As a final stage, each country can be given an overall score by pooling the scores of all the representatives. Credit can be given to the highest scoring individuals, and the highest scoring teams.

A few costumes, flags and pantomime accents never go amiss!

Stage 4: Comparing to the historical reality

The teacher should not proceed to go through each of the key issues and outline what was actually decided in historical reality at the conference. For each one, students should discuss who would have been most satisfied with this outcome, and whether it was (a) too harsh, (b) fair, or (c) not harsh enough. They can then collate evidence in these three categories using a Venn diagram. Similarly, they could create a Venn diagram of three overlapping circles designed to highlight how different terms of the Treaty pleased each of the Big Three to different degrees.

Taking it further

- Halfway through the conference discussions, the teacher could pause the class and tell them that if there are issues they are particularly struggling to reach an agreement on a particular issue, a compromise solution could be proposed which is halfway between two of the national objectives for that issue. In such instances, each team gaining part of their objectives get HALF of the points they were playing for on this issue.

- Rather than having multiple groups of three people all conducting simultaneous negotiations, the teacher could instead seat three team leaders in the centre of the classroom to lead the discussions. The other members of the class sit behind their national leader and can pass notes / whisper in their ear during the discussions but cannot contribute directly. This allows the teacher to monitor proceedings more closely and to act as chair if the discussions grind to a halt.

Which part of the body were you?

As a plenary exercise at the end of a group task, ask each member of the team: "If the group was likened to a human body, with each member of the group representing one part of that body, which part of the body were you?".

Start by listing a few obvious body parts on the board (e.g. heart, eyes, hands, nose, ears, muscles) and asking students what qualities we associate with each one (no rude answers are allowed!)

Then, students reflect on this question individually and in silence. Each team has a few minutes to discuss their ideas, with the stipulation that each member of the team must represent a different body part. Finally, each student should share with the class their answer to the key question and explain their answer using this template – one of which should be completed by each group.

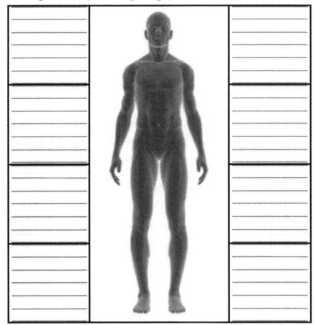

Template available at www.tarrstoolbox.net

Image jigsaw

As an alternative to of dividing the class into groups using the random name picker (page 213), take a series of images relating to the topic and cut each one up into however many people you want in each team. Shuffle the pieces, and then hand one piece to each student in the class as they enter the room.

Next, challenge the students to find out who else is in their group by matching their pieces with other people in the class to reconstruct the image.

Once they have done so, they should then consider what the meaning or relevance of the image is and be prepared to share their thoughts with the rest of the class – ideally, each student should focus on a detail within the segment of the image they were originally allocated.

After this starter activity is completed, students can then proceed to the main group work activity of the class as planned. The visual nature of this exercise lends itself particularly well to a 'Big Picture' activity (page 184).

A simple example of an 'image jigsaw'

Case study: Mughal India

A great way to improve upon the basic premise of the "image jigsaw" approach is to keep aside TWO particularly interesting pieces of each image, and then jumble the remaining pieces of the pictures and spread them on desks around the room.

I do this with six key portraits of sixteenth-century Mughal emperors. I give my class two minutes of silent time to walk around the room looking at (but not touching) the pieces of images. As they move around, encourage them to consider what they they these fragments tell us about the Mughals (e.g. clothes, weaponry, entertainment, food). When the time is up, pause the class and have an initial discussion around these issues.

Next, divide the class into six groups (or however many portraits you have used in your own exercise). Each team should be given ONE remaining piece from different portraits. Each group should look at this carefully, then share with the class what this new image segment tells us.

Then, each team has to locate the remaining pieces which match their image and reconstruct the entire portrait.

Remember that each image still has one missing piece. Students should try to guess what will be in this space. These ideas will be shared with the class from each group. It's a good idea to place this gap in an intriguing spot:

Next, the teacher will show the six remaining pieces, and each group has to claim the piece which they think belongs to their image. Did any of the groups guess correctly? Does this missing piece raise any fresh questions?

The missing piece shows the emperor presented with the decapitated head of his own brother!

Finally, the teacher will provide the class with six titles and six descriptions. Each team has to claim the title and the description which they think matches their image.

Each group could then talk through the meaning of each painting to the class, focusing on providing an answer to the question "What do portraits of the emperors tell us about the Mughals?". The teacher will make notes on the board and, when this process is complete, discuss how these could be categorised and linked ready to answer the key question.

Peer assessment slips

When conducting group work, there is always a danger that certain students might take a bit of a back seat and let their teammates do all the work. To avoid this, provide the students in advance with a 'peer assessment' slip. At the end of the activity, each student should complete the slip by dividing 100% between the members of the team to reflect their contribution to the task, and explain their reasoning.

These can then be collected by the teacher, who can quickly determine if there were any 'passengers' in the group. From my experience students tend to do this very fairly and there is little disagreement between the judgments of different team members.

PEER ASSESSMENT SLIP		
Team Number =		
TEAM MEMBERS' NAMES	% contribution	What did they do?
TOTAL =	100%	

Suggested layout for a 'peer assessment' slip

Random group generator

To quickly arrange the class into teams, simply input a class list into the random group generator at www.classtools.net, choose the amount of teams required, and let it do the rest.

I coded this particular application when I realised that doing the same sort of thing using the random name picker (page 213) took a little too long and that an instantaneous group creation facility would be a useful addition to my classroom armoury.

I deliberately added a feature so that when "create groups" is clicked, the cards spin around several (random) times with different groupings before stopping. This helps students realise that the entries are being shuffled in a random manner.

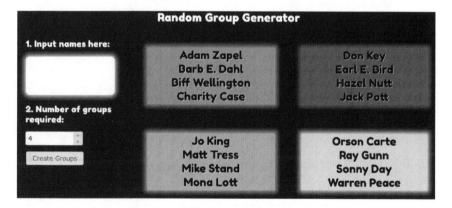

If a group leader is required, take the first name that is listed in each of the suggested groups.

Collate student feedback on your schemes of work

Giving students with the opportunity to provide feedback about your teaching is an invaluable way of deciding how to develop your schemes of work and your teaching approaches.

Case study

At least once per year, or more frequently when I am teaching a range of new topics, I gather feedback from students in each year group about what I am covering with them, and how I am doing so. For example, are they finding my subject difficult or easy? Interesting or dull? What approaches do they find particularly effective? What topics would they have liked to study instead?

History Questionnaire									

Compared to other subjects this year, have you found history....

Too Easy								Too Difficult

Interesting								Uninteresting

Useful								Not useful

Topics	
Which topics have you found **most** interesting this year? Why?	Which topics have you found **least** interesting this year? Why?
Teaching Styles	
Has there been a particular type of lesson you **have** enjoyed? If so, give details – ideally, about one particular lesson.	Has there been a particular type of lesson you have **not** enjoyed? If so, give details – ideally, about one particular lesson.
Are there any history topics which you would like to have studied that haven't been covered? If so, give details.	

Template available for download from www.tarrstoolbox.net

Secret agent

At the start of the lesson, quietly provide one student with a slip of paper which tells them their mission as a "Secret Agent". This mission will involve offering a constructive and helpful comment about some aspect of the lesson at the end of it.

The simplest way to allocate the mission is to ask all students to close their eyes and put their heads on the desks. Tell them as you walk around the room that you will tap one student on the shoulder and they should hold out their hand for the mission slip.

Case study

Some examples of a "secret mission" might be:

- Who demonstrated good teamwork skills in today's group task?
- Who contributed most effectively to the discussion?
- What was the most interesting question raised by a member of the class?
- What is the most interesting thing I learned in today's lesson?
- What one thing would I like to find out further?

At the end of the lesson, announce that this has been a lesson involving a 'Secret Agent'. Ask the rest of the class to anticipate who they think it may have been. Then the 'Secret Agent' reveals themselves and tells the rest of the class what their 'mission' was.

Taking it further

- Get the rest of the class to anticipate what they think the answer was before the 'Secret Agent' gives their answer. Use the strategy regularly to keep students on their toes and encouraging them to reflect on the purpose and content of the lesson!

Biased words knockout challenge

Students need to be able to spot writing which is designed to persuade rather than merely inform. To do this, get students to produce a list of biased adjectives in the form of a quick-fire competition.

Each member of the class takes turns to contribute a fresh word to the list without hesitation or repetition. Students failing to do so have to sit down, with the overall winner being the last person standing. The pool of words can be left on the board for students to draw from in their written piece.

Case study: the Norman Conquest

At the end of a detailed study of why William of Normandy won the Battle of Hastings in 1066, I ask students to take a basic written account of the event and transform it into a biased newspaper report. The account they are given as a starting point is written in bullet points in a deliberately dry present-tense format. In Stage 1 of the activity, students first use their word processors to convert this into one neat paragraph of text – using punctuation and linkage words as appropriate to make the narrative 'flow'. They might end up with something like this (past tense and linkage words highlighted in bold):

Edward had promised the throne to William of Normandy. **Also**, Harold was shipwrecked in France and swore to help William get the throne. **However**, Harold became King the moment Edward died and the Pope supported William. **At the same time**, Hardraada of Norway said he should be the next king. William could not invade because the wind was blowing from the north, **but this meant** Hardraada invaded England from the North. **So**, Harold marched north and defeated Hardraada at Stamford Bridge. **Then**, the wind changed direction so William was able to invade from the south **and** William was able to rest his army before battle. Harold quickly marched his army back down to the south coast and it got tired, **but** Harold's army took up a position on the top of Senlac Hill. William's army charged up the hill several times, but Harold's army held firm. There was a rumour that William was dead, but he lifted his helmet to show he was alive. William's army **then** retreated down the hill, and Harold's army chased it. **However**, William's army **suddenly** turned around and killed many of Harold's soldiers. Harold was shot in the eye with an arrow. **After this**, William marched to London and declared himself King on Christmas Day.

In Stage 2, they are put into two teams (Anglo-Saxons and Normans) ready to insert some bias into the narrative: "good" words about their favoured ruler, "bad" words about his enemy:

Anglo–Saxon Chronicle	The Norman News
Group A: An Anglo-Saxon newspaper. This will see the defeat of Harold as a terrible disaster. It will talk about how brilliant Harold was, and how William was cruel, evil, and only won because of luck.	**Group B: A Norman newspaper.** This will see William's victory as a good thing. It was talk about how evil and stupid Harold was, and say that William was clever and deserved the throne all along.

The biased words knockout challenge

At this point, students are told how the game will work. Each student will be given five minutes to produce a list of positive adjectives, then a further couple of minutes to memorise as many of them as possible. Then, the whole class stands up and the teacher makes it clear who will start by giving the first word, and then the order that other students will follow (it therefore helps to have students standing in a ring as far as this is possible).

The teacher then invites the first person to start. The teacher repeats the word, writes it on the board, and then points to the next person to continue. Any student who hesitates, or repeats a word already on the board, has to sit down. Repeat the process until there is one overall winner left standing.

Then, immediately move to round two (the "bad" words). This time, start with the person who came last in the 'ring' in the previous round, and work around the group in the opposite direction, to keep things fair.

At the end of the process, students will be left with a list of useful words to make use of in their final piece of persuasive writing, both positive and negative.

Taking it further

- As well as incorporating adjectives, more able students could add adverbs too. A final piece of writing should add images and an alliterative headline.

7
TESTS & REVISION

Teaching effectively through the use of classroom games is something I have always been fascinated with. Here are some examples of how fun and entertainment can be brought into the history classroom without sacrificing rigour and focus.

Revision leaderboard

Rather than treat each factual test or quiz as a discrete assignment, foster a sense of competition and tension over the revision period by building up a leaderboard and awarding a prize to the winner.

During revision time I start every lesson with a short factual test, arcade game (page 238) or 'Fling the Teacher' quiz on the topic covered in that lesson.

Prior to the lesson, I warn students what the topic will be so they can revise. At the start of the lesson, I outline the main task for the lesson so they know what to do as soon as they finish the quiz.

I then direct students to a 'Fling the Teacher' quiz on this topic. Students have 10 minutes to complete the quiz.

Any student finishing within that time gets points into their 'leaderboard' (which is an Excel spreadsheet which builds up throughout the revision period) based on the amount of minutes left on the clock. They can then proceed to the main task outlined at the start of the lesson.

It's a great way of encouraging students to do a bit of intensive revision prior to each lesson – especially if prizes are awarded in the final lesson before study leave starts.

Create your own "Fling the Teacher" quizzes at www.classtools.net

Keyword challenge

This is a simple game to revise important terms, concepts and people. It is particularly effective just before students have to produce some written work making accurate use of key vocabulary.

Before the lesson, the teacher should put together a list of key terms from the most recent topic of study. When the lesson begins, divide the class into teams of around four or five students.

The first member of the first team sits in the hot seat at the front of the class, with their back to the interactive whiteboard or projection screen.

The teacher inputs the list of key terms into the "Random Word Picker" at www.classtools.net and uses this to display one entry at random on the interactive whiteboard behind the student.

The rest of the team have thirty seconds to get their teammate to guess what word is on the screen behind them by giving a definition.

A correct guess gets points for the team based on how many seconds are left on the clock (e.g. 25 points if they correctly answer after 5 seconds). If 30 seconds elapses without a correct guess, the round is over and the team gets no points.

The teacher should then provide a short outline of the significance of the term, and all students should make a note of it.

The process can the be repeated for the other teams, and the game can then carry on for as many rounds as is the teacher considers appropriate. A prize can be given to the highest-scoring team at the end of the game.

Case study: Was life good or bad in the Middle Ages?

After playing the online interactive Medieval Time Machine adventure at www.activehistory.co.uk and completing the accompanying worksheets, I gave students a list of the main jobs of people that they met in the simulation (scribe, bailiff, apprentice, moneylender…).

Each group had five minutes to work together to revise what each job entailed. They were then told that points would only be won by teams which could not only define the job, but could also explain why it should be regarded as evidence of 'bad' or 'good' conditions. They were then given a further five minutes to consider which jobs fitted which category, and why.

At the end of this period, each student had a list of characters, a brief description of each, and also an inference about what they suggest about the quality of life in the Middle Ages. After we played the game, this then provided useful raw material for either a 'Travel Brochure' for a holiday to the Middle Ages (the task for one half of the class focusing on 'good' elements) or a complaint letter about how the holiday turned into a disaster (the task for the other students focusing on the 'bad' elements).

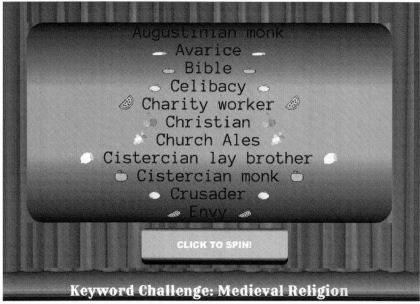

Keyword challenges can be generated using
www.classtools.net/random-name-picker

Share possible test questions in advance

Sharing a long list of possible questions with students in advance of a test in exam conditions is a simple way of ensuring that their revision and reflection is focused and effective.

When I tell my students that a forthcoming lesson will be a timed essay or a structured question based on their recent studies, I make a point of sharing with them a list of possible questions that have come up in previous examination papers. I also promise them that the question(s) chosen will be taken directly from that list. Students are then given homework time to reflect on how they might approach each and every question if it turns out to be the one selected. In the following lesson, we spend time discussing approaches to particular questions which they are less confident about. The test then takes place the following lesson.

From my experience, this is more effective than simply announcing that 'next lesson we will be having a test on this topic' and leaving them to revise in an unfocused manner. By giving students a 'long list' of questions they end up preparing much more thoroughly and from many more angles than they otherwise would have done. Moreover, they are able to spot their areas of weakness and have a chance to develop and improve their understanding of these before the test takes place.

Example: World War One structured question (40 minutes)

Instructions: The teacher will choose one (a), one (b) and one (c) question for this test in timed conditions. As homework, all students should therefore consider how they would approach every question in this list.

a. Who was Kaiser Wilhelm II?
a. Who was Tsar Nicholas II?
a. Who was Franz Ferdinand?
a. What were the Balkan Wars?
a. What were the Dreadnoughts?
a. What was the Daily Telegraph Interview?
a. What was the Black Hand Gang?
a. What was the July Crisis?
a. What were the Moroccan Crises?
a. What were the Willy-Nicky telegrams?
a. What was the Schlieffen Plan?
a. What was the Russo-Japanese War?

b. Why did an alliance system develop before 1914?
b. Why did an arms race develop between Britain and Germany?
b. Why did the Anglo-French Entente survive?
b. Why was the Triple Alliance formed?
b. Why did Germany issue Austria with a "blank Cheque" in 1914?
b. Why did Russia decide to defend Serbia at all costs in 1914?
b. Why did Britain declare war on Germany in 1914?

c. Why did the 1914 Balkan crisis cause European war, but earlier crises did not?
c. "No country in 1914 actually desired a general European war" – Do you agree?
c. Assess the view that the assassination at Sarajevo made war inevitable.
c. Assess the view that Russia was most to blame World War One.
c. Assess the view that nationalism was the main cause of World War One.
c. Assess the view that Austro-Serbian rivalry was the main cause of World War One.
c. "World War One began because Germany invaded neutral Belgium" – Do you agree?

Spot the mistakes

Summary sheets of key information and facts can be very helpful for students before the examination. To encourage close reading of such resources, deliberately insert mistakes into them and encourage students to find them in a classroom quiz format.

It is always an effective revision technique to provide students with model answers after they have completed an examination-style test (for example, a timed essay). For this reason, I will usually write the essay at the same time as the students, with the only difference being that I give myself 25% less time as a 'handicap' for my experience and speed on my keyboard.

However, from experience I found that one danger in simply providing students with model answers was that they simply got filed away without a great deal of reflection. Therefore, what I now do is deliberately insert factual mistakes into my answers after they are written, and make some stylistic gaffes (e.g. not using paragraphs, quotes or appropriate evidence). I then put students into teams and challenge them to spot the mistakes – which works particularly well if used as part of a 'leaderboard challenge' described earlier in this chapter.

Rules of the game

The first team has to identify and correct an error in the account. If there are a lot of these, insist instead that each team will instead identify and correct two or even three errors.

The team can choose to play for up to 10 points. If they successfully identify and correct the specified amount of errors, they win the points. However, if they fail to do so, or make a mistake, they lose the same amount of points. This rule adds a bit of interest to proceedings!

Everyone in the class corrects their own version of the model answer. The remaining teams then take their turns one after another, and the process can continue for as many rounds as are required.

Who, where, what am I?

Students have to identify the most important individuals, events and places related to the topic, then provide five key details about each one. This information is then used as the basis of an intensive group quiz.

Stage 1: preparatory revision and research

In advance of the lesson, students prepare quiz cards designed to challenge the other people in the class to guess a key character from the topic about to be revised.   The quiz cards require the student to provide five statements about the character, each one of which is progressively more obvious who it relates to.

Stage 2: conducting the quiz

After collecting the quiz cards, the teacher arranges the class into teams and shuffles the pack. The "50 point" statement will be read out from the first card to the first team (obviously, the teacher will need to choose a card that wasn't designed by a person within that team). If they wish to 'pass', they get further (easier) clues but the points available steadily decline (40 points for a correct guess after the second question, 30 points after the third, and so on).

An incorrect guess at any point means they automatically get zero points for that round and the card is placed back into the pack – so it usually a good idea for each team to nominate a 'captain' who is the only person allowed to give the quizmaster the final answer after conferring.

The game is played over several rounds; the winning team is the one with the most points.

Taking it further

The rules of the game are flexible. Most simply, each team could take it in turns to guess a different character from the five statements they are provided. However, another approach is to adopt a 'first on the buzzers' approach using some quiz buzzers. I also record the scores from these quizzes in a revision leaderboard which builds up over several weeks of revision to build up a bit more tension, as outlined at the start of the chapter.

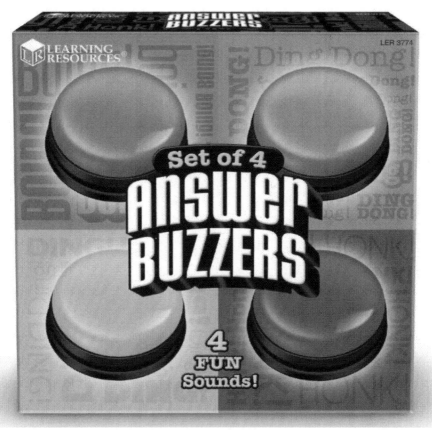

Answer buzzers add an extra layer of tension to a classroom quiz and can be purchased online.

Arcade game generator

The arcade game generator at www.classtools.net allows you to submit one set of questions and answers and then converts these into a range of interactive revision games. Each of these can be shared as web links or embedded in a website, blog or wiki.

To create a game, simply input a series of questions and answers into the interface (these can easily be copied and pasted directly from an existing worksheet).
At the time of writing, the games generated currently include:

- Manic Miner
- Pacman
- Wordshoot
- Matching Pairs
- Flashcards
- Asteroids (2-player option available)
- Pong! (2-player option available)

Several of the games include a leaderboard so that at the end of the allocated time the teacher can see the highest scores attained by each student.

Taking it further
- Create a leaderboard during revision time (page 230).
- Get students to create their own revision games on different subjects ahead of the revision period. Use this databank of quizzes as starter/plenary exercises during revision time, and compile a revision leaderboard to build up a sense of competition.
- There are other game generators available at www.classtools.net, including Only Connect, and a Crossword Generator.

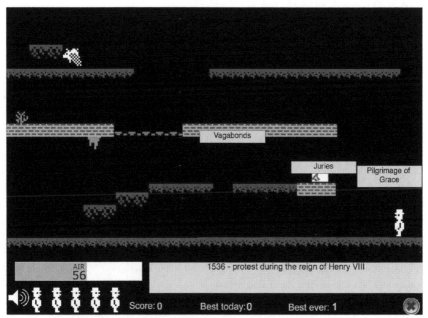

Manic Miner: Jump onto the correct answers to move up a level

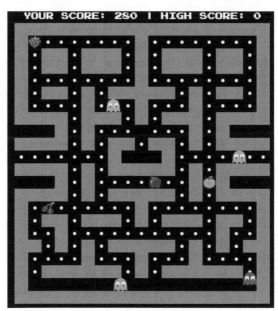

Pacman: win lives by answering questions after getting captured by a ghost

How certain are you?

To add an extra layer of drama to factual tests, require students not only to provide an answer, but also to choose how many points to play for to reflect their confidence. If they're correct, they win that amount of points, but if not they lose them!

Case study: the civil rights movement

This image shows the start of a factual test on the civil rights movement. Students have to choose first whether they are confident enough to answer the question. If they do, they play for up to three points, knowing that an incorrect answer will mean their score being reduced by the same amount.

The Civil Rights Movement 1945-1965 (25 questions)				
For each question, play for 1, 2 or 3 points to reflect your confidence. If you're correct, you **win** those points. If not, you **lose** them.	Points played for			Score
	1	2	3	
The name of the Chief Justice of the Supreme Court throughout this period	☐	☐	☐	
The NAACP lawyer who represented black families in the Brown v. Board of Education case	☐	☐	☐	
The name of the woman whose refusal to give up her seat started the Montgomery bus boycott	☐	☐	☐	
The SCLC was formed during the Montgomery Bus Boycott by MLK and Ralph...?	☐	☐	☐	
The NAACP leader who recruited the "Little Rock Nine" to force the desegregation of schools in Arkansas	☐	☐	☐	
The Governor of Arkansas whose refusal to desegregate his schools forced Eisenhower to send in federal toops	☐	☐	☐	
The "Sit-Ins" began as a protest against segregated lunch counters at which deparment store?	☐	☐	☐	
In which city did Diane Nash force Mayor West to admit that segregated public services were racist?	☐	☐	☐	
The Sit-Ins spurred the creation of SNCC, whose most prominent early leader was John ..?	☐	☐	☐	

'How certain are you?' template available from www.tarrstoolbox.net

The maximum score is obviously if they play for 3 points for every single question and get the answers right (75 points). But by the same reasoning, the worst score would be -75. Therefore it's a good idea to add 75 onto the final score to get a total which can range instead from 0-150. This format removes the element of guesswork to a large extent, and produces a much wider spread of marks because the test measures not just factual recall, but also how securely the students felt they were with their knowledge acquisition.

Plot holes in history

During revision time, get students to identify the most outlandish coincidences and unlikely events they have learned about: things which, if they appeared in a Hollywood movie, would be regarded as lazy 'plot holes'. Convert these into posters and give credit for the best examples.

Case study: modern world history

After reading an amusing blog post on this theme ("Assume all of world history is a movie. What are the biggest plot holes?"), I decided to narrow the question down to the modern world history topics I teach to older students. Without too much thought a few ideas quickly suggested themselves:

> • I stopped watching that film about "Stalin" when, after spending several years killing millions of people for being 'Fascist counter-revolutionaries', he then formed a non-aggression pact with HITLER. Yeah, right. Like that would have happened.
> • I thought it was particularly lame when the whole "Hitler delivering a barnstorming speech at the trial designed to discredit him" thing was ripped off almost word-for-word in "Castro". Very unimaginative.

Taking it further

With a little more work, each scenario could be adjusted to turn the exercise into a quiz, with students asked to deduce which event / individual is being referenced. For example, who is being referred to in the following example?

> • There's that film where an American President wins a long, bloody Civil War, then the director pulls on the heartstrings just a little too obviously by having him assassinated basically minutes afterwards. That's not pathos so much as second-rate scriptwriting.

Spiced-up "cloze" exercises

"Fill the Gaps" ("Cloze") exercises help students build up vocabulary and to learn fresh information through focused, methodical reading. Here are several ways to 'spice up' cloze exercises.

1. Don't provide the list of missing words straight away.
• Instead, challenge students to fill the gaps purely from their own background knowledge.

2. Include extra 'rogue' words in the list of possible words that students can use to fill the gaps. For example:
• Use familiar key terms from earlier topics: this is a nice way to remind students of earlier vocabulary that they have learned!).
• Use new key terms that students will learn in the new topic, and then challenge students to research the meaning of each of these.

3. Don't just remove nouns – cloze exercises can also be used to help students enrich their vocabulary in other ways. For example:
• Remove adjectives and adverbs from the account and challenge students to insert the appropriate term from their own judgment or from a list.
• Remove the occasional piece of punctuation to get students thinking about when to use commas, semi-colons, hyphens and so on.
• Remove linking words and phrases (e.g. However, Therefore, Nevertheless, Additionally, Hence) from the start of paragraphs to help students think more carefully about how writers join paragraphs:

Nevertheless | Moreover | In some ways | However | On the other hand

Could you get justice in the Middle Ages?
In the Middle Ages, the guilt of somebody accused of a crime was determined in a range of ways.

these methods were unfair and they are no longer used. For example, was unfair because . In addition, was unfair because [etc]

, we should not be too harsh on people in the Middle Ages, because they did not have the sort of science and technology that we have today to help them. For example, in the Middle Ages they did not have which helps catch criminals today by [etc]

, in other ways, these methods were fair and are still used today. For example, was fair because . [etc]

Alphabet challenge

Challenge students to produce a list of words from A-Z, each of which has something to do with the topic being revised. If time is available, these can then be converted into a rhyme or song. Ideas can then be shared in the format of a team competition.

The case study that follows was inspired by the existence of genuine 'slavery alphabets' I discovered that were used by the abolitionist movement in the early nineteenth century, but the concept can be adapted for any topic whatsoever.

Case study: the slavery alphabet

As part of our studies about the Transatlantic Slave Trade and the abolition movement, students are challenged to produce a "Slavery Alphabet" poem to raise awareness of the horrors of the middle passage and life on the plantations. I start them off by reading out the first two lines of a genuine 'handbook against slavery' produced at the time:

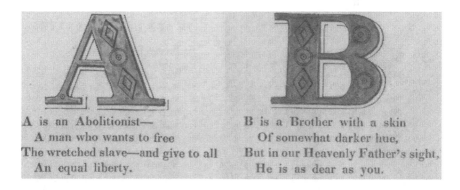

A is an Abolitionist—
　A man who wants to free
The wretched slave—and give to all
　An equal liberty.

B is a Brother with a skin
　Of somewhat darker hue,
But in our Heavenly Father's sight,
　He is as dear as you.

The remaining 24 letters of the alphabet are then divided between the three teams (C-J, K-R, S-Z). Teams are then given a limited amount of time to decide upon which words are most powerfully associated with the topic, and (if they are given sufficient time) to turn these into full lines of the poem – ideally, with rhyme incorporated.

Taking it further

- The "A-Z" approach can be used to help students to consolidate or revise knowledge for any topic.
- Different students could focus on different pairs of letters and produce two illustrated (and rhyming) lines of a poem which can be collated together as a whole class display (page 247).
- The teacher could conduct a team challenge where letters of the alphabet are randomly chosen from the ClassTools name picker (page 213) and teams score points if they can successfully nominate a relevant word starting with that letter and explain its relevance to the key question being studied (in the example above, this was 'What were the most inhumane aspects of the slave trade?').
- Another quiz format could be a 'blockbusters' board with letters of the alphabet placed within it. Each team takes it in turn to nominate one letter, give a word starting with this, and explain its relevance to the topic, to 'shade' it their colour. The 'white' team has to join up a chain of hexagons vertically, the 'blue' team (which should be a bit larger as there are more to join up) horizontally.
-

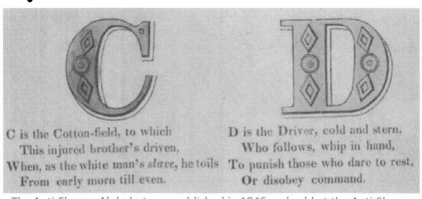

C is the Cotton-field, to which
    This injured brother's driven,
When, as the white man's *slave*, he toils
    From early morn till even.

D is the Driver, cold and stern,
    Who follows, whip in hand,
To punish those who dare to rest,
    Or disobey command.

The Anti-Slavery Alphabet was published in 1846 and sold at the Anti-Slavery Fair in Philadelphia. It can be found easily online using a search engine.

Exam questions from hell

One of the best ways to prepare students for examinations is to get them to design their own questions using the established format of past exam papers: the more difficult the better.

This helps familiarise them with the demands of the syllabus which is way more focused on the final examination. It is particularly good practice to encourage students to produce the most challenging questions they can imagine (within reason!) so that they are continually stretching themselves to develop their knowledge and understanding.

In most exams for history, there are only a limited number of command terms that can be used (e.g. "Compare and Contrast", "Evaluate", "Analyse", "Examine", "To what extent"). This means that in a subject area like rise and rule of dictators, it is quite straightforward to generate random questions – especially given the fact that the factors to be covered (e.g. social, political, economic) are generic too: here's an example of some questions generated by my own students in revision season:

Origins of the Cold War: Possible questions

1. Compare and contrast the role played by ideology and fear and aggression in the breakdown of the Grand Alliance between 1943-1949.

2. To what extent do you agree with the view that fear and aggression was mainly responsible for the breakdown of the Grand Alliance between 1943-1949.

3. Compare and contrast the impact of Sino-Soviet relations and detente on the course of the Cold War 1947-1979.

4. Evaluate the significance of two Cold War crises, each chosen from a different region.

5. Compare and contrast the role played by the USA and the USSR in the breakdown of the Grand Alliance between 1943-1949.

6. Discuss the causes of two Cold War crises, each chosen from a different region.

7. Compare and contrast the role played by ideology and economic interests in the breakdown of the Grand Alliance between 1943-1949.

8. Discuss the view that the US was mainly responsible for the breakdown of the Grand Alliance between 1943-1949.

9. Discuss the degree to which detente was achieved between the US and China in the 1970s.

10. Discuss the impact of two leaders on the course and development of the Cold War, each chosen from a different region.

11. Examine the degree to which detente was achieved between the US and the USSR in the 1970s.

The procedure is so mechanistic that I was able to generate an online tool which automates the process entirely. I have used it on several occasions since to generate a random question for a timed essay exercise and students then used it during revision season to help them prepare more effectively for the examination.

Authoritarian States: question generator

Rise and rule of authoritarian states: IB History Paper 2 sample question generator

This tool is designed to help teachers and students prepare for the IB Paper 2 exam by generating possible questions to practice and discuss. It is based on the command terms and syllabus bullet points provided in the IB syllabus.

Use this tool to generate a random question for a timed essay, or to sketch out various essay plans during revision season to keep minds open, flexible, and prepared for anything!

"To what extent do you agree that ideology formed the basis of control in two authoritarian states, each from a different region?"

Random question generator available at activehistory.co.uk

Taking it further

- Formulating the exam questions should really be just the first part of the learning process. These questions can then be swapped around so that different students have to design a mark scheme, complete with indicative content, for a fresh question that they had not considered.

- Next, the questions could be shuffled around the class again and each student has to provide a response in exam conditions.

- Then, pairs of students are given two responses to mark – firstly individually, and then comparing their thoughts as part of a moderation system. These results can then be discussed with the class as a whole in order to help fine tune the mark scheme and even write an "examiners' report" for each question highlighting good practice and common pitfalls.

- Finally, the entire batch of responses – or at least the better ones – can be shared with the entire cohort as a revision resource and made the subject of a "tell us something we don't know" quiz (page 77).

Rhyming timelines

At the end of a unit of study, divide a list of key words, terms, dates or individuals among the class. Challenge each student to create a rhyming couplet to make memorising the essential facts easier. Join these together as a class to make an overall revision poem or song and record this as a revision resource.

Although the following examples here focus on a chronological approach, it can just as easily be used thematically: for example, the assessment of the successes and failures of a particular ruler could be broken down in the same way, as could the main beliefs of a particular ideology, religion or society - although you may wish to adopt the "Alphabet challenge" approach for these sorts of topics instead (page 243).

Example 1 - People: Roman emperors
Following a debate on the subject 'Who was the most interesting Roman Emperor?', students sum up each emperor in a couple of rhyming lines, using this one as an example:

> "Augustus, the first Emperor, the best some might say:
> Left Rome made of marble after he'd found it as clay".

Example 2 - Events: modern world history Revision
The same approach can be adapted for revising a detailed chronology of events. At the end of the examination course for the Modern World History course, I remind students of the first event we studied, which was the outbreak of the Franco-Prussian War (1870). I use to start them off with this example:

> "In 1871, the French lost Alsace:
> Screamed 'revanchisme!' at Germans, would not let it pass".

I then challenge students to identify the most important events from the rest of the syllabus, all the way up to the fall of the Berlin Wall (1989). Each student then produces a rhyming couplet for their allocated event, and these are then collated into an overall rhyming timeline.

Taking it further

- Conclude the exercise by lining students up in date order to read out their couplet as the teacher moves along the line, filming them step by step. This can then be shared with students as a revision resource.
- To boil down the detailed rhyming timeline further for revision purposes, students should be encouraged to do something creative with the material. For example, they could use design a DVD inlay (page 271) to draw some conclusions ("Who was the most interesting Roman Emperor?", "What were the most important turning points in Modern World History?"), or use their timeline as the basis of a board game (page 122).

Personalised number plates

As a revision exercise, get students to design personalised number plates for historical characters they have studied. Accompany each one with a series of quiz questions which can be used to review the course in an engaging way.

To help students review key dates, people, places and relevant quotes, provide students with a list of key people they have studied (historians as well as historical characters). Divide these between the members of the class and give everyone a copy of a template which they can use to design a personalised number plate for each of the characters they have been allocated. This will require them to consider carefully what they will include to help them answer the following five questions:

- **Who**: Whose initials are shown on this number plate?
- **When**: What significant event occurred on the date shown?
- **What**: What is the significance of the picture that has been chosen?
- **Where**: What is the significance of the place stated under the picture?
- **Why**: Why has the particular quote been chosen?

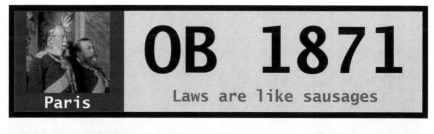

Once these have been collected in, they can be used as the basis of a revision quiz: the class can be divided into teams, and each team shares the number plates that they have produced with each other.

The first team chooses a number plate produced by one of their members, then challenges the second team to answer the five key questions outlined above in relation to it to obtain a maximum of five points. The second team then does the same for the third team and so on, until the final team poses its questions back to the first team. The quiz could proceed over several rounds.

Taking it further

- To ensure that all students are encouraged to revise the material during the lesson (not just the cards they personally produced), make it clear that any question which is not answered correctly will immediately be 'bounced back' to the team which asked it – and that the teacher will nominate a random student within this team to provide the correct answer. Failure to do so will result in one point being deducted from the team. With this new rule made clear, provide all the teams with sufficient time before the quiz starts to discuss their number plates with each other so that the whole team is confident to answer any questions relating to their team's material.

- The teacher could award a bonus point for the team which provides the best answer to the question "What car do you think would suit this person best? Explain your answer!".

Personalised number template available for download from
www.tarrstoolbox.net

Tarsia puzzles

As a refreshing change from straightforward factual tests, provide students instead with Tarsia puzzles. These consist of triangles where questions and answers are provided on different sides of opposing triangles. Joining them all together produces a pyramid, hexagon, or other shape, depending on the number of questions provided.

To help teachers and students create these puzzles easily, I have provided a generator at www.classtools.net which allows question and answer sets to be transformed with the click of a button into a printable Tarsia puzzle worksheet.

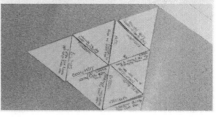

Students could work in pairs or small groups to cut up the triangles and to complete their puzzle.

Once students have successfully completed the puzzle, they should then take the time to copy down the questions and answers for revision purposes.

Taking it further

- Teachers could leave the sides of one or more triangles blank and challenge students to provide the missing question or answers.
- Tell the students in advance that there are a certain number of answers which are deliberately incorrect. Challenge them to identify these correctly.
- Get students to make their own Tarsia puzzles as a revision exercise.

Fling the Teacher

Working on the same principle as the popular TV show "Who wants to be a millionaire?", students are challenged to answer 15 questions of increasing difficulty to test their knowledge.

They have three 'life lines' to help them succeed. If they answer all the questions successfully, they then get the chance to "Fling the Teacher" at a target on the screen, Angry-Birds style!

You can create your own Fling the Teacher quizzes (or get your students to do so) using the free online generator at www.classtools.net. Simply input your question and answer sets, then click a button to get a unique web link to your quiz that can be shared with the class. You can also input your own face as the "Angry Bird"!

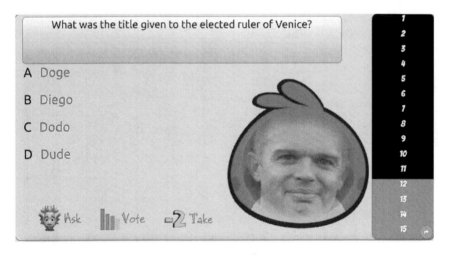

There is also a facility to set the quiz as a classroom test: in this instance, students are given a fixed amount of time by the teacher to play the game as many times as they wish, and at the end of the designated time the class leaderboard can be viewed, which immediately reveals how close each student came to completing the quiz. This information can then be inputted into the markbook.

Z to A: word association quiz

The Z-A quiz format involves revealing a series of words or phrases, letter by letter, in reverse alphabetical order. Students, organised into teams, win points if they are the first to identify what all the words/phrases have in common.

As soon as a hand is raised, the teacher 'stops the clock' to hear the answer. If the team answers incorrectly, it is frozen out of further play and the game resumes.

I have coded a simple Z-A quiz generator at ClassTools.net to enable students and teachers to quickly generate their own Z-A quizzes.

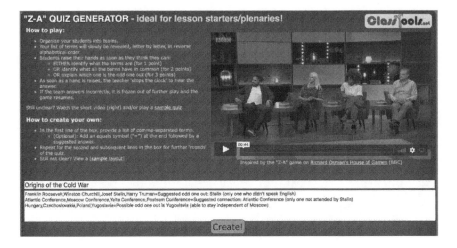

Case Study: The Origins of the Cold War

In the sample game provided freely on www.classtools.net on the Origins of the Cold War, the first set of terms is Winston Churchill, Franklin Roosevelt, Harry Truman and Josef Stalin. The students might identify them all as leaders of key states at the end of World War One (2 points for 'something in common'). Another team may have played though for three points with "Stalin was the only one who didn't speak English". If you are playing the version of the game where each team is challenged to identify such a connection and the teacher judges the most sophisticated, another team might trump this by saying instead "Stalin was the only one who wasn't at least half-American" or "Stalin was the only one who attended both the Yalta and Potsdam conferences from start to finish"). It's up to the teacher (or a special team of student adjudicators!) to decide which of these is the most useful/sophisticated points when deciding who to judge the winner!

Taking it further

To add further interest to the game, the rules can be developed by rewarding students when they:

- EITHER identify what the terms are (for 1 point)
- OR identify what all the terms have in common (for 2 points)
- OR explain which one is the odd one out (for 3 points)

If a team successfully for only one or two points, the clock can be started again to allow teams to try to score by aiming for the remaining (higher-scoring) options. So for example, Team 1 might successfully identify what the words are (1 point); Team 2 might then a few seconds later 'buzz in' to say what they all have in common (2 points); and then either team might buzz in a little later to identify which one is the odd one out (3 points).

Another format could be as follows: the first team to correctly identify what the words/phrases are gets a point. With the terms now identified, all the teams are challenged to identify the most impressive explanation of what they have in common. The teacher judges the winner and awards a point accordingly. Finally, all the teams are challenged to produce the most impressive explanation as to which one is the odd one out, with the teacher again judging the winner and awarding points.

8

CLASSROOM DISPLAY

Classroom displays, even when changed regularly, often have little educational value since students regard them as the equivalent of wallpaper or visual static. What follows in this chapter are a variety of suggestions about how to make your history classroom displays both visually appealing and educationally valuable.

Who tall are you?

The 'Who tall are you?' poster is designed to be printed off on A3 paper, laminated and then placed at the appropriate height in the classroom.

Students are invited to stand against it and write their names at the appropriate height to find out which historical celebrities they match.

The 'who tall are you?' resource can be downloaded at www.tarrstoolbox.net

Lesson / activity idea

Each student in the class should measure themselves against the 'Who tall are you?' chart. Each student then has to choose one of the names corresponding to their height to research in more detail.

The teacher will then conduct a 'balloon debate' between the different characters over several rounds to determine the most important character chosen.

Taking it further

The "Who tall are you?" chart can be taken down at the end of each academic year and replaced with a fresh version. As students make their way through the school it will be interesting to chart their growth over the course of their time at school over several years.

WHO Tall are YOU?

Write your name here!

			cm	
		Roald Dahl	**198**	Michael Jordan
			197	Mick Fleetwood
		French President: Charles de Gaulle, Paul von Hindenburg	**196**	John Cleese, Blackbeard
		Rock Hudson	**195**	Usain Bolt, , Christopher Lee, Vince Vaughan, Peter Tosh
		John Kerry	**194**	Stephen Fry, Aldous Huxley
		Rasputin, Idi Amin, Osama Bin Laden US Presidents: Abraham Lincoln, Lyndon Johnson	**193**	John Wayne, Josh Homme
		Malcolm X	**192**	Snoop Dogg, Ben Affleck, Gotye
		Prince William, Muhammad Ali US Presidents: George Washington, Fidel Castro, Reynard Heydrich	**191**	Sacha Baron Cohen, James Stewart, Oscar Wilde, Jesse Jackson
		Tsar Alexander III of Russia, Bismarck	**190**	Prince William
		Bashar al-Assad French President: Jacques Chirac US Presidents: Thomas Jefferson	**189**	Hugh Laurie
		US Presidents: Franklin Roosevelt, Bill Clinton, King Henry VIII, Neville Chamberlain	**188**	Maria Sharapova, George Orwell
		Boris Yeltsin	**187**	Peter Cook, Jay-Z, Johnny Cash, Cary Grant
		Saddam Hussein	**186**	Keanu Reeves
		David Cameron, Nick Clegg, James Callaghan, King Charles II US Presidents: Reagan, Obama	**185**	Ronaldo, Robert Plant, Clark Gable, Brigitte Nielsen, Oliver Hardy
		Benjamin Netanyahu	**184**	Benedict Cumberbatch
		US Presidents: Kennedy, Ford, Edward Heath, John Major Nelson Mandela, Ernest Hemmingway	**183**	Tony Blair, Wyatt Earp, Gadaffi, David Beckham, Sojourner Truth
		US Presidents: George W. Bush, Herbert Hoover Eleanor Roosevelt, Che Guevara	**182**	Harry Styles, Will Smith, Elvis Presley, Neil Young
		US Presidents: President Nixon French President: Georges Pompidou	**181**	Larry Page
		Mao Zedong, General Sherman, Mary Queen of Scots, John Major, Gordon Brown, Rowan Atkinson	**180**	Jimi Hendrix, Jim Morrison, John Lennon, Bach, Warhol, Dr. Seuss
		Al Capone US Presidents: President Eisenhower	**179**	Dean Martin
		US Presidents: T. Roosevelt, Coolidge Edison, Ford, WE Gladstone, William the Conqueror, Nehru, Goering	**178**	Princess Diana, Prince Charles, Michael Palin, Sitting Bull, Ozzy
		US Presidents: Jimmy Carter Paul Newman, Eddie Murphy, William Shatner	**177**	Kurt Cobain, Freddie Mercury, Robert de Niro, Cindy Crawford
		Albert Einstein	**176**	Robert Downey Jr.
		Gorbachev, Henry Kissinger, Robert Kennedy Sylvia Plath	**175**	Justin Bieber, Kate Middleton, Mariah Carey Mark Zuckerberg
		German Chancellor: Gerhard Schroder, Mark Twain, Trotsky Subhas Chandra Bose, JRR Tolkien	**174**	Marissa Mayer, Cameron Diaz
		German Chancellor: Hitler, Winston Churchill, Josef Stalin, Stan Laurel, Ulysses Grant,	**173**	Sheryl Sandberg, Ned Kelly, Billy the Kid, Edgar Allen Poe, Dickens

The 'who tall are you?' resource can be downloaded at www.tarrstoolbox.net

"Inspirational quote" posters

Get students to locate a thought-provoking quote about a topic, theme, or by a person related to the current topic, then turn it into a classroom poster. Display one poster per week on your classroom door to provoke some reflection and discussion.

Case study

As a development of my study unit on "Who is your history hero?", I challenged my students to locate a thought-provoking quote by or about their chosen character, or alternatively a quote about one of the 'heroic' qualities which they identified (determined, creative, principled and so on). Students can easily locate inspirational quotes from websites like www.brainyquote.com. Next, students used the free service at www.canva.com to turn their quote into a poster. I then rotated the best posters as a "thought for the week" display on my classroom door.

Taking it further

Students could be encouraged to provide an observation on the quote by leaving a block of post-it notes nearby. These can then be turned into follow-up quotes from the students themselves so that the "quote of the week" turns into an on-going conversation. I've started doing this with the display outside my own classroom after one of our students wrote a post-it note in reply to a Martin Luther King quote, and I then turned this into the following week's poster.

As an extension activity, students could research the author of the quote and provide a brief biographical summary as part of the poster and a web link or QR code with further information.

Dozens of free posters can be downloaded from www.activehistory.co.uk

Classroom windows as word walls

With classroom space limited, consider building up a 'Word Wall' on available windows or glass doors.

Window crayons can be purchased cheaply at online stores such as Amazon. Whenever a new or interesting word crops up in discussion or through reading, add it to the wall.

Taking it further
- Consider having separate word walls for different year groups.
- The word wall can be used for regular lesson starters.
- With younger classes, invite a different student each lesson to ask for a definition of one of the words added by the older classes.
- With older classes, challenge students to construct a sentence using different words from the wall in relation to the topic currently being studied.

"Currently being studied" posters

Maintain a 'currently being studied…' area outside the classroom, with separate A3 laminated posters outlining topics being studied by each year group.

Each poster consists simply of the key enquiry question and a relevant image. When one topic finishes, simply take down the old poster, keep it aside ready to use again next year, and replace it with the new one.

This display technique not only gives younger students an interesting insight into the sorts of things that they will study later on in their exam years, but also enables colleagues in other departments to spot potential overlaps with their own study topics.

This in turn can inspire fruitful conversations leading to cross-curricular projects between various subjects.

Taking it further

Ask students themselves to design the poster as an extension task. What image will they choose? What key question will they identify? Students could design the posters using the 'Breaking News Generator' at www.classtools.net.

Sample 'currently being studied' posters

Share video projects with QR codes

Many students enjoy the challenge of producing a video project to consolidate their learning. QR codes are a simple way of sharing these with the wider school community.

The main drawback with video projects, in comparison to posters or written work, is that they do not easily lend themselves to display.

To get around this problem, simply save the video on the web or on a page of your school's virtual learning environment. Next, use a URL shortening service (e.g. www.tinyurl.com) to get a short web address of this location. Even better, when you click the 'details' option you are given a QR code that you can copy directly into a document.

Print this information onto a piece of paper, place it on display and then students can scan the code to watch the film (QR scanning apps can easily be found for free in the ITunes store or similar). These can then be placed on your classroom door.

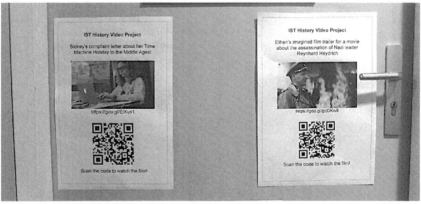

Students scan the QR code with their mobile phones to watch the video

"In the news...!" debate posters

In order to reinforce the relevance of History, and to encourage students to engage with current affairs, have a regular "In the news..." notice pinned up on the door outside your classroom.

I set aside a regular slot each week where I check my favourite blogs and newspaper websites for articles relating to my subject (I collate these using the excellent online service www.feedly.com), then print out the most interesting and stick them up on the classroom door along with a suitable "yes/no" question for consideration, such as:

- Should Santa Claus always be white?
- Should this History teacher be fired for comparing Trump to Hitler?
- Does Fidel Castro deserve to be remembered as a hero, or a villain?

Students will often read these during their break periods of when they are waiting to come into class, and this will generate discussion at the start of lessons. They should then write their name in the "Yes" or "No" box underneath the article, and the totals can be announced at the end of each week and placed on display:

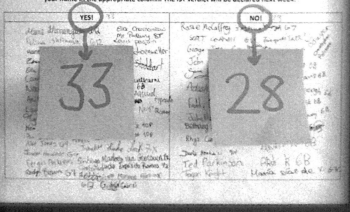

Example of a weekly "History in the News Debate"

"Open me" display pieces

When producing a display poster summing up several ideas, students should identify a 'cover image' for each main part of the piece. This should be 'lifted up' to expose the written detail.

These sorts of display pieces are a good way of associating an essential image with each piece of relevant information, and of encouraging students to engage with the display rather than ignoring it as if it were simply wallpaper.

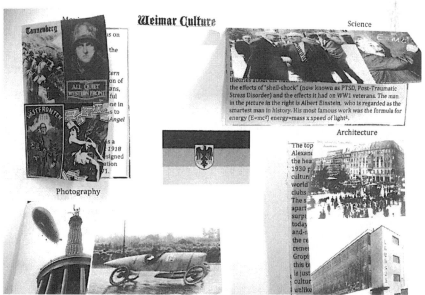

A sample 'open me' display piece on the culture of the Weimar Republic

Taking it further

An even simpler method is to take a piece of A4, fold it in half to create a greeting card, and place the image on the front with the written information inside. I have done this when students researched the origins of superstitions: a bold illustration on the front (e.g. of a four leafed clover) and an explanation on the front.

Acronyms and icons

For revision purposes, creating memory words, with each letter representing the first letter of another key word, helps students construct an effective way of recalling a larger amount of information.

At the start of a topic too, it can also be used as a technique for encouraging students to read the text more closely and actively reflect on fresh knowledge.

Step 1: Summary words
After identifying key factors, events, causes or effects, challenge students firstly to provide a one-word summary for each one.
For example, here is a summary of 6 problems facing the Peacemakers in 1918. Students need to add a heading in each box to summarise its message (e.g. "Rash bargains", "Deadly Disease" and so on).

Problems facing the peacemakers in 1919	
??	??
The war ended very suddenly. This meant that there was no agreement between the allies about how Europe should be reorganised. It also meant that ordinary Germans were left completely "shellshocked" by their defeat?	The War had created political chaos across Europe. The monarchies of Russia and Germany had been overthrown. The Austrian and Ottoman Empires had disintegrated.
??	??
The Allies had made rash bargains with countries such as Italy and Japan, promising territory after the war in return for their support. Would they have to stick with this?	Voters put pressure on the democratically elected leaders – the English and French public wanted to "Hang the Kaiser" and the Americans wanted a return to "Isolationism".
??	??
The war had completely changed the balance of world power. The war cost Europe $260 billion dollars, much of which had been loaned by the USA, which emerged as the world's first and only superpower.	An influenza pandemic was raging across Europe. Ultimately, this killed more people (c. 30 million) than the war itself! Half of the US soldiers who failed to return died of the 'flu, not from enemy action!

Step 2: Acronym for revision

An acronym is a word made up of letters, each of which symbolises another word. For example, the ADVENT verbs in French are those which take "Etre" in the past tense (aller, devenir, venir, entrer, naitre, tomber). Students have to now produce their own acronym of 6 letters to summarise the six titles they came up with earlier. They may have to change some of these so that they have a selection of letters from which you can make a word (i.e. a combination of consonants and vowels).

Example: The Treaty of Versailles
For the Treaty of Versailles, I get students to remember the acronym "TRAWL' (**T** = Territory | **R** = Reparations | **A** = Armaments | **W** = War Guilt | **L** = League of Nations)
Then within this, I encourage students to remember the "SCRAP" over Territory (**S** = Saar | **C** = Colonies | **R** = Rhineland | **A** = Alsace-Lorraine | **P** = Polish Corridor).

Step 3: Adding an icon

Students can add an appropriate icon in each box to summarise its message. I encourage students to think in terms of road signs and map symbols. For example, how can you summarise each of these factors as an image?

Problems facing Hitler after he became Chancellor in 1933		
Parliament	**Party**	**Presidency**
Hitler was only chancellor of a coalition government – of its 11 members, only 3 were Nazis!	The SA was becoming difficult to control. Its leader, Ernst Rohm, was starting to challenge Hitler's leadership	President Hindenburg had ultimate control. He deeply distrusted Hitler.

Knowledge cubes

When students conduct research on key individuals, get them to write up their findings on a cardboard cube, with each of the six faces covering a different theme, quality or contribution.
After the class has exchanged its findings in the form of a debate or similar, collect the cubes in and, as an extension activity, invite pairs of students to arrange these into a pyramid with the most significant characters placed towards the top.

Take a photo of the completed pyramid with the students behind it, and get them to summarise their reasoning on a large sticky note.

When you have a number of these photos and sticky notes, pin them all on a display board outside your classroom, then place the cubes on a table and invite other students (and teachers) to do the same thing.

Case study: who is your history hero?

In this project, students are guided towards identifying and researching a character from history that they will not only find personally inspiring but also totally novel.

Students start by deciding the personal qualities they most admire in others, then decide upon which area of achievement they are personally interested in (e.g. ballet, basketball, politics, music, horse-riding, boxing, football, feminism....).

They are then in a position to search the internet for such targeted things as 'Most determined scientist' or 'Most principled ballet dancer' and so on. Once they have found a suitably heroic character, I then get them to summarise their findings on a cardboard cube (which can be bought online in batches for postage purposes), in the following format:

Face 1: A picture of their chosen hero
Face 2: A picture of themselves
Face 3: Why this character is significant (how they affected lots of people, over a wide area and a long period of time: the who/where/when approach)
Face 4: First 'heroic' quality (e.g. 'Principled')
Face 5: Second 'heroic' quality (e.g. 'Caring')
Face 6: Third 'heroic' quality (e.g. 'Creative')

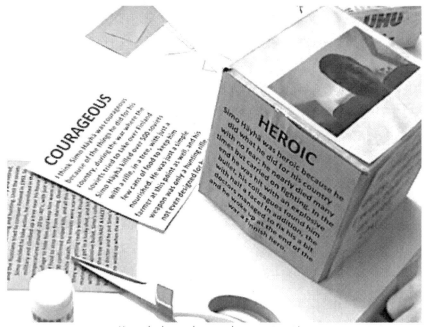

Knowledge cubes under construction

We then had a debate to determine a whole-class "History hero" for the year, before I then invited different students (as an extension activity in different classes from different year groups, over several days) to arrange the cubes in a pyramid of their choosing, with the characters towards the top to reflecting the people they personally found most impressive.

These photographs were placed on display, with the cubes left on a table for other students and teachers to do the same thing with at break times.

Students are invited to stack the cubes into a ranked pyramid

Taking it further

- Students could create an online 3D version of their cube using the "BrainyBox" generator at www.classtools.net.
- Once there are a range of photographs of pairs of students with their pyramids, encourage the school to look closely at these rather than just treat them as decoration by placing these sorts of questions around the display:
  o Do boys and girls rank the same sorts of people?
  o What about different ages?
  o What about different nationalities?
  o What does this tell us about the sorts of qualities that different ages, genders and nationalities regard as being most heroic?

Design a DVD inlay

As a way of consolidating or revising knowledge and understanding, challenge students to design a DVD inlay for a fictional documentary film. They should give careful thought to the images to include, the cast list, the reviews and the 'blurb' at the back.

I have created this editable template to be used in class. When printed off onto A4, it is exactly the correct size for a DVD case. It can be downloaded directly from www.tarrstoolbox.net. A completed set of such DVD inlays could form the basis of an interesting classroom or library display.

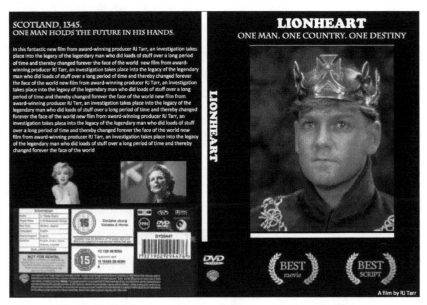

Editable DVD inlay template available at www.tarrstoolbox.net

Rice above the statistics

Statistics are a particularly useful source of evidence to help students form opinions and illustrate their arguments, but can too easily become meaningless numbers lacking in persuasive force (as Stalin infamously put it "One death is a tragedy. A million deaths is merely a statistic").

As seen earlier, an effective way to combat this is by challenging students to "guess the statistic" in advance of being given the data to generate an element of surprise or even shock when they are presented with the correct numbers (page 84). However, to impress these statistics more effectively upon the memory, it is worth getting students to then present them in a visually engaging way. Infographics are a great way of doing this (page 117), but another way is to use grains of rice to create physical representations of the statistics.

By working from the principle that one kilogram of rice contains 50,000 grains, this method can be used as a starter exercise for one particular statistic. It can also be used as a revision exercise when challenging each student to produce a different rice-based display piece to represent something covered over the course of the syllabus, or even as a whole-school competition open to all year groups.

Possible focus points

Start by placing one grain of rice upon a piece of black paper and telling the class that this represents one person. Alongside this, place a small pile of rice matching the amount of people in the class (you may prefer to place this into a small pot to prevent things getting messy!). Next, give students a cup and a bag of rice and challenge them to create a pile which accurately reflects the amount of people in the entire school.

Now that students are getting to grips with how the method works, invite them to consider how this could help them to visualise a key aspect of something they have studied. They may need some prompting here – for example, one pile of rice can represent the people involved in a particular event or in a particular place; alternatively, several piles of rice could represent how the amount of people involved/affected changed over time. Proceed after this discussion to conduct a quiz using the "Guess the Statistics" format (e.g. "How many people were killed when the Titanic sank?", "How many people were involved in the Salt march with Gandhi?"). After providing them with the answers and comparing scores, each student should then take responsibility for producing a rice-based representation of their chosen statistic.

To avoid the exercise simply becoming a process of students weighing /counting out grains of rice onto pieces of paper, challenge them to see this simply as the first and most simple step of the process. Their main challenge is to take this further by doing such things as:

- Sculpting the shape of the rice pile into something connected to what it represents;

- Providing an associated image / information panel to accompany the rice display;

- Using brown and white rice within the pile to represent two clear sub-groups;

- Producing a second pile of rice for comparative purposes (e.g. the capacity of Wembley stadium v. casualties of a particular battle).

Population density and land distribution in Apartheid South Africa

Taking it further

There are several further ways in which students can be encouraged to "rice above the statistics". The rice could be used to represent:

- **Change over time** – for example, the amount of people killed by certain diseases in particular years to represent the fight against disease; the size / distribution of population in different cities over time when studying the impact of the Industrial Revolution.

- **Comparing themes** – for example, the amount of people involved in different protest marches and demonstrations (e.g. Mussolini's March on Rome, Hitler's Munich Putsch, Gandhi's Salt March, the civil rights Selma March).

- **Objects, distances, weights and currencies** – although the rice approach is most powerful when representing individual people, it could also be used to represent other things. Each grain of rice could, for example, be used to represent a bullet used in a battle, a brick used to build a medieval cathedral, a vote used for or against a key issue debated in Parliament, a Euro or dollar which something cost, a kilometre or a kilogram.

Display organised at the International School of Toulouse

Affordable props

Artefacts, props and gadgets can serve as a great 'hook' into lessons. Over the years I have built up quite a collection in my own classroom, some of which are surprisingly affordable and obtainable. What follows is a list of some of my favourites, starting with the cheapest.

"Hard Boiled Humanities" entries

The 'Hard Boiled Humanities' competition takes place at Easter each year (page 336). As these eggs are 'blown' rather than strictly 'boiled', they can be placed on display indefinitely to provide inspiration year on year.

"Hard Boiled Humanities" entries in a dedicated glass cabinet

Roman dice

When studying the Romans, I have designed a game where students research different gladiator types, produce playing cards based on each, and then 'fight' each other in pairs using both their knowledge and chance (factored in by the dice) to help them to victory. As a result I purchased these Roman numeral dice so that I could start the lesson with a short exercise in how Roman numerals work.

Roman dice

Sugar cane

I purchased a piece of sugar cane from a supermarket several years ago and it's still going strong. It's useful at the start of my study of the Transatlantic slave trade (and before I tell students what we about to study), when I show it to students and have it passed around the class, ask them to guess what it is, and then encourage the students once they have correctly guessed – or, more frequently, been told – to 'guess the topic'. I usually give them a series of clues (the British Empire was built on this…it was grown in large plantations…it was harvested by slaves in terrible conditions…).

Soviet medals

The Soviet Union, to put it mildly, had a bit of a thing for medals. Just about any contribution to Soviet life beyond getting out of bed in the morning was likely to be rewarded with a lapel badge. As a result they can be bought very cheaply on Ebay, and I have build up quite a collection. They are a good way of getting students to start understanding the social fabric of the USSR as well as the attributes and achievements it valued.

Weimar Germany hyperinflation notes

The story of hyperinflation in Germany is central to any study of the fragility of the Weimar Republic after World War One. A dramatic story in itself, it is infinitely improved if the teacher is able to show a series of notes which chillingly reflect the declining value of the Germany currency in 1923 – from the point where each note represents a few Marks, to when each note represents billions (and is still unable to purchase anything whatsoever of value). Precisely because they were printed in such gargantuan quantities, these hyperinflation notes are now easily purchased online at a very affordable price and forming a collection can be quite addictive (especially when combined with a collection of beautiful German Notgeld). The following photo shows some examples from my own collection, along with an original Dawes Plan loan bond from 1924 and government bond stamps from 1922.

Hyperinflation notes, Dawes Plan loan bond and government bond stamps

Codd bottle

At the start of my unit on "Who was the Greatest Person of the Industrial Revolution?" I ask students two questions about this "Codd" bottle (right), named after its Victorian inventor, Hiram Codd. Such bottles are easily and inexpensively obtainable online. First, I challenge the class to explain how this Codd bottle works. It's a cheap example of Victorian ingenuity: the marble acts as the seal to the bottle and is kept in place by the pressure created by the fizzy drink inside. Children would frequently smash the  bottles for the marbles inside. Second, I ask them why a blue version of the bottle is so incredibly rare (it would sell, if genuine, for thousands of pounds). The answer is that blue was associated with poison bottles, therefore manufacturing a fizzy-drink bottle in blue glass was a marketing disaster.

Topic-themed mugs

As an Englishman abroad, my mug of builders tea is a permanent fixture of my classroom. To keep the historical theme alive I have a collection of themed mugs, my favourites among which are Churchill ("If you're going through hell, keep going"), American Civil War generals (Stonewall Jackson being a favourite), Napoleon and – in homage to the 1980s arcade games I recreate at ClassTools – my Manic Miner mug.

Judges' wig and gown

As a big fan of role-play exercises, I have built up quite a collection of various hats to represent different nationalities. I use these when, for example, we debate the Origins of World War One. The costume that gets the most use, however, is a wig and gown which is worn either by me or a student when we need somebody to act as a judge during a debate.

Glass-bottomed tankard

I received a pewter tankard, illustrated with a scene of the Battle of Trafalgar, as a birthday present a few years ago, and it sits on my desk as a pencil holder for the most part. However, when teaching the British Empire I empty it out and start by asking students to explain why they think it has a glass bottom. This leads me into a discussion of the 'King's Shilling': a bonus payment of a shilling was offered to tempt lowly paid workers to leave their trade. Once the shilling had been accepted, it was almost impossible to leave the army. Sometimes the 'King's shilling' was hidden in the bottom of a pewter tankard (having drunk his pint, the unfortunate drinker found that he had unwittingly accepted the King's offer). As a result, some tankards were made with glass bottoms so that drinkers could check it hadn't been tampered with.

Breaking news / Click bait

As a starter, plenary or revision exercise, challenge students to summarise an aspect of their most recent study topic as a 'click bait' or 'breaking news' headline.

Breaking news

Using the Breaking News Generator which I have made available at www.classtools.net, students should reflect on the key location, the title of the news channel, the headline, the ticker with related news and the most appropriate image. The completed designs can be downloaded and printed off to form an attractive display.

Click bait

A similar approach is to provide students with some of the most common formats of "click bait" headlines and challenge them to convert some of the key events from their studies into historical examples:

- [?] decides to [?]. The reason why will make you [?]
- [?] tries to [?]. You won't BELIEVE what happened next!
- This video will prove that [?]
- 10 [?] you should never [?] to [?]
- X was Y. First you'll be shocked, then you'll be inspired
- 10 [?] that look like [?]
- 10 [?] that you won't believe [?]

Teacher Network The Secret Teacher

Boston Flash Mob takes a tea break
You won't BELIEVE what happens next!

Created using the headline generator at www.classtools.net

Taking it further

- Produce a timeline of events (e.g. from a historical event, or a novel being studied in literature) and then divide it between different students so they can produce one screenshot each. The finished results can be displayed as a timeline in class.
- Encourage students to adopt a biased editorial tone. For example, a newsflash on the Battle of Hastings could be produced from both a French ("Norman News!") and an English ("Anglo-Saxon Herald!") perspective (see page 226).
- During revision, secretly allocate different students a different topic to produce a click bait headline for. Other students then have to guess what topic is being referred to.
- The "Breaking News" generator can also be used to show off photographs of students' achievements.

Meme posters

As a closing exercise, or a fun activity or competition during the revision period, get students to design a meme poster related to the topic or the subject that you teach.

The best posters – those which most effectively use humour as well as an 'inside joke' demonstrating knowledge of the subject – could be printed off, laminated and used as classroom posters.

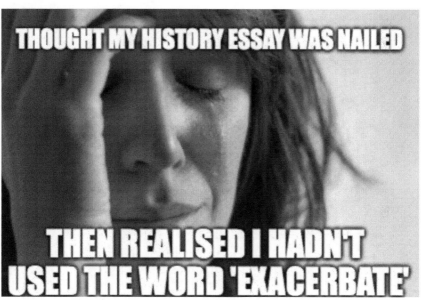

A winning meme from my annual student competition

Taking it further

- Allocate different meme types to different students, and even allocate particular topics along with them. In this way you will be guaranteed a wide range of posters on a wide range of themes.

Further examples of meme posters for the classroom. Henry VIII as 'distracted boyfriend' could easily be adapted to chart Stalin's rise to power, for example.

Turn the topic into objects

Superb podcast series such as "50 things that made the modern economy" and "A history of the world in 100 objects" reflect the growing popularity of understanding topics through key artefacts.

This approach could be adopted in a classroom setting by challenging students to decide upon the most iconic objects to symbolise a particular topic, theme or individual that they study.

At the start of my IB History course, students were presented with an overview of the syllabus and then used this to choose a topic, theme or individual to research further. They then used this research to decide upon at least one "object" which would symbolise it best.

Each student then produced an 'exhibit' as the basis of an engaging corridor exhibition. It was an effective way of giving students an overview of the entire course and the presentations were then re-visited at appropriate points in the following months.

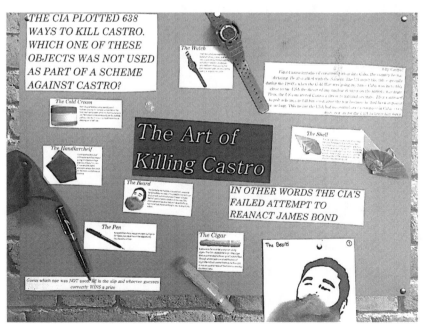

The CIA against Castro in five objects – watch, pen, cigar, shell and beard!

283

Model-making ideas

Producing a physical model can be a very engaging and stimulating way of bringing history alive.

Case studies

Medieval Cathedrals and Castles

Designing a castle is a popular project for younger students, but I prefer getting students to produce their own design for a cathedral complete with Gothic and Romanesque features as appropriate. We start by looking at the features of both styles of architecture - with a stress on the engineering and mathematical side of things as much as anything else - and then each student produces either a design or, ideally, a model of their cathedral. Although the preferred material is often cardboard, an increasing amount of students are keen to produce their models using software such as Minecraft or Google Sketchup and then export this as a video with a narrative.

Heraldic Shields

A fixed feature of my school calendar is a study with younger students of the principles of heraldic designs. Each student firstly complete an interactive simulation on ActiveHistory which asks them a series of questions about their personality, interests, family and ambitions. It uses this information to provide them with the colours and symbols to incorporate into their shield design. Students then use this information to produce their own historically accurate heraldic shield in cardboard, wood or metal and explain the meaning of each symbol in a written account which they attach to the back. I then film each student holding up their shield and reading out their account. The shields can then be placed on display alongside a QR code which links through to the video of the shield being explained by its creator.

Sample shields produced by students reflecting their personalities and interests

World War One Trench
One subject which lends itself particularly well to model-making is designing a first World War trench. Students are presented with a list of key features of a trench on the Western Front - duckboards, parapet, dugout, sandbags and so on - and are marked according to how many of these features they include in their final model. As an added twist, students could be divided into groups to produce models which represent different aspects of the trench experience: for example, highlighting how a German trench was different to a British one.

World War Two Toys
As part of a study about the civilian experience of World War Two, provide students with primary source instructions about how to 'make do and mend' by producing their own inexpensive playthings. There are several freely downloadable facsimiles of booklets provided for this very purpose during the war which can easily be located using the web, including "Toys in Wartime" (from the US) and the wonderfully entitled "Hundreds of Things a Boy Can Make" (from the UK - all of which, believe it or not, are within the capabilities of 21st-century girls too). Each student should nominate a different toy that they will produce as a homework project, and then these can be played in a subsequent lesson and peer-assessed to determine upon the overall winners.

Taking it further

- Although cardboard, plasticine and Lego are popular materials for classroom model-making, and software such as Minecraft and Google Sketchup provide a more hi-tech alternative, students could also be encouraged or instructed to produce an edible model in the form of a cake!

9

SOURCEWORK, RESEARCH AND ESSAY-WRITING SKILLS

The knack of writing a good essay in a subject like history is a skill which is a challenge to acquire for many students, but immensely rewarding and useful. The ability to carry a reader along with a well-crafted argument is no easy feat, since it involves carefully synthesising the creative arts of the storyteller with the scientific rigour of the evidence-driven empiricist. This chapter provides several techniques for helping young historians develop these vital skills.

Miscellaneous essay approaches

It is not enough to simply take in an essay, mark it and provide feedback, and then hurry on to the next lesson or activity. Much better is to take in a first draft of the essay, involve the students in some reflection and redrafting, and then take it in for final marking so that the advice is immediately being put into effect rather than going stale whilst the class awaits the next essay assignment several weeks later.

Listed here are a few activities that can be used to help students improve their essay-writing skills after their initial draft of work has been completed.

1. Analysis skills for students
The Skeleton
Students should produce an essay plan which contains merely the first topic sentence of each paragraph. This should then be passed to a partner, whose job is to suggest what evidence could be used to substantiate the point made by each topic sentence.

Objection!
The teacher takes a completed essay and reads out just the opening topic sentence of each paragraph to the class. If at any point anyone in the class thinks that an opening sentence is a narrative statement of fact rather than an analytical argument they should say "objection" and explain why. The sentence should then be developed appropriately before moving on to the next.

Flowchart
Students are organised into pairs. One student reads out the opening topic sentence of each paragraph and the partner has to summarise the overall argument in the form of a flowchart to share with the class. A poorly constructed essay will consist of simple narrative statements

and this will be more difficult to achieve, whereas a well constructed essay will consist of analytical statements, linked together in a logical way.

2. Narrative skills: "Mr. Interpretation"

One student reads out a sentence of factual detail from an essay and nominates somebody else in the class to provide an analytical point that it illustrates, for example:

- Person 1 presents a fact – "Tsarina Alexandra was German by birth"
- Person 2 the interpretation – "Provides explanation for opposition to Tsar during World War One"

If the nominated person explains the significance of the fact successfully, it is their turn to choose a factual detail of their own and nominate somebody else. If they fail to explain the significance of the fact, they are knocked out of the game. The winner is the last person standing.

3. Source evaluation skills: "Mr. Sceptical"

This is the same as "Mr. Interpretation" except a third person in each round has to show an awareness of the limitations of the evidence:

- Person 1 presents a fact – "Tsar Nicholas was 'not fit to run a village post office' (Trotsky)"
- Person 2 the interpretation – "Provides explanation for opposition to Tsar during WW1"
- Person 3 the limitations – "But Trotsky was a hostile witness", "But the Russians were deeply loyal to the principle of Tsarism".

4. Challenging the question: "Mr. Angry"

Students are provided with a list of sample questions from past exam papers. For each one, they have to explain:

- What loaded assumptions are within it.
- Why these are quite obviously completely and utterly wrong.

5. Structural skills: where are the paragraphs?

The teacher should take an article available in a digital format (e.g. from the History Today archives), paste it into a Word document, and then remove all of the paragraph marks and (as a final act of stylistic sadism) make it 'fully justified'. Students should then be presented with this essay from hell, and challenged to deduce by reading it carefully where they think that each of the original paragraphs began. This can then lead into a discussion about how a writer determines when to start a new paragraph – for example, when they are about to make a brand new point in relation to the question, or take the previous point in a fresh direction.

6. Avoiding stock responses: "Rewrite a model essay"

Students should be given a model essay or an article on a key topic. They should then examine past exam papers to determine what other questions have been set on this theme. In what ways, and to what extent, would the given essay need to be re-written and re-structured to answer these questions?

7. Focusing on the command terms: "Guess the title of the essay"

Another technique is for students to copy and paste the entire article or essay into a word cloud website such as www.wordle.net or www.tagxedo.com. If a writer has clearly focused on the command terms then these will appear at a higher frequency in the word count and therefore will be displayed more prominently in the word cloud.

8. Only use quotes you disagree with

Using quotes in essays is too often a technique used by students to avoid thinking for themselves. Worst of all is the paragraph which is effectively a potted summary of another writer's point of view. To avoid this, students should be asked to remove any quotes which they actually agree with. Instead, they should use quotes as a means of setting up a debate and demonstrating clear evidence of independent thinking ("Although AJP Taylor argued that…this does not bear close scrutiny because…").

True, false, or anachronism?

Helping students understand the concept of anachronism – the misplacing of a concept, object or individual in a time period where it could not have existed - is an important step to getting them to understand the concept of chronology, to empathise with people in the past and to understand a historical period.

Arthur Marwick argued that "anachronism is still one of the most obvious faults when the unqualified…attempt to do history". One effective technique is to provide students with a short, but informative and evocative, written account. Within this, add some deliberate anachronisms. Challenge the students to use any sources available to them to work out which parts of the story are historically accurate, and which are anachronisms.

Case studies

I constructed the following short accounts and provided them to the students with plenty of space for marginal notes. Students underlined any facts that could be checked (this in itself was an interesting discussion which highlighted the difference between fact, opinion and imagination):

Example 1: Imperial Rome
"It is a glorious day in Imperial Rome. The year is 1AD, and it is the month of August (recently named after the current Emperor, Augustus). After having a pizza for lunch, you hitch up your toga, climb onto your motorbike, and drive through city centre, admiring in particular the white marble statues and the magnificent Trajan's column (engraved with battle scenes) and the Theatre of Pompey (named after the city destroyed by the explosion of Mount Vesuvius a few years earlier). You glance at your watch and decide you have time to watch a show, so you drive alongside the Aqua Virgo (one of the

---

major aqueducts supplying the city), past the part of town recently destroyed by the Great Fire of Rome, and arrive at the Circus Maximus, which has just recently been rebuilt in stone. Here you watch a gladiator fight between two Christian prisoners, which reminds you that just last year Spartacus led a slave rebellion against the Romans"

Example 2: Victorian Britain
The year is 1895. We are in a London street, which is crowded with the new popular motor-car, the Ford Model 'T'. A newspaper seller is shouting that today Benjamin Disraeli has died, and the advertisements on the street-side announce trips to see the opening of the brand new Eiffel Tower in Paris. A man called Kevin is walking along the street eating some fish and chips, complaining that the pubs won't be open until the early evening. His wife, who is wearing a bustling crinoline, tells him to stop moaning and suggests that they go to the cinema to watch a film by Charlie Chaplin instead.

Students then listed all these facts underneath the account, and researched each one in turn to declare it "true" (in which case they had to elaborate), "false" (in which case they explained why it is factually incorrect) and "anachronism" (in these instances, they had to explain why it is something which has been placed into the wrong time period by explaining the historical time period in which it actually belongs).

This approach is a nice, simple way to engage students in a bit of targeted research and a quick blast of information about the topic from a fresh perspective. It works particularly well as a starter or extension activity.

Taking it further
- Get students to produce their own accounts in a similar way.
- Additionally or instead, they could try to sketch an imagined scene containing anachronisms.
- Older students could be challenged to research the meaning of two very different types of anachronism: parachronism and prochronism.

Visual essay-writing in groups

This multimedia approach allows students to conduct an investigation by organising various sources into categories and then linking them together to produce the basis of an essay plan.

To develop analytical and essay-writing skills in a collaborative and engaging manner, start by gathering a series of photographs relating to the topic in question:

- A pile of cartoons and photographs (maybe about 20 of these)
- Podcasts
- Video clips
- Textbooks
- Articles

Next, divide the class into groups. Within each group, three students should be responsible for organising the cartoons into meaningful categories to answer the key question for the lesson (in the photograph shown overleaf, cartoons are being organised into meaningful categories to help understand "Why was the Marshall Plan so controversial?").

Whilst the 'cartoonists' are busy discussing how to arrange the images meaningfully, another student should be listening to the podcasts, another watching the video, another reading the article, and another reading a textbook (it is a good idea to let students choose the task they are most comfortable with, as far as possible). As they spot any evidence that helps answer the key question, they should write it on a sticky-note (this helps them to keep their points focused).

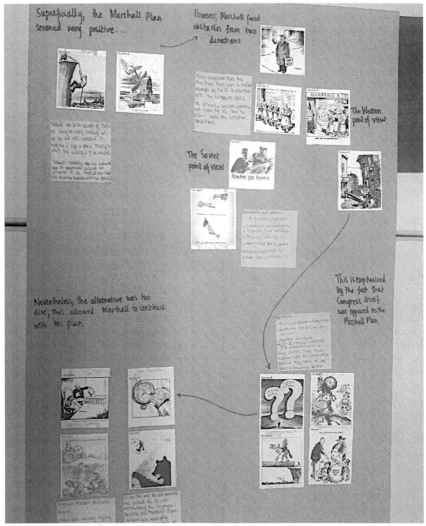

A sample outcome investigating the motives behind the Marshall Plan.

When the cartoonists have finished organising their images into categories that make sense to them, the next step is to give each category a heading, and to link the categories together in a meaningful manner by spotting causal links and natural overlaps. At this stage, I get different cartoonists to swap places with the someone in another team, the members of which then explain their diagram to their 'visitor'. Each person then returns back to their original team and makes suggested amendments based on any bright ideas gleaned from the other team or teams.

At this stage, the readers/viewers/listeners will start to be joining the cartoonists, bringing their sticky notes with them. Their job, working with the team, is to discuss the answer that appears to be emerging, and to determine where to place their sticky-notes to best effect to help provide the essential detail to give substantiation to the ideas identified in the cartoons.

Thereafter, each group can compare and contrast the answers that they have formulated, before each individual student provides a formal written response to the key question using their completed diagrams to help them.

Taking it further
The visual essay writing approach overlaps effectively with the hexagon approach (page 24) and the sticky-note approach (page 204).

Analysing the causes / consequences of the Manchurian Crisis

Write a script, not an essay

Giving students an essay to write as the main outcome of a unit of study can be repetitive and tiresome. To give students a fresh enthusiasm for essay writing, present the topic instead as a documentary-making project.

This approach has additional benefits in the sense that it stresses the art, not just the science, of essay writing. By recording themselves as part of the process of making the actual film, it also gets students to reflect carefully on how their own voices come across and the importance of speaking clearly, steadily and lucidly when presenting to an audience.

Case study: making a film on the causes of the American Civil War

Phase 1: Students gather information about the topic

My study of the causes of the American Civil War begins with a teacher lecture, then an illustrated timeline task whereby students start to build up a folder of high-resolution images based on the most interesting events and developments. They also research events in more detail by watching clips from the famous Ken Burns documentary.

Phase 2: Students think how scriptwriters construct a narrative

I do this firstly by watching Ken Burns being interviewed on "The Art of Story" (available at www.vimeo.com) which is a brilliant synopsis of how the historical writing process is a balance of science (empiricism, research) and art (imagination, emotion). We then watch the opening minute of several documentaries to see how they use silence, subtle music, carefully chosen images and a narrative 'hook' to engage the viewer from the outset (in particular, I use the opening segment of the first episode of "The World at War" which is fantastic).

Phase 3: Students select and connect the main factors

In this phase students are effectively writing their essay, but they are seeing this merely as one part of a creative process and are much more engaged. They start by choosing the five most interesting events in their timeline and explain how each one increased the tensions which erupted into war. Next, they have to connect these factors in five key sentences using "connectives" ("As a result...Nevertheless...This meant that...This highlighted...This accelerated...This was the result of...Because of this..." and so on). Following this, they have to develop each sentence into a full paragraph with substantiating explanation and detail. Finally, they have to design their own narrative 'hook' to serve as an introduction, and decide how to finish the story.

Phase 4: Students record the script create the film

In this phase, we start with a lively and humorous discussion about what usually marks out school film projects as being amateurish. Students usually identify such things as a monotonous, rushed, mumbling narration, irrelevant and low-resolution images and intrusive background music. These are clearly therefore the things to avoid! Students record their narratives into Audacity, import these into IMovie or similar, and then overlay the images they gathered in Phase 1 to produce their movie.

		Marks
Structure	Narrative structure [1-2] or analytical structure [3-4]?	1-4
	Engaging introduction and a thought-provoking conclusion	1-2
Research	Detail from classroom notes [1-2] or also from personal research [3-4]?	1-4
Visuals	Related to the narrative	1-2
	Good range, good resolution	1
	Subtle motion / transition effects	1
Narration	Clearly spoken and recorded at a sensible pace, with varying intonation to maintain viewer interest and appropriate use of silence	1-4
Music	Sensibly chosen backing track used to add atmosphere, at a suitably low volume	1-2
Total		20

Sample mark scheme for a documentary script project

Banned word list

As a history teacher there are certain tired words and phrases which make me wince when I see them being used by examination students. I therefore use my classroom window word wall (page 260) to list words and phrases which are not only useful, but also those which I do not want to see being used.

Structured questions
My key banned phrase for topic sentences in essays and structured questions is "On the one hand...on the other hand" (the ultimate 'fence-sitter' response). In this way, during test conditions and in homework, students have a ready list of useful 'balancing phrases' which express a meaningful position ('Although, in some minor respects,....Nevertheless, more fundamentally...') without creating written pieces which appear non-committal.

Source work questions
Another window in my classroom has a similar list of words to help students evaluate source material. Here, the banned phrase is 'This is a primary source so it is reliable because....this is a secondary source so it is reliable because...' - the classic stock response in source work questions for students that can't be bothered to reflect properly on the particular sources they are presented with.

In this case, I provide students with other words. During revision time I ask them to rank these from words which suggest 'most reliable' down to 'least reliable'. Once again, this helps students broaden their vocabulary and provide a more nuanced response to examination questions. For example, how would you rank these words in that manner?

Partial	Contradictory	Impartial
Biased	Ill-informed	Objective
Partisan	Well-informed	Subjective
Prejudiced	Propagandistic	Secondary
Bigoted	Censored	Primary
Vitriolic	Edited	

Rubric grids

To help students improve their essays skills, I consistently use the same rubric sheet to provide them with feedback on different aspects of their performance and progress.

Students are graded against the following separate criteria, giving an overall total out of 20 marks:

Name of Student: Title of Essay:						Comments
	L1 - 1 Mark	L2 - 2 Marks	L3 - 3 Marks	L4 - 4 Marks	Bonus Mark	
Introduction / Conclusion	Introduction 'sets the scene' and outlines what factors will be considered. Conclusion summarises the main points made in the essay.	Introduction 'sets the scene' and summarises what the essay will seek to prove. Conclusion summarises the main points made in the essay and establishes clear reasons for what this topic provides for today.				
Structure	Narrative. Although not incoherent, the essay is a narrative account of events with very little analysis.	Narrative with bolt-on analysis. There is some limited analysis, but the response is primarily narrative/descriptive in nature rather than analytical.	Opening paragraph sentences are arguments, but do not link together consistently. The response makes appropriate links and/or comparisons although these are not always convincing.	Opening paragraph sentences are arguments, and consistently link together consistently to provide a balanced 'path' of argument. Arguments are consistently clear, coherent and effective in terms of links and/or comparisons.		
Breadth	Key factors overlooked. There is limited understanding of the demands of the question. Key aspects of the topic will be completely overlooked.	Lack of balance between paragraphs. There is sound understanding of the demands of the question. The most important aspects of the topic are covered, but not in a suitably balanced manner.	Lack of balance within paragraphs. There is good understanding of the demands of the question. The most important aspects of this topic are covered in a suitably balanced manner. However, there is little awareness of different perspectives and concepts within each paragraph.	Excellent range and balance. Responses are clearly focused, showing a high degree of awareness of the demands and implications of the question. There is rigorous evaluation of different perspectives and concepts, and this evaluation is integrated effectively into a sophisticated answer.		
Depth	Limited use of classroom materials. The essay relies on partial use of classroom notes. The relevance of this knowledge is not always established.	Good use of materials. Appropriate evidence is drawn effectively from classroom notes and / or wider reading. This is used to substantiate the arguments being presented.	Excellent use of evidence, used illustratively. Plenty of evidence is also used from wider reading (e.g. quotes, historiography, statistics), but is taken at face value AND/OR a bibliography is not included.	Excellent use of evidence, used critically (its reliability is regularly questioned). The examples used are appropriate and relevant, and are used effectively to support the analysis/evaluation.	Any candidate in Level 3 or 4 gains an additional bonus mark if they include a bibliography AND footnotes in their essay.	

Full-scale template can be downloaded at www.tarrstoolbox.net

For each of these, I provide different level descriptors for 1 mark up to the maximum available for that particular essay feature. Then, it's simply a question of shading off the correct cell in the grid and providing an explanation on the right-hand side.

The benefits of this approach are that I mark the essay much more methodically, but also much more quickly. Rather than make one overall evaluation right at the end of the essay, I instead make separate, shorter but more focused comments about half a dozen features of the piece. This provides the students with feedback which is directly comparable to their previous essay rubric so they can spot exactly where they have improved, and where they need to focus next.

Use YouTube comments to spot historiographical debates

Identifying the key debates between historians on central topics is an important way of engaging students with their studies. A simple way of doing this is to direct them to the comments underneath YouTube videos. These tend to fall into two categories: those that are angry, which give an indication of the passion which the topic generates; and those which are more measured, which are useful for identifying some of the key evidence that historians use on either side of the argument.

Case study: the Spanish Civil War

In my first lesson on the Causes of the Spanish Civil War, I directed students to watch a short video clip about the exhumation of Franco last year, and then they used the comments underneath to get an idea of how divisive a figure he is, and why. They seemed to find it a really engaging 'hook' - this screenshot gives an idea of how to lay it out:

What were the causes of the Spanish Civil War?
Introduction and Overview

• In 1936, a group of Spanish army generals led a coup against their own government. Their failure to seize immediate control condemned Spain to a Civil War which lasted three years, cost half a million lives, destroyed entire communities and divided families – in some cases, permanently.
• The causes of the Spanish Civil War remain one of the most controversial topics of the 20th century.
• For those on the **left**, the Civil War between the "Nationalist" forces of General Franco (pictured) and the "Republican" forces of the left-wing government was a struggle of Fascism against democracy. This view is shared by books such as Orwell's "Homage to Catalonia" and in films such as Ken Loach's "Land and Freedom".
• For those on the **right**, the Nationalists were Spanish patriots bravely determined to stop the Republicans from turning Spain into a communist dictatorship.

Activity:
Using YouTube comments to identify the key historiographical debates about Franco
• General Franco, who emerged victorious in 1939 and ruled as dictator of Spain until his death in 1975, therefore remains a highly controversial and divisive figure – as illustrated sharply by this news video from 2019 (and the comments underneath it!):
https://www.youtube.com/watch?v=IqA7Uewhmtl

1. What happened in 2019 with regard to Franco?	???	
2. Using YouTube comments to identify the key historiographical debates:	**"HEAT"** (copy and paste a comment which shows the passion some commentators feel).	**"LIGHT"** (copy and paste comments which use arguments backed up with evidence)
Why are some commentators critical of this development?	???	???
Why are some commentators in favour of this development?	???	???

Use a selection of comments from underneath the video to complete these answers.

Nine note-taking strategies

Effective note-taking is a vital skill for students, but by no means a simple one to teach or to learn. It helps to have several approaches to share with students so they can choose the one which works for them best.

From my experience, students have to be constantly reminded to take notes during a reading, a lecture or whilst watching a video documentary. They then either take such detailed, undiscriminating notes that they miss the big picture, or make such brief and unfocused points that they serve no useful purpose whatsoever.

At the start of the lesson, the best approach is therefore to encourage students to identify the most effective note-taking strategy, and consider in advance what format they intend to transform these notes into after the lesson.

Some of the following methods are clearly 'note-taking' strategies to be used during the lesson itself. Others are 'note-transformation' strategies to be used when re-drafting after the lesson.

A. Methods suitable both for lectures and for readings
Four Box Limit
Tell students to divide their paper into four sections. If the lesson is based around a text-reading, they have to identify the main points made in the piece and write these into each box. Alternatively, if this is a teacher-led lecture, these headings might be provided by the teacher at the start of the lesson. In this way students are limited in how much space they have to write their notes. This means that they avoid simply writing things down passively and verbatim and they are more motivated to transform their notes into something more useful after the lesson.

Concept Maps

This method encourages students to break the material down into key points, secondary points and substantiating evidence. This is best suggested to students as something that they will transform their initial notes into after the session. It thereby provides them with more focus during the initial note-taking phase.

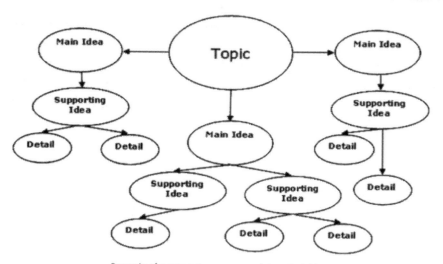

Example of a concept-map approach to note-taking

Cornell Note-Taking Method

The Cornell Method involves dividing up notes into 3 sections. Key points / questions are made in the left-hand column, and substantiating evidence / answers are provided on the right either during the lecture or directly afterwards. Following the lesson, a summary is written at the bottom.

B. Methods suitable for reading-based tasks

The following methods are specifically suited for tasks involving close reading at the students' own pace. In that sense they promote close reading of a text. They also overlap the 'live' note-taking strategies listed above, and the 'second-draft' note-transformation strategies listed below.

One Post-It Per Page

When students are taking notes from a book, provide each student with some sticky notes. They can only make notes on these, and can only include one sticky note on each page of the book to summarise its essential message (you can of course change this rule to one sticky note per paragraph if this is more appropriate). These can simply be left in the reading if it is the student's own copy; if they need to be removed then an appropriate citation should be written on the reverse of each note before they are removed and collated – they could even be stuck together with a 'covering' note to create a 'miniature book' entitled 'A gnome's guide to…'! These could certainly form the basis of an interesting display or form the basis of a "sticky notes for silent presentations" activity (page 87).

If this is the answer, what is the question?

In this method, students number each paragraph of the text. They then read each paragraph carefully and identify what question it appears to answer. Their notes then take the format of three columns: (a) The paragraph number; (b) The question this paragraph answers and (c) The answer to that question using the key evidence in that paragraph.

C. Note-transformation methods

Telescopic Topics

Students could also create notes in the form of an indented list. I developed the ClassTools "Telescopic Topic" generator to provide an interactive version of such notes, so that students can expand and contract different parts of the diagram to obtain levels of detail:

'Telescopic Topic': create collapsible summaries with ease!

- Just create a bulleted list here, or paste one from your word processor
- You can click 'preview' to see how your completed Telescopic Topic will look
  - Click each line to expand information
    - Click again to collapse
- They are a great tool for revision, or for providing an essential overview
- You can add as many items as you like...
- ...and you can indent elements as deeply as you want, for example:
  - Like this
    - Or this
      - Or this!
- You can then continue editing
    - Note that there are plenty of formatting tools in the toolbar
      - You can add hyperlinks, for example.
- You can save your work to develop later
- You can also embed and share your work in a variety of ways

---

Five-Finger Summary

Get students to trace the outline of their hand on a piece of paper. Across the palm, write the central question answered by the text. On each finger, provide a key point made in answer to that question. For further development, the 'hand' can be cut out and on the reverse side a key piece of evidence can be added to each finger as substantiating detail for the point made.

Sketch-noting

At a Practical Pedagogies Conference that I organised, I was intrigued that a number of the teacher delegates and workshop leaders were busy taking notes surrounded by a vast array of coloured pens. The results can be visually stunning and they summarise the key points in a very immediate and accessible way.

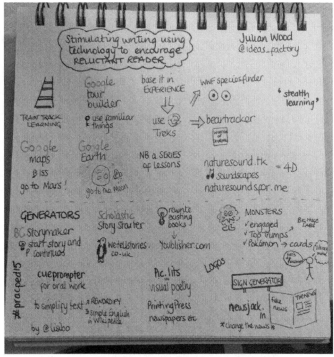

Sketchnotes by Lisa Stevens

Backward rainbow essays

When covering content-heavy programmes of study, time is always tight. Rather than delivering lengthy, in-depth lectures or getting students to deliver time-consuming presentations after conducting independent research, provide students from the outset with a model essay or article on the subject – but then get them to analyse it by colour-coding different features, and develop it with fresh, targeted research.

Finally, test their knowledge with a factual test and consolidate their understanding with a timed essay on a related question on the same topic.

Case study – the rise of Pinochet

One of my favourite topics in IB History is the Chilean Coup of 1973 which saw the overthrow of the democratically elected Salvador Allende by a military junta led by Augusto Pinochet. With its Cold War background and shady influence of Kissinger, Nixon and the CIA, it lends itself particularly well to source analysis through the study of declassified intelligence documents. For these reasons though, it also takes up quite some time to investigate thoroughly.

Therefore, as I approach the end of the examination course with my students and time is running particularly short, I choose to study the rule of Pinochet in Chile in a more compacted manner. Firstly, and with absolutely zero prior knowledge of the topic, I provide students with the model essay which in previous years I used to give to them right at the end of the study after they have finished their own essays to use for comparative purposes ("Evaluate the political and economic impact of military rule in Chile between 1973 and 1989"). We then "work backwards" from the essay by proceeding through the following tasks.

Student task 1: You are the examiner!

Step 1: Analysing the essay
- Read through the sample essay provided.
- Highlight in **yellow** the opening topic sentences and be prepared to discuss its obvious structure.
- Highlight in **green** any quotes used.
- Put into **bold** the most important pieces of evidence (names, terms, statistics) used in each paragraph
- **Underline** any interesting words / turns of phrase that are used by the author.

Step 2: Improving the essay
- Consider how this essay FAILS to incorporate any critical evaluation of the evidence. How could we improve the essay to make up for this deficiency?
- The "Missing Links" which follow are terms that are NOT included in the essay (disappointing!). Conduct your own research on how each of the following fit into the story of Pinochet's rule of Chile. Make notes on each, and then decide how to develop the essay further to incorporate them.
- Finally, add your additional research into the essay at appropriate points. Highlight all such research in red like this so that your teacher can easily identify and evaluate the improvements made.
- **The Missing Links:** Margaret Thatcher | General Leigh| General Prats | Operation Silence | Women's March 1985 | Vicariate of Solidarity | Operation Colombo | Colonia Dignidad

Student task 2: You are the student!

You will subsequently be given a factual test and / or a different essay question on the same topic to complete in timed conditions to demonstrate that you have successfully consolidated your understanding.

Taking it further
- If the essay is uploaded to a collaborative environment like Google Docs, further time can be saved by getting each member of the class to make their personal edits 'live'.

Student vocabulary bookmark

In order to help students develop a wider range of vocabulary for their extended writing, I have produced a bookmark which can be downloaded, printed and laminated to share with students.

The bookmark has proven very popular with my classes, and can be downloaded directly from www.tarrstoolbox.net.

Taking it further

- To ensure students make full use of the bookmark, ask them to suggest additional words that could be added to the bookmark which do not currently appear: for example, by creating a fresh 'row' of nine new words which could be added underneath.

- Ask students to highlight any words from the bookmark which they use in their next essay. Give credit to those students who have most clearly tried to develop their range of vocabulary by using the bookmark.

Student bookmark: vocabulary for essay writing

www.activehistory.co.uk | : @russeltarr / @activehistory

Unimportant	Less important	More important	Most important	Catalysts	Revealers	Emphasisers	Contradictors	Categorisers
Irrelevant	Minor	Major	Crucial	Accelerated	Consolidated	Moreover	Nevertheless	Social
Pointless	Allegedly	Substantial	Imperative	Hindered	Showed	Furthermore	Despite	Economic
Negligible	Superficial	Fundamental	Created	Sparked	Indicated	Indisputably	Conversely	Religious
Trivial	Indirect	Direct	Decisive	Triggered	Highlighted	Definitely	Notwithstanding	Military
Cosmetic	Theory	Practice	Essential	Exacerbated	Demonstrated	Clearly	However	Political
Insignificant	Inadvertent	Deliberate	Pivotal	Aggravated	Revealed	Obviously	Nonetheless	Long-term
Marginal	Ostensibly	Central	Vital	Facilitated	Reflected	Demonstrably	Although	Short-term

Online essay-writing tools

Although essay-writing is as much an art as a science, there are still certain key elements that characterise effective essay-writing that can be objectively measured.

As such I have developed several freely-available online tools at www.classtools.net that can be used to help students draft their essays and for teachers to then mark them.

Keyword Checker

This tool allows you to copy and paste a typed essay into one box, a list of key terms (organised under headings, if you wish) and then gives you a quick summary of which words have been included and which have not, along with an overall percentage rating.

Overall score: 51%

CATEGORY	USED	UNUSED
RELIGIOUS	Concordat / Jesuits / Gil Robles / CEDA.	Anticlericalism.
SOCIO-ECONOMIC	Depression / Latifundia / Tragic Week.	.
POLITICAL	Popular Front / Primo de Rivera / Azana / Falange / Sotelo / Two Black Years.	Alfonso XIII / National Front / Jose Antonio de Rivera / CNT / Carlists / Cortes.
REGIONALISM	Basque / Catalonia / Asturias.	.
MILITARY	Cuba / Morocco / Franco / Sanjurjo.	Annual / Half pay / Mola.

Paste keywords here (one per line) [clear]	Paste the essay here [clear]
*RELIGIOUS Concordat Jesuits Anticlericalism Gil Robles CEDA *SOCIO-ECONOMIC Depression Latifundia Tragic Week *POLITICAL Alfonso XIII National Front	What was the main cause of the Spanish Civil War? 'This is a frontier war against socialism, communism, and whatever attacks civilization' is a famous quote from Franco, after he ordered the colonial troops to bomb and shell mining towns. The Spanish Civil War was caused different parts within the country; each section has its own strengths and weaknesses, and its own causes of the war. There will always be debates between historians with different opinions as to what the main cause of the Spanish Civil War was. The fundamental cause of the Spanish Civil War in 1936 is religion. It has a major affect on the country, and the beliefs of the public. There was a week of 'workers unrest' in 1909 were 50 churches, monasteries and church school were burnt, this shows how people were against the church, their opinions and their approaches. On the 9th December 1931 the Constituent Assembly approved an amended constitutional draft, which meant that divorce was allowed, along with female

Because it is such a simple tool, it has proven very popular with my own students. The way I use it is to discuss and agree with the students in advance which are the key themes that will need to be covered (for breadth) and which particular key words, phrases, quotes and statistics we will aim to include. The students take this list away with them and can use it along with the keyword checker to help frame their own essay before handing it in.

Eyesay!

This is a development of the previous tool, providing students with particular tips regarding issues of style and structure. Once again, students simply paste their essay into the interface. This time, though, the computer then runs a detailed analysis and ratings based around the use of quotes, statistics, sentence lengths, range of vocabulary, linkage between paragraphs and so on. The essay can be edited directly within the application and continually re-assessed by the computer to provide a running commentary.

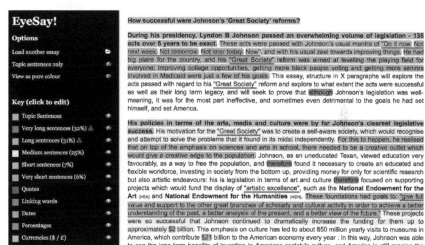

Citation Generator

Effective and accurate citations are an important part of extended essay writing and can often cause a lot of confusion and heartache for students. Although many online tools exist to create citations, I always found them rather cumbersome since they input so many pieces of information that it takes longer than writing the citation from first principles. So I coded a simple tool, through which students can simply provide a web address, author, film or book name and then obtain a citation in a whole range of formats (MLA, APA, Chicago, HAD…). There is also the facility to add a 'bookmarklet' to your web browser so that a citation can automatically be generated for any web page currently being visited.

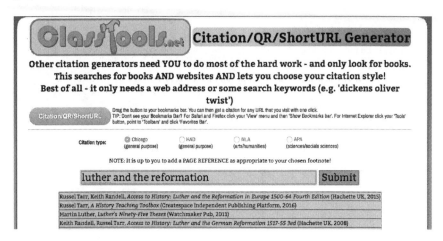

Taking it further

- The keyword checker could check not just for topic-specific terminology: consider using it also to encourage students to use linkage words (e.g. nevertheless, however, notwithstanding, consequently) within their writing.

- The EyeSay! application could be used to analyse existing articles written by professional historians and provide further insights into what constitutes good writing (not to mention the limitation of computer-based tools for measuring this!). It is also possible to view the essay's opening topic sentences in isolation. If these thesis statements are written well, then taken together they should provide a coherent overview of the entire argument. If not, they should be edited further.

Persuasive writing vocabulary matrix

As the historical writing vocabulary bookmark (page 307) proved popular with my students, I decided to produce the following matrix of persuasive writing vocabulary to help them with their essay writing.

Students could be asked to highlight words that they are not familiar with and to produce a definitions list. They could also be invited to suggest additions and improvements.

Vocabulary for persuasive historical writing		Positive			
Fortify Soothe Reassure	Restore Repair Rebuild	Relieve Pacify Courageous	Improve Progress Solve	Enrich Inspire Visionary
Stabilise Recover Calm	Traditional Familiar Reassuring	Mollify Appease Alleviate	Reform Liberalise Strengthen	Stimulate Flexible Liberate
Continuity	Entrench Buttress Bolster	Embed Reinforce Underline	Subdue Pragmatic Highlight	Transform Radical Catalyst	Revolutionary Unprecedented Cause	Change
Overlook Disregard Smother	Hardened Suppressed Restricted	Quash Cynical Muddled	Weaken Deteriorate Inflame	Destabilise Undermine Subvert
Reactionary Neglect Paralysed	Exhausted Crippled Ignore	Disastrous Catastrophic Ignorant	Counterproductive Damaging Rash	Destructive Impetuous Reckless
By Russel Tarr		Negative			

activehistory.co.uk

Download available from www.tarrstoolbox.net

Taking it further

Blank out some of the cells in the table and provide the deleted words in a separate list. Challenge students to explain where they most naturally belong. This could be set up as a team competition in a similar format to interpretation battleships (page 173).

Lotus diagram templates

Lotus diagrams are graphic organisers that help students break down a question into key factors or arguments and then summarise the essential knowledge that can be used to develop each.

In some respects Lotus diagrams are similar to mindmaps, but they are more structured because they are more constrained in terms of the numbers of factors that can be considered and the number of substantiating details that can then be added.

Case study

I have developed two templates which I initially used with IB History students to help them prepare for an essay entitled "Analyse the roots of the Cold War before the end of World War Two". The first template allows students to choose EIGHT factors. For each of these, they will then have a different segment of the diagram where they can provide eight pieces of evidence and analysis to develop the point further:

Fact	Fact	Fact	Fact	Fact	Fact	Fact	Fact	Fact
Fact	Factor 1	Fact	Fact	Factor 2	Fact	Fact	Factor 3	Fact
Fact	Fact	Fact	Fact	Fact	Fact	Fact	Fact	Fact
Fact	Fact	Fact	Factor 1	Factor 2	Factor 3	Fact	Fact	Fact
Fact	Factor 8	Fact	Factor 8	Key Question	Factor 4	Fact	Factor 4	Fact
Fact	Fact	Fact	Factor 7	Factor 6	Factor 5	Fact	Fact	Fact
Fact	Fact	Fact	Fact	Fact	Fact	Fact	Fact	Fact
Fact	Factor 7	Fact	Fact	Factor 6	Fact	Fact	Factor 5	Fact
Fact	Fact	Fact	Fact	Fact	Fact	Fact	Fact	Fact

Template freely available for download from www.tarrstoolbox.net

The second template will allow students to choose FOUR factors. For each of these, they will then have space to include a relevant memorable image (e.g. a political cartoon or similar) as well as EIGHT pieces of evidence and analysis to develop the point further:

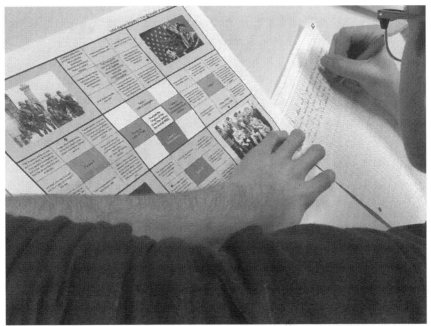

Template freely available for download from www.tarrstoolbox.net

Taking it further

- Make it a competition by organising the class into teams, and then challenging each one in turn to suggest a 'fact' to place into a box of their choice until all ideas have run out. For a further twist, award additional points for teams which use statistics or quotes in a particularly effective way.

Making the most of old history magazines

As digital archives of history articles become increasingly accessible, it's easy for print versions of magazines slowly gather dust on the shelves before being unceremoniously dumped.

But looked at more creatively, those old issues of *History Today*, *Modern History Review*, *Hindsight* and similar can be given a new lease of life in order to generate fresh topics of debate and inspiration for personal projects, presentations and extended essays.

Case Study

The following "When and Where?" approach helps to broaden chronological and regional knowledge. Provide each student (or pair of students, given how many magazines you have available) with a different edition of the history magazine. Ask them to look at the cover image and the caption associated with this 'lead article'.

Without opening the magazine, invite them to make a deduction about what is going to be the "where and when" focus of this piece (e.g. Americas, Early Modern period? Britain, 19th Century?). After discussion in groups and/or as a class, each student should then open the magazine, identify the article in question, and decide upon the actual "where and when" focus of the article.

Each student should report their findings one at a time, and the rest of the class should take brief notes. Additionally, the teacher should record the patterns that start to emerge on the classroom whiteboard in a grid like this:

	Americas	Asia	Africa	Oceania	Europe
<1450	-	XXX	X	-	XX
1450-1750	X	XX	-	X	
1750-1900	XX	X	-	-	XXX
1900-2000	XXXX	XXXXX	XX	X	XXXXX

Following from this, students should be invited to draw some observations and complete some follow-up tasks to make use of their notes and the summary grid. These might include:

- Which periods / regions appear to be most popular with historians? Why might this be?
- Are there particular topics or themes which seem to be particularly popular? Why?

From this initial starting point, students can go in all sorts of different directions. For example, the process could be deepened by students completing their own version of the grid outlined above for all the articles in their allocated magazine. These could then be compared and collated prior to further discussion and observations.

Next, students should choose one article from their own or someone else's magazine to read more thoroughly (or skim-read, depending upon the time available) and present to the class in a mini-presentation (sticking to the strict format, perhaps, of "Three interesting things and one interesting image" to present in just a couple of minutes). After finishing, provide each student with a sticky-note to summarise their essential thoughts upon and to stick onto the article ready to provide inspiration and interest for the students who follow the next year.

Taking it further

- The ideal result of this process should be that students have broadened their perspective about the breadth of history in a way which gives them a complete break from the normal scheme of work. They should also now be aware of neglected parts of the historical record, at least insofar as these magazines would suggest.

- From this point, they could then proceed to conduct their own research on one of these neglected periods, places or themes and come up with a proposed question for investigation. Each of these ideas could be "pitched" to the teacher in a "dragon's den" format (with the teacher asking such questions as "Why is this interesting? Why is this significant?").

- Alternatively or additionally, students could design their own mock magazine cover in the same style as those they have been using, drawing attention to what they consider to be the best articles from the widest range of places and periods. After providing an explanation along with their design, this could form the basis of a stimulating display piece with the magazines themselves being placed alongside for students to dip into and hopefully gain interest and inspiration from.

Compare opening paragraphs of historical books

The art of writing a good introduction to an essay is something which students need to regularly reflect upon.

I encourage students to ensure that in their essay introductions they do such things as:

- Set the scene
- Provide a bold thesis statement to summarise their argument
- Outline the main factors that will be considered to prove this point (ideally, in a way that shows how they are connected using such words from our word wall (e.g. 'therefore / as a result / exacerbated by').

Another technique I have tried is to provide students with a series of screenshots of opening paragraphs of books dealing with the topic in question. In pairs, students should read through each one and discuss such things as how it draws the reader in, what argument it makes, what evidence it uses, what creative language is used to develop mood, what aspects of the introduction are most engaging or controversial, and which one overall is the most effective in their judgment. It also raises questions about how far history is an art or a science.

This approach can ideally inspire students to take the book away and read it in full. At the very least it provides hard examples from professional writers of what can sometimes be a rather abstract concept of what constitutes good writing.

Taking it further

If you have an Amazon account, there are an increasingly large number of books that you can 'look inside' for a preview – these provide great material for collating some opening paragraphs. Similarly, Google Books is increasingly becoming a fantastic source for historical works.

10
OTHER IDEAS

This chapter provides a miscellaneous range of thoughts about such things as homework strategies, rewards and sanctions, and cross-curricular projects between history and other subjects.

Choose your own homework

Giving students the flexibility to choose the content and / or the outcome of their homework assignments increases engagement and promotes independent learning.

When the teacher gives the class an open-ended opportunity to reflect on what they need and want to learn about, and then to choose the most effective way to demonstrate their learning, students are able to take more ownership of their studies and teachers are able to cover more material in a more diverse manner. Another appealing aspect of this approach is its ease of implementation: it does not have to be adopted wholesale for all year groups and all homework assignments, but can rather be adopted to different degrees and at the most appropriate times.

Example 1: "choose your own content"

The simplest way to get started with a "choose your own homework" approach is to allows students the freedom to choose their topic of study, but for the teacher to specify the outcome. In this way there is flexibility in terms of content, but the teacher will be able to measure some distinct skills through the work that is produced. I use this approach with my older students at the end of the first half term, when I set them a holiday homework designed to get them thinking about the possible focus of their extended essay assignment. I give students a list of recommended podcasts (e.g. "Great Lives", "In our Time", "Witness" and "The Moral Maze", all of which are freely available from the BBC). Their job is to listen to at least one hour's worth of podcast material, and then use this to deliver a classroom presentation on one or more key questions raised by what they have learned. Example presentations that resulted ranged from "What are the main causes of the Arab-Israeli conflict?" to "How has game theory informed international decision making since World War Two?".

Example 2: "choose your own outcome"

My IGCSE History students reached the end of a heavily detailed and methodical study of Hitler's foreign policy in the 1930s with a desperate desire for some creative, independent work. I therefore gave them a homework which consisted of producing a resource designed to demonstrate their understanding of the key questions relating to Hitler's foreign policy in such a way that they would find it a useful revision aid. I made it plain that the only rule was that the outcome clearly demonstrated thought and effort and would prove useful as preparation for the final examination. I then gave the class some time in groups to list some possible outcomes, then we shared these in class.

The range of proposals was immense, including such things as a Google Earth Tour of the key locations of conferences and clashes relating to Hitler's foreign policy; a 'Diary of a Wimpy Fuhrer' outlining the main steps towards World War Two in the form of an illustrated children's book; a "TripAdvisor™" review of each place coveted by Hitler from his perspective, complete with rating to indicate its importance; a photo-album scrapbook of a German soldier from the 1930s charting the progress of German foreign policy; changing the lyrics of a song to cover the topic essentials in a way that would be memorable, and much else besides.

Open homework outcomes on Hitler's foreign policy

Example 3: "choose the content and the outcome"

The most open-ended method of all, of course, is to give students the flexibility to choose both the topic and the outcome rather than merely one or the other. I tried out this approach recently with a class that was studying the growth of the British Empire. I provided students with a summary grid, with the main periods of growth forming the columns and the main countries and products involved forming the rows. Their job was to produce a homework based on one cell of the table (a particular event), one row (which focused on one of the key countries involved) or one column (which focused on one particular period). In this way they had a great deal of flexibility to choose a task corresponding to their interests and abilities. For example, the students who tended to focus on a single cell (event) in the table either did so because they wanted to keep the task more manageable, whereas others who did so opted for it because it addressed a key issue that stimulated their interest: a Dutch student investigate in more depth the occasion when the Netherlands sailed its ships up the Thames in a daring raid in 1667, for example.

	When?	Where did they settle?	What products did they gain?	Who settled in this area?	Why did this happen?	Who were they rivals with?
West	1610s	**North America** They settled in Virginia (named for Elizabeth I) and married native American women like Pocahontas	**Tobacco** Tobacco and coffee was imported into Britain from North America.	**Pilgrims** The Pilgrim Fathers sailed from England on the Mayflower	**Protestants** They wanted to escape from persecution in England	**France** British settlements in North America threatened French settlements in Canada like Quebec
	1650s	**West Indies** Pirates like Captain Morgan used their riches to establish sugar plantations in Jamaica	**Sugar** Sugar was imported into Britain from Jamaica. Most was re-exported to Europe, making Britain wealthy	**Pirates** Captain Morgan stole gold from Spanish galleons coming from the "New World"	**Catholics** They wanted a Protestant Empire in the "New World" to rival that of Catholic Spain	**Spain** British pirates attacked Spanish ships in America. The British seized Jamaica from Spain in 1665
East	1660s	**Indonesia** Trade bases were established in places like Bantam in Java	**Spices** The "Spice Islands" of Indonesia sold pepper, nutmeg, cloves and tea to the British	**Merchants** The East India Company was established to establish trade links with Asian countries	**Economics** Gold, tobacco and sugar generated wealth for the British, who wanted to spend it on Asian spices and clothing	**Holland** The "Spice Wars" with Holland saw Dutch ships sail up the River Thames towards London in 1667
	1750s	**India** The British established trading bases which became the cities Bombay, Madras and Calcutta	**Clothing** India provided cotton and silk which was immensely popular in Britain	**Politicians** Robert Clive exploited and then defeated the ruler of India at the Battle of Plassey	**Politics** The Mughal rulers of India sided with the French during the Seven Years' War - so the British attacked them	**France** Britain defeated France in the Seven Years' War. Britain now "ruled the waves" and controlled trade out of India

Open homework starting point on the British Empire

Takeaway mark scheme

The decision to allow students to choose their own homework has a lot to commend it, but needs to be accompanied by an equally flexible approach to marking and assessment to reach its full potential.

This is because one of the inevitable challenges posed by the flexibility of the "choose your own homework" (page 320) approach is that standardised mark schemes cannot be applied to what will likely be a clutch of widely different homework outcomes.

To meet this challenge, allow students to design their own mark schemes so that they can be measured against the qualities and criteria which they think will reward their efforts to best advantage:

Example of a 'choose your own mark scheme' approach stemming from the "Iceman Mystery" Humanities induction project

The "choose your own mark scheme" process follows directly after students have completed the "Choose your own homework" phase by settling upon the project outcome that they will produce to demonstrate their knowledge and understanding, as per the following format.

Stage 1: students consider a range of assessment criteria

Each student is presented with a list of commendable traits that will help them achieve success in school and later life (Inquisitive, Thoughtful, Communicative, Knowledgeable, Risk-Taking, Principled, Caring, Open-Minded, Well-balanced, Reflective, Creative, Resilient).

Working individually for a few minutes, each student produces their own one-sentence definition of each word. The teacher then leads a discussion and the class settles upon agreed definitions for them all:

Design your own mark scheme

For this project, you will choose NOT ONLY how to present your research and conclusions, BUT ALSO how you would like the teacher to mark your work.

Step 1: Remind yourself of the Learner Profile attributes

As a class, come up with a simple definition of each of these words. NOTE: you will eventually choose THREE of these that you would like your project to be measured against.

	Brief Description
Inquisitive	
Thoughtful	
Communicative	
Knowledgeable	
Risk-Taking	
Principled	
Caring	

Helping students decide on the criteria for their mark schemes

Stage 2: students choose the three criteria for their projects

Each student is now asked to select just three of these qualities which they would like their "Choose your own homework" outcome to be measured against. Students who have opted to do something they have never tried before might select 'Risk-taking' as part of their criteria, for example, whereas someone else who plans to conduct some in-depth independent research might opt for 'Inquisitive' or 'Knowledgeable'. For each of these, they need to explain in a sentence or two how they think their project will allow them to demonstrate these qualities:

Student Name:			
Research Question:			
Brief Description of project:			
	Attribute	How will YOU demonstrate this attribute in the project? (TIP: start with phrases like 'I will include...', 'I will ensure...', 'I will try...').	When your project is finished, give yourself up to FIVE marks for this attribute, with '5' being the best score*
1			
2			
3			

*Your teacher will then decide if they agree with your judgment, and **extra** credit will be given to students whose self-assessment is particularly close to the teacher's.

Stage 3: students self-assess their projects against their criteria

In this final phase before handing the work in, each student marks their own work, giving a maximum of five points for each of the three attributes that they settled upon earlier. They hand in this mark sheet with their project. The teacher then judges whether the marking is fair, adjusts as necessary, and gives additional credit to students who assessed their own work particularly accurately.

Taking it further

- **Peer-assessment possibilities**: Students could be arranged in groups of three. They pass their projects and the accompanying mark sheets clockwise to the next person along, then assess them. Then the projects are passed round once more and the process is repeated so that each project has now been marked by two people. Finally, the three students can moderate the marking after discussion.

- **Demand that students develop different skills with different projects**: One possible drawback of the 'choose your own mark scheme' approach is that students might end up choosing to play safe by selecting the same three qualities every time they are given the opportunity. To avoid this, and to encourage students to develop a wider range of study skills, keep a record of their choices from previous exercises of this nature, and insist that each time they design a new mark scheme, they must change at least one of the learner profile attributes that they wish to be measured against.

A particularly impressive board game designed to teach fellow students about the growth of the British Empire.

Select a cover image for the workpack

When you provide your students with a printed work pack, or even if they have their topic notes in a ring binder with separators, ask them to decide upon an appropriate cover image with an explanation of its relevance directly underneath.

The image here shows examples from my Year 10 students, who produced front covers for their work packs on the Origins of World War One.

Taking it further

Get students to explain their choices to each other in pairs and groups. One student from each team should then be nominated to report back to the class about the image they found most intriguing, and why.

Bounce the detention

This is a simple strategy that I have used for many years when students need to work silently for a period of time. All that's needed is a prop which can be passed from one student to another (I use the large foam die that always lies around my classroom when I need to randomly choose a group to answer a question).

The rules are straightforward. The class needs to work in absolute silence. Anyone talking or otherwise disrupting anyone else in the class during the allocated time will receive the foam die and get a five-minute detention where they will have to practice sitting in silence.

However, if anybody else subsequently breaks the same rules, then the original detainee is completely off the hook and the detention (and the foam die) passes instead to the new offender, who now faces a detention that has increased to six minutes.

From my experience, the original detention sometimes 'snowballs' upwards for a little while (five minutes for Rohan...six minutes now for Noah but Rohan you're off the hook...seven minutes now for Rory, but Noah you're free...), but then hush will quickly descend as the cost of breaking the rules becomes the loss of an increasingly large slice of their free time.

Like any disciplinary strategy it is of course crucial that the rules are made absolutely clear from the outset, and applied firmly but fairly. I always deliver it with good humour, and stress that it is in order to help the students work more productively for a clearly defined period of time. As a result I often get classes asking to 'play a game of bounce the detention!' when they spot themselves that productive discussion around the tables has degenerated into irrelevant chatter.

Create bookmarks as rewards

Design a range of subject-themed bookmarks, print them off, laminate them and cut them out as prizes for good work.

The great thing about these bookmarks is that you can use a permanent marker or a pen for writing on CDs to put a brief congratulatory message on the back to pass to the student. Over time, students could be encouraged to 'collect the set' or even design some themselves as a homework project.

I have created a wide range of these bookmarks which you can download freely from www.activehistory.co.uk.

Bookmarks downloadable from www.tarrstoolbox.net

Hands up if you DON'T know

One of the most common, and maybe one of the very worst, teaching techniques is to say to students "Hands up if you can answer this question".

This is because the same (confident and able) students end up hogging the lesson and the rest of the class simply falls below the radar: either happily (because they'd rather have an easy life) or unhappily (because they might like to get involved but lack the confidence of the others). Put simply, the act of raising a hand requires a degree of self-confidence that many able but shy students – especially younger ones – lack. And if the teacher chooses to ignore the students straining with their hand in the air to encourage a less confident student to offer an answer, a sense of injustice and resentment can result.

With this in mind, consider taking a new approach. Instead of asking students to raise their hand when they DID have something to contribute, they have to raise their hand to express that they DID NOT have anything to say or to ask. This requires you to re-frame my questions: instead of "Who can tell me…?", ask instead "Who is NOT able to tell me…?". I then had to choose the students who had not raised their hands.

This might flummox the class to start with, but in a good way. Those students who wish to stay 'under the radar' now have to counter-intuitively raise their hands; those students who usually hog the discussion have to keep their hands down; but so too do the more shy students who feel they know the answer. These students can now be asked to contribute points without the more pushy students feeling they had been unfairly ignored.

One proviso applies with this method: if you frame a question in such a way that highlights ignorance, then of course nobody will be willing to raise their hands ("Read through the following passage. If there are any words you don't understand, raise your hand and I'll explain them"). So once again, reverse the question. Place the students into small teams, then encouraged them to read closely by asking the following question instead: "Raise your hand in a few minutes if you are confident you can define ALL of the words in this account. Points will be *given* to any students who can identify a word which NOBODY in the class can correctly define". All of a sudden, students will be searching for words that they do not understand with enthusiasm instead of trying to hide their lack of knowledge and understanding.

Cross-curricular speed-dating

One of the biggest challenges in a school curriculum is to break down the barriers that students and teachers set up between their various subjects. Too often, students treat each subject in isolation instead of realizing how skills acquired in one area are transferable to another.

An quick way to spot links between curriculum areas is a cross-curricular speed dating event between staff lasting for as little as one hour. The ideas generated can be fed into curriculum review discussions or used for curriculum-crossover projects.

Start by arranging the room with two chairs on either side of each desk. Divide the staff into groups of six teachers, with no single group containing two members from the same department:

		ABR	RWA	GHU	RNJ	IMA/NCO	SMO	EWH	LHA	BFO	JNO	SMA	MPO
French	ABR		1	2	3	4	5						
Maths	RWA	1		3	4	5	2						
Biology	GHU	2	3		5	1	4						
ICT	RNJ	3	4	5		2	1						
Spanish	IMA/NCO	4	5	1	2		3						
English	SMO	5	2	4	1	3							
Chem	EWH								1	2	3	4	5
Art	LHA							1		3	4	5	2
German	BFO							2	3		5	1	4
Maths	JNO							3	4	5		2	1
English	SMA							4	5	1	2		3
Geog.	MPO							5	2	4	1	3	

Each group can then be arranged into three pairs around three desks, and then simply rotate clockwise one place in a musical chairs format over five rounds lasting 10 minutes each. Each of these 10-minute sessions should be structured as follows:

- 5 minutes: Each pair of teachers aims to identify at least one key topic, and one key skill, that overlap between their subjects.

- 3 minutes: Each pair of teachers writes down their findings (even better, record them in a Google form).
- 2 minutes: Each teacher moves clockwise around their table of six people to face their new partner.

The process can then be repeated over five rounds. The results generated in the Google spreadsheet provides a rich mine of inspiration to be shared with all staff and for curriculum development, two examples of which are provided below from my own school.

Outcome 1: What was the most important development of the Renaissance?

Students are organised into teams which carousel through a series of one-hour specialist lessons (e.g. Geography, Science, Art, Design and Technology, ICT, Maths, Music). In each lesson, the teacher will address two questions:

a. What changed during the Renaissance in this subject?

b. Why did these changes take place?

The following morning, the students have two hours to produce presentations to answer the "Big Question":

c. What was the most important development of the Renaissance?

Finally, the groups deliver their presentations to the school principal, who judges the overall winner. In addition, each team "peer assesses" itself to determine who contributed most to the success of the team.

Outcome 2: Was World War Two a period of progress?

In the first week back after the summer holidays, students starting the IB are placed into teams and take part in a themed event involving six subject groups. Teachers involved in the event provide a one-hour lesson investigating the positive and negative legacies of World War Two in relation to their particular subject specialism.

Co-ordinators involved in the event then help each team of students tie these various lessons together in an overall thesis which forms the basis of a group presentation, which is judged by senior teachers. This is then followed by each student writing an essay which marked according to a strict rubric, the results of which are recorded in the student reporting system as a baseline assessment.

Local history scavenger hunts

Scavenger hunts are superb not just for developing awareness of local history, but also for team building. In this sense they are a great way to start the new school year, when many new students might be joining the school.

Stage 1: Complete the first mission

Students are taken to the centre of the local town and are divided into small teams. Each team is initially given a mission sheet consisting of a series of questions and challenges that can be answered by visiting different places hinted at in various clues. For example, the first challenge for our students in Toulouse is "Go to the gardens nearby which are named after the French Resistance leader during World War Two who later became President".

Toulouse Treasure Hunt		
Tick the final column for any tasks you achieve!		
As your first task for 5 points, take a photo of your team in front of the Mairie.	📷	
Proceed to the gardens behind the Mairie. This square is named after the man who led the Resistance Movement in World War Two and who then became President afterwards.		
Take a photo of yourself in front of the monument to this man.	📷	
Locate the modern sculpture of the mother and child in the same square. What is the name of the sculptor?	.	
Locate the monument to a Toulouse mayor assassinated in 1914 for 'non-patriotism' when he resisted the drift to war with Germany. What was his name?		
Head straight through the middle of the gardens until you reach the main road named after a province of France regained from Germany		

Opening tasks in the scavenger hunt used as part of the induction process for IB students at the International School of Toulouse

Once they arrive at this spot, they are asked to complete two tasks. Firstly, they are asked to answer a factual question by looking around the place in question ('Find a monument in the gardens dedicated to a local mayor assassinated for refusing to support France's war against Germany in 1914, and write down his name here'). Secondly, they are asked to take a group photo at a particular spot nearby ('Find the sculpture of Resistance leader after whom these gardens are named, and take a group photo alongside it'). For each task completed, the team will gain a point.

Stage 2: Complete the remaining missions

From this point, the 'proceed to a place' format can be repeated indefinitely: I used Google Maps to identify 10 key places around the city within walking distance, and then created a series of questions which guides them through clues from one place to another ("Proceed through the gardens till you reach a road named after the province regained by France at the end of World War One. Head West down this until you reach a square named after England's patron saint" – and so on). It is a good idea to ensure that each question, as far as possible, works in isolation rather than requires successful location of the previous spot: in this way, if students are unable to work out where they need to go they can cut their losses and move on to the next challenge instead.

Stage 3: Beat the clock!

One crucial ingredient of the treasure hunt is to provide a strict time limit. Teams have to hand their completed sheets back to their quizmaster at the designated location before a specified time (so that we can all get on the coach on time, as much as anything else!). Failure to do so incurs a heavy penalty or even disqualification. In this way, an element of urgency is built into the event. There is always one teacher based at a central location in case students need to locate them urgently, and we also provide each group with the school mobile phone number.

Taking it further

- It is not helpful to have all the teams following each other around in one large clump. Therefore, design the route in a broadly circular format consisting of several mystery locations (e.g. "Location A" through to "Location F"). Then, give each team a slip of paper which gives the actual name of a different particular place in the mission, and the question that it corresponds to in their activity pack. Each team then proceeds to its nominated locations and then works through the questions from that point forwards (with the final question in the mission pack directing them back to "Location A"). In this way, all students rotate through the locations independently and the chance of them following each other around is minimised.

- Include useful bits of trivia about the places in question so that when groups arrive there they can learn additional interesting things about them. In particular, names of streets, buildings and squares are a rich and generally untapped historical source.

- Set some 'selfie challenges': provide students with a photograph of a local landmark – complete with some interesting information about it - then ask them to take a group photograph at this spot to earn bonus points. One particularly fun task is to get students to find a statue in the area commemorating a famous figure, then use a 'face swapping' app on their phones to take a bizarre picture alongside it.

Build history into the school calendar

For key moments in the year, line up special lessons for each year group that provide a full context not just for historical events like Holocaust Memorial Day and Remembrance Day, but also providing a historical twist to moments like Christmas, Valentine's Day and Easter.

Example 1: Whole-school competitions - Easter and Valentine's Day

a) Easter: Produce portraits on eggs

At Easter Time, have fun by challenging students to produce a 'Hard Boiled Humanities' portrait of a key figure in history painted on a boiled egg (even better is to use a blown egg so they can be kept on permanent display).

Anne Boleyn, Thomas Crapper and William Wallace

I run this as an open competition across the school every year and we award a prize to the best entry - voted upon by creating a Facebook poll on the various teacher groups I belong to and then collating the results so that there can be no accusations of favouritism.

b) Valentine's Day: Design historically-themed cards

Another popular activity I open up to students is to design an historically-themed Valentine's Card. This idea was inspired by Ben Kling, who created a series of such spoof cards which can be found on the web ("Quit Stalin and be my Valentine", "Roses are red, so is the state, let us be Comrades, because you are great"). After showing students some of these examples, brainstorm a list of key people, terms and events on the board.

Then challenge them to come up with some suitable word-play to create captions for Valentine's cards. For example, my modern world history class came up with such examples as "When I'm with you, I Dreadnought" (Jackie Fisher), "Will you be Goering out with me this weekend?", "Haig girl, let me give you Somme love" and "I don't want to Putsch you into anything, but my heart burns for you like the Reichstag Fire" (Rise of Hitler). Finally, invite them to design the card itself as a competition challenge, with the winning entry getting a box of chocolates or similar.

Example 2: Separate lessons for different year groups

Another approach is to design a series of lessons, one for each year group, so that every year students get a different layer of knowledge for a key anniversary as they work their way upwards through the school.

a) Christmas

The final days before the Christmas holidays begin in particular are often accompanied by my students excitedly wanting 'fun' lessons and otherwise charging me with being Scrooge. Keen to oblige but without sacrificing valuable education time, I designed one lesson for each year group with a suitably festive theme. For example, younger students learn how Medieval Christmas evolved from the rowdy Roman feast of Saturnalia. This raucous heritage was reflected in the ceremony of the "Boy Bishop" who we elect in class and who randomly "marries" pairs of people in the class. The following year, the same students will learn about how and why the Protestant Reformation led to the emergence of a 'Puritan' movement which banned Christmas altogether. This cycle continues onwards through the different year groups, with lessons on such things as "How the Victorians invented Christmas" (focusing on the development of Christmas cards, trees, Santa and 'A Christmas Carol'), "Have Yourself and Very Nazi Christmas!" (how effectively Hitler used propaganda to manipulate the message of Christmas so that it promoted Nazi ideology), "A World War Two Christmas" (comparing different speeches made by politicians, actors and heads of state at Christmas time during World War Two).

MAY DED MOROZ SMITE YOUR KULAK ENEMIES WITH THE FORCE OF YEZHOV, BRING COLLECTIVE JOY TO SOVIET HEARTS, AND A FATLLY COLD WINTER FOR THE BOURGEOIS COUNTER-REVOLUTIONARIES IN THE GULAG

Students designed Stalin-themed Christmas cards to share with each other (Ded Moroz being "Grandfather Frost, a Slavic equivalent of Father Christmas).

b) Remembrance Day

The same format can be adapted for other key historical anniversaries. For example, Remembrance Day (11th November) enables the school community to think about the tragedy of war, reflecting on how it can be avoided and how its victims should be commemorated and supported. It is nevertheless a challenge to provide a fresh assembly and follow-up materials every single year (and for every single year group). With this in mind, I have designed a framework which can be used every single year but with appropriate modifications and flexibility to ensure it is different each time. It once again works on the principle that each year group works on a different project, so that as students progress through the school they are approaching the subject from a different angle every year. Such activities include the following:

- Peace Charities: Which should our school support?
  - o This exercise involves students researching a range of different charities, debating their respective merits and deciding which should be the 'official' charity that the school should support this year.
- Current Conflicts
  - o "Remembrance Day commemorates not just past wars, but also current ones too. In this activity you will research a current conflict, produce a one-slide summary using a PowerPoint template, and then compare it to others in order to reflect on the most common causes of warfare"
- Statistics and Infographics
  - o "One death is a tragedy, a million deaths is just a statistic" said Josef Stalin. In this exercise students are given some of the key statistics relating to World War One, and consider creative ways in which they can present those statistics to make them more powerful.
- Art and War
  - o Why do governments employ war artists? What makes a great work of art? What is the difference between art and propaganda? Students consider a range of different paintings, then compare and contrast their findings.
- The Nature of Remembrance: The White Poppy / Red Poppy Debate
  - o "Although Remembrance Day is an established day on the international calendar, there remains a great deal of debate about what exactly we should "Remember". People who wear the Red Poppy have one opinion, and those who wear the White Poppy have a different view. In this activity you will talk through the different points of view and reach your own independent point of view". This activity is accompanied with a PowerPoint Presentation and a YouTube Video Discussion.

Fake news

Newspaper reports including extracts from political speeches and interviews are useful primary source material for the history classroom. To help students evaluate the reliability and usefulness of such reports, provide them with the original, full speech and then require them to produce edited versions which demonstrate how selective reporting skews our understanding of what was actually said and meant.

This "quote them out of context" approach works well with any source which can be interpreted in different ways, and particularly those from individuals with controversial reputations.

Case study: Kaiser Wilhelm II

Kaiser Wilhelm II of Germany had a policy of approaching every question with a loud, open mouth, scandalising and delighting his listeners in equal measure and making him a journalist's dream.

Wilhelm claimed that the media misrepresented him through selective editing and what we would call "fake news". Considering how much truth there is in these claims is central to assessing how far he was really responsible for poisoning international relations before 1914.

One good example is Wilhelm's speech to the North German Naval Association, 1901 – known, for obvious reasons, as "The 'Place in the Sun' Speech". Start by reading out the following extract to the students, after asking them to focus on whether it creates the impression of a Kaiser who is peaceful or warlike in his intentions:

> "In spite of the fact that we have no such fleet as we should have, we have conquered for ourselves a Place in the Sun. It will now be my task to see to it that this place in the sun shall remain our undisputed possession, in order that the sun's rays may fall fruitfully upon our activity and trade in foreign parts, that our industry and agriculture may develop within the state and our sailing sports upon the water, for our future lies upon the water. The more Germans go out upon the waters, whether it be in races or regattas, whether it be in journeys across the ocean, or in the service of the battle flag, so much the better it will be for us. For when the German has once learned to direct his glance upon what is distant and great, the pettiness which surrounds him in daily life on all sides will

disappear...As head of the Empire I therefore rejoice over every citizen, whether from Hamburg, Bremen, or Lübeck, who goes forth with this large outlook and seeks new points where we can drive in the nail on which to hang our armour..."

After some initial discussion about its message and tone, divide the class into two teams. Half will be 'friendly' journalists, half will be 'hostile'. The task of the 'friendly' team is to underline any quotes which create a benign view of Wilhelm; the 'hostile' team the opposite. Students can compare their choices with a partner from the same team, then in larger groups.

Next, they have to produce a précis of the speech using just those quotes: this is a great opportunity to remind students how to use "..." to indicate to the reader that text has been removed, and [square brackets] to replace text with a brief summary. Again, students can work on this individually and then compare their work with other members of the team.

Finally, bring out a person from each team to read their work out to the class, and follow this with two questions:

[1] What does this teach us about the strengths and weaknesses of news reports as sources?
[2] How far does this particular source prove that the Kaiser had warlike intentions?

Subsequent speeches by the Kaiser himself – in particular the notorious Daily Telegraph interview of 1908 ("You English are mad, mad as March hares!") could be immediately consulted after this exercise for a fuller judgment on Wilhelm's character and policy.

Taking it further

Rather than providing students with the full speech first and challenging them to provide a biased version, consider instead reversing the process. Provide half the students with a 'friendly' speech on a slip of paper each, and half with a 'hostile' version, without telling them that their are different versions being given out. Students then read the source in silence, then the teacher leads a discussion about what impression they get from them. Quickly it will become obvious that their are sharply divergent views, at which point the full speech can be read out and the same process of reflection takes place regarding the utility of such reports.

History podcast database

To help students and teachers locate the very best podcasts relating to topics of study, I have developed a searchable database which contains links to more than ten thousand episodes.

The database can be searched directly from a web browser at www.activehistory.co.uk/library/podcasts, where you will the ability to search by period, topic or theme. Alternatively, the facility can be accessed in the form of a web application at www.podcasts.activehistory.co.uk, which organises the podcasts into the most popular themes of study in the IB History syllabus such as Authoritarian States, Twentieth Century Wars and The Cold War.

Taking it further

As a holiday homework exercise, I ask student to listen to at least one hour of podcast material on any topic and from any sources of their choice, and then share their findings in the form of a short presentation with the rest of the class. I find this is an excellent way to help students settle upon a topic for their Internal Assessment (the personal research essay which forms a major part of their final exam grade). I give the students information about my favourite podcast series:

"People who lived through moments of history bring you a personal perspective on world events" **(10m each)**	"Matthew Parris interviews an eminent guest and an expert to reveal the truth behind their history heroes" **(30m each)**	"Melvyn Bragg and his guests discuss topics drawn from philosophy, science, history, religion and culture" **(40m each)**

Wheel of emotions

When assessing the values and limitations of sources, get students to use Plutchik's Wheel of Emotions to explain the tone of the author and thereby evaluate its reliability with a more sophisticated use of vocabulary and reasoning.

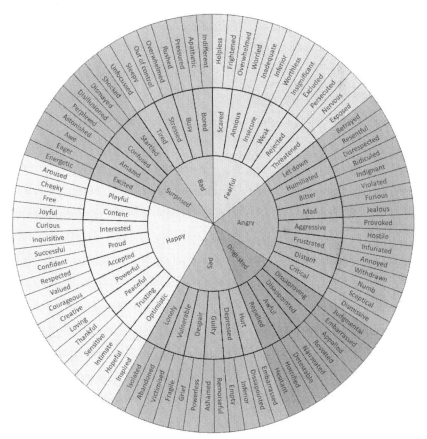

Plutchik's "Wheel of Emotions"

Case study

When analysing historical sources, students often treat their content and provenance as two completely distinct features. By this logic, the content can be used to provide information and to help us make deductions, whilst the provenance alone can help us put it into context and thereby decide how reliable this content actually is.

In reality, however, one of the most useful ways of determining the reliability of a source is through its content, not its provenance. After all, the tone of a source is a useful indicator of the objectivity and detachment of the author, or conversely of his or her emotional involvement and subjectivity.

To get students thinking about analysing the tone of sources in a more sophisticated manner during source work analysis exercises (for example, during a silent discussion activity), have an image of Plutchik's Wheel of Emotions on the board and instruct them that only words listed within it can be used in their annotations and later answers. The teacher can then circle each one off if and when it is used by somebody in the class during discussion, with the rest of the class being given the opportunity to challenge its use and suggesting something more appropriate. Once a word has been settled upon, it can no longer be used that lesson. Special credit could be given to students who are deemed to have used the widest and most appropriate range of adjectives by the end of the lesson.

Taking it further

- The use of Plutchik's Wheel of Emotions can be combined with a banned word list to restrict them from using basic adjectives ("biased", "happy", "angry").
- Students could be presented with various emotions from the different rings within the diagram, and challenged to provide a word which lies inbetween them.
- Students could also use Emojis (page 345) to label appropriate parts of the diagram, or use a Venn diagram to help them identify some of the most important overlaps between the 'strongest' emotions towards the center of the piece.

Using Emojis

Emojis are handy little images representing a particular feeling or concept in visual form that can often be seen in text messages. There are several ways to use them for concrete learning outcomes.

Sets of magnetic emojis can easily be purchased online to use on a whiteboard

Idea 1: Make an emoji vocabulary chart describing tone

To help students develop a richer vocabulary for source analysis, provide students with a range of emojis of different facial expressions. Students have to arrange these from the most positive emotion to the least positive, and then provide a one-word summary of each one.

Idea 2: Use the emoji vocabulary chart to analyse cartoons

To help students analyse cartoon sources, replace (or annotate) the faces of key characters or visual metaphors in cartoons with emojis. Students then have to provide a key which explains these choices.

Idea 3: Use the emoji vocabulary chart to analyse written sources

When presented with written sources, ask students to sum up the tone of the writer and/or their attitude towards the event or individual described using one or more emojis from the list.

Idea 4: Sum up the lesson content in five emojis

As a plenary or homework activity, students could be challenged to summarise the lesson material in five emojis – some of which might be emoticons to indicate such things as degrees of success and failure, some of which might be more generic object-based icons to refer to particular themes, policies and events.

Biographies beyond the syllabus

When considering the motives, actions and consequences of key individuals, it is too easy to simply treat them as cardboard cut-outs that appear on the stage at the start of our story and then disappear again at the end of it.

By challenging students to anticipate and/or research the lives of these people outside of the time constraints of our topic of study, they will gain a more rounded view of their motives and significance.

Example 1: The Big Three at Versailles
After recently re-reading "Peacemakers" by Margaret MacMillan, I was struck by how an understanding of the motives and actions of key figures in Modern World History is enriched by an appreciation of their lives and careers leading up to, and not just during, the events in question. For example, the "Big Three" at Versailles (Lloyd George, Clemenceau and Wilson) cannot be fully and properly understood without reference to their social background and formative experiences: yet too often this 'juicy' biographical detail is treated as irrelevant by the textbooks even though it helps students form important judgments about the genuine significance of other, more famous, characters.

Example 2: Soviet Russia
There is also a tendency to regard Stalin as being wholly and personally responsible for all the achievements and abominations of his rule if the henchmen that surrounded him are little more than a list of near-unpronounceable names (Kaganovich, Voroshilov, Ordzhonikidze…) hiding in the background. However, if students devote a little time to researching each one of them – for example by reading the excellent "Court of the Red Tsar" by Simon Sebag Montefiore - they emerge from the shadows and students are suddenly in a much better position to challenge the assumption in the examination question "How successful were Stalin's policies for…?" that Stalin was the only individual worthy of consideration.

Example 3: Weimar Germany

Similarly, the future destinies of key characters provide added interest and insight: a great example of this is when my students watch "The Blue Angel" (a classic 1930s film which is an allegory of the crises facing Weimar Germany) and are then challenged to find out what happened afterwards to some of the key actors in the movie. In a classic case of life imitating art, some ended up collaborating with the Nazis; some became resistance fighters; some tragically ended up in death camps.

		Life and career up to "The Blue Angel"	Life during and after Hitler's Nazi Regime	Any other interesting facts?
Emil Jannings as Prof. Emmanuel Rath				
Marlene Dietrich as Lola Lola				
Kurt Gerron as Kiepert, the magician				
Rosa Valetti as Guste, the magician's wife				

Students research the lives and careers of key actors from 'The Blue Angel'

Example 4: The Titanic

Individuals studied outside of the narrow time constraints of the syllabus do not even need to be well-known in their own right, but might simply be recognisable from appearing in iconic photographs; the stories behind these people too are sometimes very powerful and illustrative too. For example, as part of our studies about World War One, I get students to conduct research to learn more about the fascinating life story of Ned Parfett, famous as the boy selling newspapers on the day that the sinking of the Titanic became public knowledge.

Tastes and smells

The benefits of using audio-visual sources in the history classroom is well-established. However, it is much rarer for teachers to make use of sources which appeal to the sense of taste and smell, even though these are just as thought-provoking and evocative and perhaps even more so. Obviously take care though to have due consideration for food allergies when using such sources in class.

Case studies

Example 1: Rationing in the World Wars

Necessity being the mother of invention, the World Wars saw civilian populations having to 'make do and mend' not just in terms of clothes, but in terms of foodstuffs. To illustrate this point, have a range of examples of such foods placed around the room (or at least images of them). Next, place a series of sticky notes or cards around the name with the names of the foods upon them, and another series which describes the historical origins of each one. Students should then be challenged to match the food to its name and its description.

For example, in World War One, Germany developed margarine as a butter substitute as the allied blockade reduced the civilian population to starvation, whilst at the wars' end the jelly sweets now known as "jelly babies" were rebranded as "peace babies" after previously being known by Victorians as "unclaimed babies". In World War Two, tinned SPAM (Spiced Ham) gained popularity as a cheap and easy source of nourishment for soldiers and civilians alike (Nikita Khrushchev even declared: "Without SPAM we wouldn't have been able to feed our army"). At about the same time, M&Ms were developed by Frank Mars for the US army as an chocolate energy sweet that wouldn't melt so easily, and it was towards the end of the war that many Italians were eating eggs and bacon supplied by troops from the United States, giving birth to spaghetti carbonara (first recorded in

1950 as being a dish sought by the American officers after the Allied liberation of Rome in 1944).

Example 2: Voyages of Discovery

The early modern European voyages of discovery are a fantastic way of bringing non-European history into the study of the 16th century. They also present great potential for learning about (and tasting) some of those foods brought back from faraway lands which were once worth many times their weight in gold despite being so commonplace in our kitchens today.

In terms of delicacies brought back to Europe from the spice islands in modern Indonesia, it is easy to obtain cloves, mace, nutmeg, black pepper and cinnamon to bring into class to examine and sample. The modern cost of each one could be compared to the price they commanded in the Tudor period. The scent of cloves in particular were believed to have the ability to ward off plague, and were pinned into oranges in pretty patterns and held to the nose as a pomander for that reason: it's great fun to get students to make one of their own as a project task.

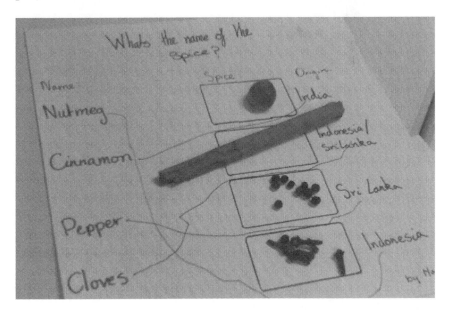

Looking instead to the New World, students are most likely to be attracted to the story of chocolate coming into Europe from the Americas, although the traditional recipe including chilli is unlikely to be as popular as the milk chocolate variety. This form of chocolate was developed during the industrial revolution by Quaker families like the Cadbury and Rowntree families, who originally marketed it as a drink as a substitute for alcohol as part of their Quaker mission for social improvement.

Taking it further

- All cultures have their own feast and fast days, and national dishes. The origins of these could be researched and examined to give an international flavour(!) to your classroom's history studies.

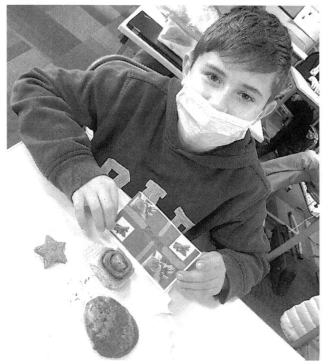

The "Spice Wars": Cinnamon cakes and biscuits made to share with the class as part of a "choose your own homework" project (page 320).

Five ways to use music effectively

Popular music provides some of the richest, but most under-utilised, sources of historical interpretation that can be used in the classroom. By analysing the meaning of lyrics and placing them in their proper context, students are able to consolidate their knowledge and understanding in a highly engaging way.

Moreover, collections of relevant songs can be organised into classroom playlists for use as atmospheric music during subsequent lessons or as a study aid during revision time.

Strategy 1. Provide a musically-themed timer to keep students on task

In lessons consisting of short bursts of activity on a regular basis, having a relevant piece of music to act as a timer is particularly effective to help students with time management. For example, I teach the Nazi school curriculum by getting students to write school reports for each other for a variety of subjects using various primary sources. This involves an intensive blast of factual information, a short amount of time to write a report using the key terminology just provided, and then passing the reports around the class ready to write the next one for a different student.

To maintain this pace, I start the activity with the report for 'music' and analyse the lyrics of the 'Horst Wessel Song' – the anthem of the Hitler Youth movement – as the central focus. I then give students three minutes to write their report, which is the length of the piece itself, and have the song playing in the background. As the exercise proceeds, students quickly get into the rhythm of how long they have left from the increasingly familiar tune. At the end of the exercise, the lyrics of the song itself should be analysed in their own right.

I have also coded a dedicated classroom timer at ClassTools with 20 pre-loaded popular instrumental tracks of various lengths that you can bring up on your whiteboard. You can upload your own choices of music to it as well (www.classtools.net/timer).

ClassTools countdown timer (www.classtools.net/timer)

Strategy 2: Instrumental Music (for atmosphere and mood)

Classical music can be very helpful for creating a calm and purposeful working atmosphere, when a bit of Chopin or Debussy sets the tone perfectly. Even better, though, is when there is a relevant story around the composer to accompany the music and bring the topic into sharp focus. For example, when studying World War Two, give students a bit of background to the life – and tragic end – of Glenn Miller before playing some of his music (e.g. "In the Mood") as the soundtrack for the main lesson.

Another piece I recommend is Elgar's Cello Concerto in E Minor, made famous through its performance by Jacqueline du Pré (whose life story is gripping in its own right). Although now a well-established national favourite, fewer people are aware that it was inspired by the composer sitting on the cliffs watching British troop ships of the BEF heading off into the mist towards France in 1914. Less well-known, but perhaps equally moving, is "On the Banks of Green Willow" by George Butterworth, a wonderfully elegiac piece by a young composer of the "Lost Generation". A charismatic member of the "Bloomsbury set", Butterworth joined the war to test his own mettle and quickly distinguished himself as a particularly fine soldier, but was tragically killed during the Battle of the Somme and is now commemorated on the Thiepval memorial for the missing.

There are many other pieces of instrumental music whose historical context can be outlined at the start of the lesson and then used to provide a backdrop to the main activity. The best way forward with this technique is to start with a piece of music from the place or period being studied, then do some basic research around the context in which it was produced. Some notable pieces worthy of a listen in this respect include Beethoven's Third Symphony (dedicated to Napoleon until he declared himself emperor, at which point the composer furiously scratched his name from the dedication), Shostakovich's War Symphonies (arguably a subtle protest against Stalinism) and Tchaikovsky's 1812 Overture, with its booming cannon commemorating Russia's defence against Napoleon's invading Grande Armée in 1812.

Strategy 3: Individual Songs (for starters / plenaries)

Occasionally, a historical topic will be associated with its own clear corpus of music. Notably, slave songs and many blues pieces can be analysed for historical meaning. For example, "Amazing Grace" was written by John Newton, a former slave trader keen to share how he came to see the error of his ways; "Redemption Song" by Bob Marley is a wonderfully evocative tale not just of being kidnapped into slavery, but also the challenges faced down the centuries by subsequent Afro-Americans.

The most fruitful individual performer in this respect is perhaps Hughie Ledbetter, better known by his stage name of Leadbelly. His "Pick a Bale of Cotton" is a classic example of a song which was designed to help the slaves stay motivated and maintain momentum in the fields. Moreover, as with the classical composers outlined earlier, the life story of Leadbelly is worthy of study in itself for highlighting the hardships and injustices suffered by black Americans in the segregated south, and race relations in the United States as a whole in the period before the Second World War. Leadbelly, a convicted murderer, was recorded performing in prison by legendary musicologist Alan Lomax, and his songs include such superb material as "Bourgeois Blues", "Midnight Special" and "Where did you sleep last night?" (covered by, of all people, Kurt Cobain of Nirvana, who described Leadbelly as 'our favourite performer').

Over the years I have built up a large repertoire of songs which have a strong historical dimension to use at particular points. Some of my favourites include:

- "William the Conqueror" (DMX Krew): Why was King Harold defeated at the Battle of Hastings?
- "Cult of Personality" (Living Colour): How important is the role of the individual?
- "Sophiatown is Gone!" (Miriam Makeba): In what ways did black South Africans oppose the apartheid regime?
- "Political Science" (Randy Newman): What impact did the Vietnam War have upon American society?
- The Ripper (Judas Priest): What do the Whitechapel Murders reveal about working-class life in Victorian London?

Strategy 4. Write lyrics for an "ANTI-protest" song

Protest songs by definition are packed to the hilt with strongly expressed opinions and perspectives. These sorts of songs can be analysed in the manner just described, but another challenge could be to rewrite the lyrics of a song to provide the opposite perspective. Occasionally, history provides us with ready-made examples of such "Anti-Protest Songs" that can be used as an example. One illustration of this is when Neil Young's derogatory "Southern Man" provoked the writing of "Sweet Home Alabama" by Lynyrd Skynyrd ("Watergate does not bother me...does your conscious trouble you? Tell the truth!").

After considering both of these songs, students could then be produced with a whole range of different songs relating to the topic in question. After analysing each one on its own terms, students should summarise the main protests being made overall, then consider how the most important of these could be challenged in fresh lyrics matching the tune of one of these songs. For example, after considering a range of Vietnam War protest songs (e.g. "Ohio" by Neil Young, "Eve of Destruction" by Barry Maguire, "Fortunate Son" by Credence Clearwater Revival to name but a few), students could produce the lyrics for an "Anti-Protest Song" supportive of American involvement in the war and the policies of a particular administration. This approach is not limited to bona fide protest songs: any song with a clear agenda (from "Victoria" by The Kinks to "Rasputin" by Boney M) could lend itself to the same treatment.

Strategy 5: Complete playlists (for in-depth projects)
This technique moves students still further from being consumers towards being creators, and brings the music itself to the forefront of the exercise. It can also be used in conjunction with the analysis and writing of lyrics already described. I use this method when studying the civil rights movement in the USA. Students are firstly presented just with the lyrics with a couple of songs from 1968 ("Trouble Every Day" by Frank Zappa and "If I Can Dream" by Elvis Presley) and asked to anticipate, based on the tone of the lyrics, what style of music and instrumentation they expect to hear. After a classroom discussion, play the first verse or two of each song to see how far their assumptions were proven correct.

Next, I provide students with a long list of civil rights-era music and divide this so that each student gets three or four songs to consider. Their job is firstly to locate the lyrics of each song using the internet, and decide which two of these are historically the most valuable in terms of the references they make to genuine events and circumstances. Next, they use YouTube or Spotify to listen to each song, and make a final selection on their "best" song based on a combination of the music and the lyrics. Each student thereby nominates one song for the class 'compilation'.

All of the research should then be completed and shared. Google Presentations are particularly good here, since each student can simply add their research into a separate slide.

If there are a large amount of students in the class, a balloon debate format could be used to reduce the total songs down to a streamlined compilation of perhaps 15 songs overall.

Thereafter, students are given the opportunity – perhaps as a homework exercise – to read the lyrics and listen to all of the songs that have been researched. In a subsequent lesson, each member of the class should then vote on their favourite three songs overall. These songs are then ranked by popularity and ideally turned into a collaborative playlist using an online music service such as Spotify. As an extension exercise, students could decide upon a running order and produce a "CD Inlay" providing brief context for each song as well as a suitable cover image.

This approach works well for a wide range of topics such as the American Civil War, the two World Wars, the Cold War, and apartheid South Africa. For further inspiration, take a look at my wide collection of freely accessible playlists for history topics at www.activehistory.co.uk.

I have collated a wide range of playlists at www.activehistory.co.uk/spotify.htm

Taking it further

- Challenge students to add a final verse to their chosen song covering an aspect of the topic which is not addressed.

- Rather than allocating songs out to each student and asking them to research the lyrics, simply print off the lyrics to each song in advance of the lesson. Place these around the room and then conduct a "Silent Discussion" exercise (page 62) to identify some of the key themes and issues that appear to be raised. Then allow each student to choose one or more songs to research further.

- A full list of more than 50 such songs, complete with suggestions about when they might be used, can be found at www.activehistory.co.uk/spotify/top_songs.php.

ABOUT THE AUTHOR

Russel Tarr has a degree in Modern World History from Lady Margaret Hall, Oxford University and a History teaching qualification from Birmingham University. He has been a full-time teacher of History and Politics since 1997 and is currently Head of History at the International School of Toulouse in France.

His previously published works include *Luther and the Reformation in Europe 1500-64* and *Essays in Modern World History*. He writes regularly for the international press, delivers freelance training courses to history teachers, has been a keynote speaker at numerous teaching conferences and has organised several major international educational conferences.

Russel is also author of www.activehistory.co.uk, which provides a vast range of innovative teaching resources, worksheets and online simulations for the history classroom, www.classtools.net, which provides online game generators and learning templates, and www.tarrstoolbox.net, which contains links to many downloadable templates mentioned in this book.

If you are interested in working with Russel, or have any comments or questions about the strategies suggested in this book, you can contact him directly at **russeltarr@activehistory.co.uk**.

Made in the USA
Columbia, SC
10 May 2024

35525955R00202